THE DISMISSAL OF MISS RUTH BROWN

*Civil Rights, Censorship,
and the American Library*

BY LOUISE S. ROBBINS

UNIVERSITY OF OKLAHOMA PRESS : NORMAN

ALSO BY LOUISE S. ROBBINS

Censorship and the American Library: The American Library Association's Response to Threats to Intellectual Freedom, 1939–1969 (Westport, 1996)

A portion of this work was previously published in Louise S. Robbins, "Racism and Censorship in Cold War Oklahoma: the Case of Ruth W. Brown and the Bartlesville Public Library," *Southwestern Historical Quarterly* 100 (July 1996): 19–48 (Austin: Texas State Historical Association, 1996), and is used with permission. Chapter 5 was previously published as "'Fighting McCarthyism through Film': A Library Censorship Case Becomes a Storm Center," *Journal of Education for Library and Information Science* 39 (Fall 1998): 291–311, and is used with permission.

This book is published with the generous assistance of the Wallace C. Thompson Endowment Fund, University of Oklahoma Foundation.

Library of Congress Cataloging-in-Publication Data

Robbins, Louise S.
   The dismissal of Miss Ruth Brown : civil rights, censorship, and the American library / by Louise S. Robbins.
      p.   cm.
   Includes bibligraphical references (p.   ) and index.
   ISBN 978-0-8061-3314-0 (paper)
     1. Bartlesville Public Library (Bartlesville, Okla.)—History—20th century. 2. Afro-Americans and libraries—Oklahoma—Bartlesville—History—20th century. 3. Libraries and communism—Oklahoma—Bartlesville—History—20th century. 4. Brown, Ruth Winifred. 5. Civil rights workers— Employment—Oklahoma—Bartlesville—History—20th century. 6. Public librarians—Employment—Oklahoma—Bartlesville—History—20th century. 7. Public libraries—Censorship—Oklahoma—Bartlesville—History—20th century.
   I. Title.
   Z733.B283R63   2000
   020'.896076696—dc21
                                          99–38926
                                             CIP

The paper in this book meets the guidelines for permanence and durability of the Committee on Production Guidelines for Book Longevity of the Council on Library Resources, Inc. ∞

3   4   5   6   7   8   9   10

The Dismissal of Miss Ruth Brown

Ruth W. Brown, ca. 1950.
Courtesy Ellen Brown Ericksen.

In loving memory of four strong and
courageous women in my own life:
my mother, Nancy Booth Stevens,
my grandmother, Anna "Nan" Roe Booth,
and my models in the skirmishes for
racial equality in Ada, Oklahoma,
Marguerite Hawkinson and Ethylene Harris

CONTENTS

ILLUSTRATIONS

PREFACE

During my many years in Oklahoma, a number of them as a school and academic librarian, I cannot recall hearing about Ruth Brown and the Bartlesville Public Library. When I started research for a doctoral dissertation, a process that immersed me in the library literature of three decades, Brown's 1950 dismissal from her position as librarian in Bartlesville emerged from the pages as an intriguing episode in the history of the development of American librarians' credo of intellectual freedom. Those who are usually spoken of as heroes of intellectual freedom are men; many, if not most, are academic librarians. While it is certainly true that men played important roles in developing and articulating the American Library Association's commitment to intellectual freedom, as often as not it was women who tested that commitment—and their own. Ruth Brown was one such woman.

But Brown tested another commitment as well, her own and her neighbors' commitment to racial equality. It is this that makes her story especially noteworthy. More than ten years before the American Library Association began to deal with access to libraries by African Americans as an intellectual freedom issue and ten years before the student sit-ins at an all-white lunch counter in Greensboro, North Carolina, escalated the campaign of nonviolent direct action against segregation in public accommodations, Ruth Brown and her friends, Mary Ellen Street and Clara Cooke, went to Hull's

Drug Store in their small community in northeastern Oklahoma and asked to be served. This event would ultimately lead to Ruth Brown's dismissal.

The story of Ruth Brown and the Bartlesville Public Library has many characters and more than enough plot twists. Discovering it has been an adventure; telling it has become a labor of love. Fortunately, it is a labor that many others have shared, some long before I knew about Ruth Brown. To them I am grateful first and foremost for foresight and persistence; to that I add my gratitude for papers and time shared. Among them is Russell Davis, a member of the library board ousted with Brown in 1950 who saved all his papers and—on the urging of Jason Talley, a teenager from Joplin, Missouri, who literally ironed and then organized the papers—donated them to the library at Pittsburg State University, Kansas. There they joined Brown's own papers, placed there by her close friend Margaret Varvel. I am also grateful to Russell Davis and Margaret Varvel for hours of interview time in Bartlesville and in Corvallis, Oregon. My thanks also to Jason Talley for preserving the papers and for sharing stories of his History Day research. Frances Kennedy, the first person to conduct an on-site investigation of a censorship case on behalf of the American Library Association's Intellectual Freedom Committee, pointed me to her complete set of papers at the Oklahoma State Archives and allowed me an interview as well. Ellen Brown Ericksen, Brown's adopted daughter, answered many questions and generously shared letters and photographs. Ellen's sister, Mildred Holliday Dryer Creasy, and her children, Tom Dryer, M.D., and Ellen Dryer, D.V.M., shared two days of their lives with me at Tom Dryer's home in Cincinnati.

Many others also took time out of busy lives for interviews. Their names are listed in the bibliography. To them I also extend my profound gratitude. The DouglassAires, the triennial reunion group of graduates of the segregated Douglass School, allowed me and my husband–research partner to crash their party and evoke sometimes painful memories. Thanks to the director of the Westside Community Center, James Abraham, and Bernice Brown, who suggested it, we were able to meet with the group and ask questions about life in Bartlesville under Jim Crow. Without that opportunity this book might have happened, but it would not have been authentic. Rose Bean Hicks, Bernice Brown, Eva Chambers, Ida Dailey, Marlene Gilkey, Marie Littles, and Arnetta Nash were especially open, and I am grateful.

There are many others who assisted my research. Anne Million, reference librarian (retired) extraordinaire at the University of Oklahoma and my old friend, got me off on the right foot by sharing information she had gathered in the past. Susan Box, then archivist at Phillips Petroleum, shared a graduate school paper, her knowledge of Bartlesville, and the library and photo archives of Phillips Petroleum. The Bartlesville Public Library's director, Jan Sanders, put me in touch with Russell Davis, sent me the library's file on the Brown episode, and allowed me to set up headquarters in the History Room for many weeks one summer. Joan Singleton, local history librarian, was always one step ahead of me in my search for materials and was an encouraging presence to boot; she is the ideal reference librarian. Each office I went to in Bartlesville made an effort to help me locate the information I needed. George Jones, city clerk, remembered my search months after I had left and when he accidentally found something he thought would be helpful, took it to the library and asked them to send it to me. The Bartlesville Women's Network, especially Joan Dreisker and Harriet Guthrie, provided an unexpected support system, not only giving me names of likely people to interview but also allowing me to check perceptions and test ideas on them. They gave me their fine oral history books and hosted our evening showing of the film *Storm Center*. And late one night in Bartlesville, one of their number, Celeste Cleary, called to offer a videotape about Ruth Brown called "Red Herring," made by her mother's students in Marietta, Oklahoma. It, too, was a History Day project. Wayne and Shirley Wiegand allowed us the use of their Norman, Oklahoma, home for part of a summer, and Henry and Jo Runnels, of Bartlesville's Travelers' Motel, provided not only a good headquarters and a skinny pillow but an excellent messaging service and directions to the tornado shelter as well.

How far the news of this case spread is illustrated by the presence of primary source materials in archives from Laramie, Wyoming, to Princeton, New Jersey. The late Gene de Gruson, Special Collections librarian at Pittsburg State University, was one of those rare people who inspires others with the excitement of research in primary sources. It was he who told Jason Talley about Ruth Brown and sent him on his search for more material. And it was he who sent me copies of both the Ruth Brown and the Russell Davis files in their entirety. Rick Ewig of the American Heritage Center, University of Wyoming, carefully answered my questions and evaluated the many boxes of Daniel Taradash Papers to send me just the things I needed. Janet Lorenz sent materials on *Storm Center* from the Academy of Motion Picture Arts and Sciences. Nina Myatt stayed late and helped man the photocopy machine at Antioch College, where we used the Paul Bixler Papers. John Lovett did not reprimand me too much when I got excited about my finds in the E. R. Christopher Papers in the Western History Collection at the University of Oklahoma. The folks—many of them—at the Oklahoma Department of Libraries deserve a special thanks for helping me in the Archives, allowing me access to the working files, and sharing my enthusiasm for my research. Thanks also to the staffs of The Bancroft Library, University of California at Berkeley; the Library of Congress Manuscript Reading Room; the Seeley G. Mudd Manuscript Library at Princeton University; the Ponca City Public Library, especially the director, Holly LaBossiere; the American Library Association Archives at the University of Illinois–Urbana-Champaign; the State Historical Society of Wisconsin Library; and the Wisconsin Center for Film and Theater Research.

This work would not have been possible without two Summer Research Grants from the Graduate Research Committee of the University of Wisconsin–Madison and, in addition, the Jane Anne Hannigan Research Award of the Association for Library and Information Science Education. For three years I was the fortunate recipient of the Jean Deuss Research Assistant Professorship, awarded by the Executive Committee of the School of Library and

Information Studies (SLIS) at the University of Wisconsin–Madison, which allowed me to hire a succession of able research assistants. Arden Sujewicz, Gregory Pringle, Gretchen Revie, Dee Grimsrud, and Michele Besant were invaluable. Lee A. Bowman did the indexing. Andrew Wertheimer helped me find a title. Those who read or heard various parts or stages of this work and helped me to improve it were audiences at the 1995 Southwest Historical Association meeting, the 1996 Berkshire Women's History Conference, and the 1996 Library Research Seminar I, as well as colleagues Michele Besant, Christine Pawley, Christine Jenkins, Jim Carmichael, Wayne Wiegand, Steve Vaughn, and Paul Boyer. They can take credit for improving my work, but its inadequacies are mine alone.

Finally, Peggy Green, my colleague in the SLIS Laboratory Library, uncomplainingly kept the library running during long summers without much help, gave me some leeway when I needed a little extra writing time, and still managed to share smiles and offer support. Only my husband, Orville, has contributed more to the successful completion of this book. He drove, manned a tape recorder, checked addresses, photocopied, cooked, cleaned, and commiserated to enable the telling of this story. To these two, a special thanks.

This book is dedicated to the memories of four strong, courageous women reminiscent of the protagonist of this story. The first two, my mother, Nancy Frazier Booth Stevens, and my grandmother, Anna "Nan" Roe Booth, shared with me their conviction that we must leave our piece of the world better than we found it. The other pair—one white, one black—were elders in the skirmishes for racial justice in which the Robbins family was privileged to take part in Ada, Oklahoma. Marguerite Hawkinson and Ethylene Harris would like this book. I hope you do.

LOUISE S. ROBBINS

Madison, Wisconsin

The Dismissal of Miss Ruth Brown

ABBREVIATIONS

AAUW	American Association of University Women
ABC	American Business Consultants
ACLU	American Civil Liberties Union
ALA	American Library Association
CLA	California Library Association
CLD	Catholic League of Decency
COPD	Committee on the Practice of Democracy
CORE	Congress of Racial Equality
DAR	Daughters of the American Revolution
HUAC	House Committee on Un-American Activities
MPAPAI	Motion Picture Alliance for the Preservation of American Ideals
NAACP	National Association for the Advancement of Colored People
OLA	Oklahoma Library Association
UDC	United Daughters of the Confederacy
WPA	Works Progress Administration
YMCA	Young Men's Christian Association
YWCA	Young Women's Christian Association

INTRODUCTION

We feel that it is essential that the facts of this controversy be published, in order that the citizens of this community may be advised of what has transpired, and in order that those responsible may understand that the denial of Constitutional rights to our citizens has significance beyond the boundaries of our town.

—DARLENE ANDERSON ESSARY,
"Hush-Hush in Bartlesville"

Even at a distance of nearly half a century many residents of Bartlesville, Oklahoma, still feel strongly about Ruth W. Brown, the single, middle-aged public librarian who lost her job of thirty years in 1950 amid charges that she circulated communist and subversive materials—the *Nation*, the *New Republic*, and *Soviet Russia Today*. The charges, a red herring in the view of many, masked the real reason that Brown was suspect in this conservative community: her efforts to achieve racial integration. Brown's activities, the actions taken against her and the library, and the responses of those who took up her cause form the substance of this book.[1]

This story of a brief episode in a small city in a sparsely populated state nearly half a century ago does more than recall an interesting local event. It reveals, in addition, much about movements and countermovements during that part of the cold war that we call the McCarthy era and foregrounds the kinds of people—mostly women—who labored for racial justice, sometimes at great cost, before the civil rights movement. Set in the middle of the country, in the middle of the century, this story allows us to examine the dynamics of a community at odds with itself over the changes and challenges that confronted it.

Many of the changes and challenges confronting Bartlesville were local manifestations of national changes. New Deal programs of the 1930s and early 1940s, which emphasized the social and economic welfare of all people, and World War II, which heightened citizens' awareness of racism at home as the United States fought racism abroad, invigorated the struggling movement for racial integration.[2] In this atmosphere the National Association for the Advancement of Colored People (NAACP) accelerated its legal battles to overturn segregation in public accommodations and schooling—the "separate but equal" Jim Crow laws of the southern states. Two of those cases fought by the NAACP on its way to the 1954 landmark *Brown v. Board of Education* decision pertained to the integration of graduate and professional schools at the University of Oklahoma. The cases were in the courts and the headlines from 1946 through 1950.[3] Although the NAACP made progress through the courts, some people were frustrated by the slow pace of legal action and organized to find faster ways to achieve integration. One of these groups, formed in 1942, was the Congress of Racial Equality (CORE). Between 1942 and 1954 CORE pioneered the methods of Gandhian nonviolent direct action such as bus rides and sit-ins that would later become the hallmark of the Southern Christian Leadership Conference and the Student Nonviolent Coordinating Committee.[4]

Not only did such groups gather steam in the 1940s, but, in 1946, immediately after the election that saw Congress turn sharply to the right, President Harry S. Truman came out flatly in support of integration and recommended many proposals abhorrent to southern conservatives: the elimination of the poll tax, the establishment of a permanent Fair Employment Practices Commission, and the abolition of segregation in the military, among others.[5] The conservative Southern Democrats, who had come to ascendancy in Congress during World War II, vowed to fight to maintain white supremacy and backed Strom Thurmond's breakaway Dixiecrat party against Truman in the 1948 election. Thus, while the move toward integration achieved support from within the administration, it elicited strong negative reactions as conservative groups strove to maintain segregation and protect their power.[6]

Strong negative reactions often greeted women's postwar efforts to forge new roles for themselves as well. Although Rosie the Riveter had been welcomed on assembly lines during the war, when men began to return from the front women were encouraged—or mandated—to return to their traditional private sphere within the home and family. Containment was not just foreign policy applied to the U.S. effort to keep communism corralled within a tightly defined Soviet sphere, it was domestic policy applied to society's efforts to keep women confined within the domestic sphere as well. The new independent woman who had emerged during the 1920s and had gained self-confidence as a worker during the war was perceived as threatening to the sanctity of the home and family. Women's patriotic duty now was to help their returning men adjust to peacetime life, to exercise their creativity by making homes in the towns, cities, and newly burgeoning suburbs, and to take advantage of the remarkable new appliances that were appearing in the booming postwar market. Earlier steps toward greater freedom and independence for women were stymied by a narrowed sense of women's "place."[7]

The cold war and its concomitant anticommunism and pressure to conformity complicated the sometimes painful movements toward change and created tensions in the social fabric. Just as the United States emerged victorious from World War II, the sole possessor of the amazing power of atomic weaponry, it became increasingly aware of the menace of Soviet communism, which appeared to be encircling an ever-widening area of Eastern Europe. As one of two opposing superpowers, the United States was in new and uncharted territory. For the first time the United States launched a massive foreign aid program to rebuild Europe and forestall communism's advance. The nation perceived itself as threatened, not only by foreign military might, but also by an insidious foreign ideology that appeared to be spread, like rumors and the common cold, through casual contact. In response to conservative Republican charges that the Democratic administration was soft on domestic communism, in March 1947 Truman issued an executive order requiring all administrative branch employees to undergo loyalty screening.[8] Later that year the attorney general issued a list of organizations past or present membership in which could disqualify individuals for federal service.[9] Many states and cities followed suit.[10] Teachers were special targets of loyalty probes, not only because teachers dealt with ideas, but also because they were in a position to influence young people.[11] When Alger Hiss, a member of Franklin Delano Roosevelt's New Deal administration, was accused of spying for the communists and was tried and finally convicted of perjury, the ideals of the New Deal appeared to be convicted as well.[12] By September 1949, when Truman announced that the Soviets, too, possessed the secret of the atomic bomb, the stage was set for a period of virulent anticommunism.[13]

As Richard Fried points out in his *Nightmare in Red*, much, if not all, of this anticommunism was "functional": it "dovetailed closely with the aims of economic interest groups."[14] Conservative businessmen in particular used the cold war anticommunist crusade to diminish the strength of labor unions and to combat liberalism generally. The U.S. Chamber of Commerce was especially effective in pushing such an agenda.[15] No doubt some individuals were sincere in their belief that those who worked for racial justice or for higher wages and better working conditions for laborers were, if not communists, at least their dupes or fellow travelers. After all, the communists had been among those most active and effective in those causes.[16] It is no coincidence, however, that the social reforms associated with the New Deal or with Truman's Fair Deal were tarred by their opponents with the communist brush. Those who worked for integration, for example, were frequently subjected to loyalty investigations or to damaging rumor and innuendo in attempts to end their effectiveness and thus their threat to the economic, social, and political status quo.

It is also no coincidence that the activities that women considered their special concern—peace, consumer protection, social reform, advancement for women and minorities, for example—should be labeled subversive. Achieving their goals would require changes in the social, economic, or political structure. In addition, by engaging in activity in the public sphere women transgressed the boundaries of their traditional roles.[17] Thus Ruth Brown, an unmarried middle-class woman who had worked all her adult life, was already somewhat outside the domestic sphere—although library work was seen as a suitable profession for a single woman. She became even more vulnerable when she began public political activity on behalf of racial integration, hardly a popular cause in a conservative community with southern roots.

Bartlesville was also dealing with an evolution in local business conditions that were related to national trends, especially the growth, bureaucratization, and professionalization of its largest and most influential employer, Phillips Petroleum Company. Since the New Deal, when unions began to have more influence over company operations, and World War II, which took the company heavily into petrochemical research and changed the kinds of people moving into the community, Phillips's metamorphosis from a family-run company to a bureaucratically managed corporation with worldwide holdings had accelerated. The leadership of the firm was passing into the hands of a second generation of managers, better known for ambition, perhaps even ruthlessness, and hardheaded business sense than the colorful and benevolent dictatorship of Frank Phillips.[18] As Bartlesville was virtually a company town, the changes were bound to have an impact.

Events that appear to threaten the cultural fabric—and good press—of a community often lead to a search for villains, for a source of contagion on which all the community's discomfort can be blamed. The result is at best an intolerance of difference, a pressure to conform, and at worst something like the witch-hunting brand of anticommunism we call McCarthyism. A perception of threat can also lead to a fear of new ideas that challenge the status quo or cast a valued institution in a bad light.[19] Books, as vessels for ideas, and libraries, as institutions charged in part with the preservation and communication of culture, are vulnerable when the discourse becomes contested or constrained. Like schools, libraries received much unwanted attention during the cold war. Groups such as the American Legion and the Daughters of the American Revolution (DAR) monitored libraries for their alleged un-American biases. In response, in 1948 the American Library Association (ALA) pledged itself to fight censorship on behalf of library users' intellectual freedom. The ALA's reaction to the attack on Brown was part of its attempt to defend libraries and the professional prerogatives of librarians to build collections.[20]

The ALA's attempt to assist Brown focused almost exclusively on the censorship aspects of the case. Ironically, in attempting to defend librarians' professional jurisdiction, the ALA helped to obscure the cause of racial integration for which Brown fought. It is part of the complexity of this deceptively simple story that Brown's friends, as well as her enemies, chose to focus on library materials rather than on the actual cause of the attack on Brown, her interracial activities. When the Hollywood screenwriter Daniel Taradash used some of the story's elements in fashioning the film *Storm Center*, his answer to the investigations of Hollywood by the House Committee on Un-American Activities (HUAC),[21] he, too, shied away from the racial theme. Opposing censorship and character assassination was risky enough. This conflation of issues, this masking of motives and concerns, is one of the aspects of the Ruth Brown story that makes it most pertinent to our time, as cultural values are again perceived to be under siege, as fear of difference—race, gender, class, national origin, sexual orientation—once again is exploited, as discourse is again constrained and contested, and as conservative groups have again escalated their challenges to materials in library collections. Perhaps this case study can help us to understand the dynamic matrix of personal, community, state, and national forces that help to create the conditions and the concerns that lead to censorship, intolerance, and suppression of the rights of others.

CHAPTER ONE

"America's Ideal Family Center"

Its Librarian, and Her Library

> *Bartlesville has been indeed a fortunate town in having such*
> *a person at the helm of the public library, and I would like to*
> *express my gratitude that my own children, who are almost*
> *grown-up now, have come under her influence. Because of*
> *her, they have a deep love of fine books, with all that means in*
> *a hectic modern world.*
>
> > *It is much easier to destroy than to build. Miss Brown is*
> *a builder and has built with love and faith.*
>
> > —ARGYE M. BRIGGS,
> > letter to the editor, *Bartlesville Examiner-Enterprise*,
> > July 29, 1950

"Frontier and Stronghold of the Oklahoma Oil Industry"—in its front page ear the *Bartlesville Record* in 1950 rehearsed the city's identity for its residents. Located less than twenty miles from the Kansas border in the Cherokee and Osage hills of northeastern Oklahoma and the county seat of Washington Couty, Bartlesville was steeped in the lore of its origins as an Indian trading post and its growth as a capital of the oil boom. The town took its name from Jacob Bartles, who bought Nelson Carr's mill on the banks of the Caney River in 1875 and built it into a trading post and settlement. But the town itself grew up around the rival store established by

William Johnstone and George B. Keeler on the river's opposite bank. In 1897 the newly incorporated town of two hundred residents celebrated the completion of Oklahoma's first commercial oil well, the Nelly Johnstone. Two years later the arrival of the Santa Fe Railroad made possible the shipment of oil and thus doomed the already fragile way of life of the resident Indians—transplanted there between 1830 and 1870 by the U.S. government—and brought a population boom to Bartlesville, which was already bristling with oil rigs.[1]

Bartlesville's oldest families, like the Bartles, Johnstones, and Keelers, were those who married into the Osage, Delaware, or Cherokee tribes whose lands yielded the oil. Others came to the area seeking opportunity after the federal government opened much of Indian Territory to settlement starting in 1889. In the early decades surrounding Oklahoma's 1907 statehood, the oil fields lured many a wildcatter, and the town was full of colorful and rowdy characters. Names like Getty, Sinclair, Skelly, and Foster would be associated with oil for decades to come.

UNCLE FRANK'S TOWN

Among the early wildcatters was Frank Phillips, an uneducated Creston, Iowa, barber who had married Jane Gibson, the banker's daughter. He arrived in Bartlesville in 1905 with his brother, Lee Eldas (L.E.), to speculate on the oil bubbling from the ground in Indian Territory. After three dry holes they hit eighty producing wells in a row and joined the ranks of the wealthy. Nevertheless, in 1916, having also achieved success in the more stable banking industry, the Phillips brothers tried to get out of the oil business. They were unable to sell their last remaining lease in the Osage Hills just to the west of Bartlesville, and with World War I and its predictable need for fuel fast approaching, they began drilling again. Phillips Petroleum Company was born in 1917 and quickly expanded. With luck and hard work, the company remained independent and afloat through the Great Depression, which struck

Oklahoma especially hard. World War II brought new opportunities for the petroleum industry. In 1945, as the war ended,
Phillips had profits of more than $22.5 million—double its 1940
profits—and was producing petroleum, natural gas, and numerous
petrochemicals. Phillips grew rapidly in the postwar years, with
operations across the United States and, increasingly, abroad.
Although the company had long had New York offices and Frank
Phillips had long kept a residence in a prestigious Manhattan hotel
(as well as a lover as manager of the New York office), the company
maintained its corporate headquarters in Bartlesville. There Frank
and Jane Phillips not only renovated their sumptuous town home
but also developed Woolaroc, a large ranch complete with bison
and several varieties of exotic animals. Woolaroc was Frank
Phillips's retreat; it was also his place to introduce stockholders,
directors, and friends to his version of the Wild West at huge Cow
Thieves and Outlaws Reunions, complete with genuine outlaws,
real and Hollywood cowboys, and Osage chiefs such as Bacon
Rind.[2] These gatherings of ruggedly individualistic characters
reinforced the heavily masculine frontier culture of the oil field.[3]

"Uncle Frank" ran Phillips, and, to an extent, Bartlesville, like
an extended patriarchal family. He appeared to care genuinely,
albeit paternalistically, about his employees.[4] Each Christmas, for
example, Phillips would present a sack of fruit and candy and a
silver dollar to all the children of Phillips employees, as well as
other Bartians, as the residents called themselves.[5] He kept a doctor
on retainer to deal with the injuries roustabouts and drillers sus-
tained in the brawling oil field camps such as Burbank, Webb City,
and Whizbang. Although he gained a reputation for being tough
but fair and for working as hard as he asked his workers to, he also
demanded absolute obedience and loyalty and hated to have anyone go against his wishes.[6] But by 1939, when the whole town as
well as hundreds of out-of-town guests turned out for a huge sixty-
sixth birthday party for "Mr. Phillips 66," the company was
becoming bureaucratized.[7] Modern production methods coupled
with regulations associated with expanding size and New Deal
programs necessitated more formal rules, policies, and practices.

Phillips had to give up some of his control to professional managers who could keep track of requirements and the burgeoning number of employees. Although he remained chairman and chief executive officer, Phillips began to relinquish power to the ambitious K. S. "Boots" Adams, whom he had anointed company president just the year before. Phillips regretted his loss of close contact with employees as well as his loss of control.[8] By 1946, however, he was not nearly so active in the management of the company he founded, and following the death of "Aunt Jane" in 1948, he withdrew more and more to Woolaroc, under the watchful eye of his Japanese valet, Dan Mitani, until he died in 1950.[9]

By 1950 Phillips Petroleum Company effectively dominated the city of nearly twenty thousand, not only with its high-rise buildings, but also with its large number of employees and its complex hold on the city's social, cultural, and economic life.[10] Phillips and the less influential Cities Service Oil Company—the successor to both the Indian Territory Illuminating Oil Company and the Empire Oil and Gas Company—occupied a large portion of the business district that lay to the east of the railroad tracks. To the east and south of the business district, on streets such as Cherokee (the best address), Osage, Delaware, Johnstone, and Dewey, and toward the Caney River lived the white middle and upper classes: shopkeepers and businessmen, along with clerks, attorneys, accountants, executives, engineers, and scientists who worked for National Zinc, Cities Service, and Phillips. Price Pipeline Company, Reda Pump, and other oil-related industries also bolstered the economy. In 1950 Bartlesville boasted the highest median family income of any urban area in the state.[11]

The Chamber of Commerce touted Bartlesville as "America's ideal family center," a small city with the advantages of a larger one, a good place to rear children.[12] With its scenic location on the Caney River, it was a tree-filled oasis on the windswept prairies. It sported parks in which young people picnicked and played. Many of the wealthier Bartians, and those who aspired to be, belonged to the Hillcrest Country Club, southeast of town, where golfing was a popular pastime and appropriate evening wear was required.

Central Bartlesville from the southwest, August 1950. The railroad tracks are on the left. At middle on the far right is the Civic Center. Ruth Brown's home is hidden in the trees north of the Civic Center on the same side of the street. On the opposite side, in the 300 block, are the YMCA and the YWCA. Courtesy Archives, Phillips Petroleum Company.

There Boots Adams and his second wife, Dorothy Glynn, reigned. Four theaters and one drive-in lured moviegoers. The Phillips 66ers, the company's semiprofessional basketball team (where Adams got his start in the company), usually put on an impressive winning display. To the west of town Phillips maintained and managed the city airport. The Civic Center, on Johnstone, housed the Bartlesville Public Library and an auditorium. Active groups of volunteers sponsored the Town Hall series of speakers, played in the orchestra, or performed in community theater. There were piano teachers such as Alberta Bradstreet and dance teachers such as Betty Frey. Not far north of the library on Johnstone were the Young Men's Christian Association (YMCA) and the Young Women's Christian Association (YWCA), both with programs for all age groups. Many other clubs and activities occupied the leisure hours of Bartlesville residents. There were Kiwanis, Lions, Rotary, Elks, Masons, the Junior Chamber of Commerce, the Frank Phillips Men's Club and the Jane Phillips Sorority, the Cities Service equivalent Doherty Girls' Club and Doherty Men's Fraternity, the Business and Professional Women, the League of Women Voters, the American Association of University Women (AAUW), the Daughters of the American Revolution, the United Daughters of the Confederacy (UDC), and the American Legion. It was a community full of joiners and doers.[13]

Bartlesville was a "family center" in other ways. Phillips Petroleum occupied first place in the pecking order, with Cities Service employees regarded as somewhat second rank, as even newcomers and children came to understand. A representative of each of the major companies—Phillips, Cities Service, National Zinc—was sure to be on the city commission, which usually worked without much visible controversy in a city manager–commission form of government. Phillips built the swimming pool and allowed non-Phillips people to use it several days a week. Said one resident, if Phillips, especially after Adams became president, wanted the stripe on the street painted, "the merchants . . . would all say what color and how soon?" Since so many of the community's elite and middle class worked for the two large oil companies, their children tended to marry children of other oil company employees. Nearly everyone worked for or was related to someone who worked for Phillips or Cities Service, or both. As one woman resident said, it was deemed unwise for married women to work, because working either for the same company as one's husband or for its competitor could cause problems. Another commented that the intermingled family and business relationships, both economic and social, made many people very cautious about expressing themselves about anything controversial lest they experience economic or social repercussions. It was very unlikely that the city commission or the school board, for example, would take actions opposed by Phillips.[14]

Some people felt that the churches would not take stands opposed by the oil companies either. The Phillips family and the Adamses belonged to the Presbyterian church. The president of Cities Service, H. R. Straight, and his family attended the Episcopal church. These mainstream Protestant denominations that reminded many residents of their midwestern roots were among the most prominent of the thirty-five or so churches Bartlesville boasted in the late 1940s and early 1950s, but there was strong representation, too, of more fundamentalist churches like the Baptists and Nazarenes that had moved with residents of the Old South into Oklahoma. Nearly every Christian faith, from the Christian Scientists to the Latter-Day Saints to the Roman Catholics, was represented. There was no synagogue, although there were Jewish families in the community. Bartlesville was blessed with more churches than gas stations—even here in the "frontier and stronghold of the oil industry."

The city was blessed also with a thriving business district centered at Third (later to be named Frank Phillips Boulevard) and Johnstone. On Johnstone were located some of the offices of Phillips Petroleum and the Phillips's First National Bank and the Burlingame Hotel; Third Street from Johnstone east boasted offices of many of the city's doctors, Union Bank, Home Savings and Loan, Eng's popular Chinese restaurant, and Hull's Drug Store, as well as women's clothing stores, shoe shops, and department stores. Washington County Memorial Hospital, farther east on Third Street, was served by twenty-one physicians, more than one per thousand Bartlesville residents. One parochial and eleven public schools—ten white and one separate African-American school—educated young Bartians. Both the Missouri, Kansas, and Texas (Katy) Railroad and the Atchison, Topeka and Santa Fe Railway provided passenger and freight service from the depot just to the west of the downtown business district.[15]

Downtown Bartlesville in the 1950s, near the corner of 4th and Dewey, looking toward 4th and Johnstone. City Hall is on the right; the Burlingame Hotel and Cities Service are on the left. Courtesy Archives, Phillips Petroleum Company.

THE OTHER SIDE OF THE TRACKS

In the "Y" made by the Santa Fe and Katy tracks and to the west, under the plume of smoke from the National Zinc Company's smelters, on such streets as Elm, Hickory, Bucy, Cass, and Santa Fe, lived Bartlesville's poor whites and African Americans. A mere 5.5 percent of the population, the African Americans lived for the most part in small, dilapidated houses, more than half without indoor toilets or running water. Many of the homes were owned by white landlords who made a good return on low rents by investing nothing in upkeep. The median nonwhite family income—a median skewed by the wealth of oil-rich Indians—was about a third that of the overall median family income. The vast majority of African Americans, regardless of their educational level, worked as domestic servants or day laborers. They crossed the tracks in the morning to tend the children, homes, and gardens of white Bartians and crossed them again in the evening to tend their own children, homes, and gardens. The segregated Douglass School, serving children from kindergarten through high school, employed many of the twenty-five African-American college graduates.[16]

Although Bartlesville's Chamber of Commerce touted its parks, theaters, schools, and other cultural and natural benefits as ingredients that made the town "America's ideal family center," African Americans could not take advantage of these benefits. Most parks, movie theaters, restaurants, and hotels were closed to them, and their school was outfitted with leftovers from Bartlesville's white schools. The hand-me-downs included not only textbooks and typewriters. For example, although the Douglass School colors were purple and white, the marching band wore College High School's old black-and-gold uniforms.[17]

Medical care was virtually nonexistent. The few white doctors who would treat African Americans saw them at the back office door after hours; the hospitals relegated African Americans—when it admitted them at all—to beds by the basement furnace room. The conditions under which Bartlesville's African-American community lived and labored demonstrated clearly that Oklahoma, traditionally regarded as a western state, had much in common with its Deep South neighbors as far as ideologies of race and class were concerned.[18]

Oklahoma's history and politics reveal these commonalities. The Choctaw, Chickasaw, Cherokee, Seminole, and Creek Indians removed by the federal government to Indian Territory in the 1830s were dubbed the Five Civilized Tribes, in part because, like their "civilized" white neighbors, they owned black slaves. The tribes differed from one another in their attitudes toward their slaves. The Seminoles and the Creeks, for example, frequently intermarried with them, whereas the Cherokee forbade intermarriage and had severe slave codes. In the period between their removal and the Civil War, the tribes used slave labor to till the fields in Indian Territory. By the Civil War Indians held more than eight thousand slaves; they sided and fought with the Confederacy. At war's end the slaves gained their freedom and citizenship in the tribes; later they were supposed to gain land allotments and annuities like other tribal citizens, but the tribes frequently resisted their claims.[19]

Thus, even before Indian Territory was opened to non-Indian settlement, a southern racial pattern prevailed. Nevertheless, African Americans were among the settlers who migrated to the new territory when it was opened for an opportunity to live free in a new land. Many were fleeing the post-Reconstruction South; the new state offered African Americans a chance to escape the system of legally mandated separation of the races known as Jim Crow and to enjoy full citizenship, including the vote. Therefore African Americans came into Oklahoma and Indian lands to claim, clear, and plant the land, to enter trades and practice their professions. In fact, the Bartlesville settlement's first physician, even before Indian Territory was officially opened, was a Dr. Tann, an African American. By Oklahoma's 1907 statehood African Americans made up almost 8 percent of the population.[20]

Unfortunately, black settlers' hopes of full citizenship in the new state would shortly be dashed. Men of southern ancestry who dominated the constitutional convention wanted to make the new state in the image of the South they had left. Although President Theodore Roosevelt indicated he would veto a constitution that included a full range of Jim Crow laws, the constitution still mandated separate school systems for African Americans. In addition, as soon as the constitution was approved the legislature promptly enacted Senate Bill 1, which required segregated public transportation and waiting rooms, and passed a stronger miscegenation law. In 1910 Oklahoma voters approved a legislative referendum that deprived African-American citizens of their right to vote, a right they would have to fight all the way to the Supreme Court to regain.[21]

Segregation did nothing to ease tensions between the races, and in 1921, amid a statewide—and indeed a nationwide—resurgence of the Ku Klux Klan, a race riot erupted in Tulsa, just fifty miles south of Bartlesville. Rumors that a black man—dubiously accused of assaulting a white orphan girl—would be lynched brought a group of armed African-American men to the jail to protect the accused. A white mob gathered, and in spite of attempts by law enforcement to keep the groups apart, a gun was fired and the white mob chased the African Americans back into Tulsa's Greenwood district, known to whites as "Little Africa." The following day whites attacked the area with a vengeance, even dropping flaming kerosene bombs from airplanes onto the neighborhood below. They ransacked, looted, and set fire to homes and businesses and shot at men, women, and children. The African Americans tried to defend their homes and families, but when the riot finally ended three days later, sixty-eight blacks and nine whites were known dead. Greenwood—thirty city blocks of well-established businesses and institutions, including the library, and homes for fifteen thousand African Americans—was a pile of rubble and ashes.[22]

Although white Bartians believed that the Tulsa race riots had no effect in Bartlesville, the city's close proximity no doubt made Bartlesville's African-American community very much aware of their vulnerability. In fact, newspaper articles from 1921 through 1924 testify to the Klan's presence in Bartlesville as well as in nearby Copan, Ochelata, Ramona, Dewey, and Pawhuska. One photograph in the possession of the Bartlesville History Room depicts a group of hooded Klansmen standing on the running boards of a car participating in a funeral procession, and another depicts an initiation ceremony in which several dozen men were welcomed into the Klan. The newspaper reported that the throngs of spectators on the hill above the initiation scene clogged the roads for some time when the ceremony was over. Thousands were said to have watched a "spectacular" Klan parade in Bartlesville in 1923, and a 1924 *Enterprise* article reported the burning of a cross "in the Negro district." When the sheriff asked one of the Klan leaders at the scene what was going on, he reportedly was admonished that he would know if he attended meetings more regularly. Other articles reported that well-known and highly placed members of the Bartlesville community were Klan members. "Ku Klux Klan No. 20" even had an office in the Civic Center, along with the American Legion, the Boy Scouts, and the Chamber of Commerce, according to the 1924 *City Directory*. Although much of the Klan activity in Oklahoma appears to have been directed at the "immorality" of the oil towns, on at least one occasion the Bartlesville papers reported that the nearby Pawhuska Klan ordered "idle negroes" and those living in servants' quarters in white residential areas to leave the community. As virtually every job depended on a white employer, Bartlesville's African Americans guarded their tongues and their actions and waited for a better time to press for redress of their grievances.[23]

Although black Oklahomans continued to put survival before redress during the depression and its terrible dust bowl days, the hard times—because they brought about the New Deal—lit the fires of hope for African Americans. The New Deal not only aimed to improve the economic lot of all Americans, it shook up old political and economic relationships in the South, leaving the door open for greater participation by African Americans. The racial liberalism of Franklin and Eleanor Roosevelt was reflected in the significant number of young black and progressive white professionals appointed to posts in the administration and also in Eleanor Roosevelt's frequent symbolic actions in support of racial equality. On one occasion in 1938, for example, forced by Sheriff "Bull" Connor of Birmingham to move from her seat among black delegates at a meeting of the Southern Conference on Human Welfare, Mrs. Roosevelt refused to sit with the whites but instead placed her chair on the line dividing the two sections.[24] Although the New Deal programs were still discriminatory, more than four thousand African-American families in Oklahoma benefited from Works Progress Administration (WPA) programs alone.[25] Roscoe Dunjee, editor and publisher of the Oklahoma City *Black Dispatch*, the state's leading black newspaper, not only reported on all these developments but also encouraged the NAACP to bring its national convention to Oklahoma City in 1934; it was the group's first convention in the South since 1921.[26]

Although the spirit of equality that some saw infusing the New Deal did not have an immediate, visible impact on race relations in Oklahoma, in the state as across the South it energized African-American communities and organizations like the NAACP. The U.S. entry into World War II added both urgency and opportunity to the struggle for racial equality. All across the nation the awareness of the incongruity of fighting fascism abroad while maintaining and sustaining racism at home began to prick the consciences of white liberals. At the same time the NAACP stepped up its organizing in the South and its campaign to overturn *Plessy v. Ferguson* in the courts. In Bartlesville in 1940 African Americans reactivated their dormant NAACP chapter. By 1942 eighty-six black Bartians, including Roosevelt T. Gracey, hired only the previous year as Douglass School principal, were paid members. In 1944 fifty current members called in outside help to try to secure jobs for African Americans at the zinc smelter. The annual report summed up their effort cryptically: "None has gone to work." This may not have been the Bartlesville NAACP's first effort at improving the employment situation. One Phillips employee's widow remembers African Americans trying to get jobs in the construction of the Phillips research facilities in the late 1930s or early 1940s.[27]

Although Bartlesville's NAACP efforts did not bear fruit, the pages of the *Examiner-Enterprise* and the *Bartlesville Record* carried stories of the barrage of social forces that were pushing Oklahoma, like its Deep South neighbors, reluctantly toward change. They traced the progress through the courts of Ada Lois Sipuel's challenge to segregated higher education in Oklahoma. Sipuel, a highly qualified graduate of Langston, the African-American land grant college, sought admission to the University of Oklahoma Law School. When the U.S. Supreme Court decided in January 1948 that the State must provide her with a law school education equal to that for which she had applied, the State invented a makeshift separate law school. Sipuel returned to the Court to force the university to enroll her. Her case was still big news in 1948 when the courts ordered George McLaurin admitted for doctoral study in education. Forced to sit in specially designated areas of classrooms, the cafeteria, and the library, McLaurin appealed to the Supreme Court. Not until June 1950 did the Court rule that McLaurin's treatment by the State denied him access to education equal to Oklahoma's white students. These cases, part of the NAACP's plan to overturn *Plessy v. Ferguson*, made headlines in Bartlesville from 1946 through 1950 and served notice that African Americans no longer believed that separate would ever be equal. Coupled with reports of court action extending voting rights, President Truman's Civil Rights Committee, his 1948 executive order ending segregation in the military, and famed African-American singer Paul Robeson's negative comparisons of the United States with the Soviet Union, these headlines no doubt raised the ire and fear of Bartlesville's conservative power structure.[28]

Fear and anger were compounded by the intense anticommunism and distrust of nonconformity ushered in by the cold war. After the 1946 congressional election, conservatives—both Republicans and Southern Democrats—accused the administration of harboring communists and fellow travelers. In response, in March 1947 President Truman instituted a program to check the loyalty of every federal employee. Many states and local jurisdictions followed suit. In the South advocates of racial integration were the most frequent targets of investigations of allegedly subversive or disloyal activities. Because the Communist party had been vocal in support of racial equality since the 1930s, segregationists felt justified in accusing supporters of integration of following the "party line." Aubrey Williams, for example, publisher of the *Southern Farmer* and former New Deal official as well as outspoken president of the pro-integration Southern Conference Educational Fund, was subpoenaed in 1954 to testify before the Senate Subcommittee on Internal Security as an alleged leader of the communist underground. Virginia Durr, another native Alabaman who was active in the fight to abolish the poll tax, a device used to keep blacks (and poor whites) from voting and thus to assure that a minority of whites kept power, was accused as well. In highly publicized hearings conducted by Sen. James Eastland of Mississippi in New Orleans, paid informants swore that Williams, Durr, and her husband had been communists and that Durr had introduced top communists into White House circles. Although the accusations were false and the hearings resulted in no legal charges against any of the individuals called, the suspicions injured their reputations and their means of livelihood. And later Williams's *Southern Farmer* was virtually put out of business as a result of an American Legion *Firing Line* article repeating the unfounded accusations aired at the hearing.[29]

Anticommunism, as Fried points out, served a number of purposes—frequently economic ones—other than the defense of the nation. Those who feared loss of cheap black labor, or having to contest for scarce jobs, or changes in the status of blacks and women wrought by depression and war used charges of subversion or disloyalty to keep the threats at bay, to keep blacks and women in their place. In Oklahoma calls for loyalty oaths and investigations at the University of Oklahoma—where a number of students, including Harold and Carolyn Price from Bartlesville (son and daughter-in-law of the pipeline manufacturer), vocally supported the admission of Sipuel and McLaurin—sounded in the 1949 legislature. The following fall the American Legion called for an anticommunist oath for public employees, especially those in higher education. Even while African Americans pressed forward to claim their rights, reaction and fear established roadblocks.[30]

Against this backdrop of national tension, Bartlesville was growing and changing. Phillips Petroleum had been instrumental in meeting the World War II demand for synthetic rubber. Stimulated by the war, it moved even more vigorously into petrochemical research. As it began to develop plastics, fertilizers, and fibers from its mineral resources, its ranks swelled with young scientists and engineers recruited to work in its research and development effort. Between 1940 and 1950 Bartlesville's population jumped 18.2 percent, and the number of residents with at least four years of college jumped 68 percent. Nearly 11 percent of the population, more than in any Oklahoma community except the major university centers, boasted college degrees. Along with their educations, some of the scientists and their civic-minded wives brought liberal social perspectives. Many of the women poured their creative energies into civic, volunteer, or organizational work with such groups as the AAUW and the YWCA. They and their families frequented the Bartlesville Public Library and engaged in lively conversations with its librarian, Ruth W. Brown, a voracious reader and unconventional thinker.[31]

THE LIBRARY

The Bartlesville Public Library, serving the city of approximately twenty thousand, developed in much the same way as libraries in other communities across the United States. Public libraries in general began as private or membership-funded organizations designed for the middle and upper classes, then moved to privately funded but somewhat more generally accessible "free" libraries, and finally became publicly supported through tax dollars as public libraries with a mission of education or uplift, or, some would say, social control or hegemony.[32] Started in 1898 by a Bartlesville women's group as a part of the effort to civilize the oil boomtown, by 1908 the downtown reading room, known as the Tuesday Club Public Library, was open for several hours on Friday afternoons. Chafing under the expense and effort of maintaining the reading room, the women asked the city for a tax levy to support a library and solicited Andrew Carnegie for funds for a building. After two years of negotiations the city and Carnegie reached agreement, and in 1912 construction began.[33]

The Carnegie Library opened its doors in 1913, just six years after Oklahoma became a state and sixteen years after the town was incorporated. By 1927 the collection had grown from two thousand to ten thousand volumes, and the library had outgrown the Carnegie building. Bartlesville citizens passed a bond issue to finance an addition, but the vote was thrown out on a technicality.

The Bartlesville Civic Center, showing the north wing area occupied by the Bartlesville Public Library, early 1950s. Courtesy Archives, Phillips Petroleum Company.

When the city agreed to give the library space in the newly constructed Civic Center, Frank Phillips agreed to contribute $5,000 for furnishings. The Bartlesville Public Library opened in the north wing of the Civic Center at 103 East Sixth, on the corner of Johnstone Avenue, just three blocks from the central business district, in 1928.[34]

In 1937 the library's interior was pictured in a booklet celebrating thirty years of the Oklahoma Library Association (OLA). Light walls and incandescent globes hanging from the ceiling brightened the dark oak of the crowded shelving. On round and rectangular oak tables surrounded by bentwood straight chairs sat dictionaries or stereopticons and slides. A white sculpture stood

Interior of the Bartlesville Public Library, 1937. Courtesy Oklahoma Department of Libraries.

on its pedestal beside one of the two magazine racks. The large circulation desk stood between two columns in a central location adjacent to the card catalog.[35]

The Bartlesville Public Library was not especially well supported. In 1946–47, for example, Bartlesville and neighboring oil city Ponca City had nearly identical populations, but Ponca City's public library had an income of more than $19,000 while Bartlesville struggled along on just over $7,600, despite the fact that Bartlesville's tax valuation was about $3 million greater than Ponca City's. Ponca City's staff of eleven kept the library open sixty-six hours a week while Bartlesville's staff of five managed to serve the public for sixty hours. Brown reported a collection of more than 24,000 volumes to Ponca City's 28,000, with more than 1,000 new items added that year—somehow nearly equal to Ponca City's additions. She indicated that the library enjoyed a circulation of almost 95,000 items to only 1,267 registered borrowers, whereas Ponca City's 8,711 borrowers checked out nearly 110,000 items in 1946–47. In addition, although Ponca City's African-American population numbered only 850, the city supported a separate Community Branch library. In 1950, when Brown was accused of having subversive materials in the library, the Bartlesville Public Library had known only three librarians: Mabel Blakeslee, Myrtle Weatherhold, and Ruth Brown. Brown had served since 1919, most of her—and the library's—life.[36]

THE LIBRARIAN

Ruth Winifred Brown was born in Hiawatha, Kansas, on July 26, 1891, to Silas and Jennie Brown, transplanted New Englanders; her brother, Merritt, was two years her junior. The family spent some time in California, where Brown went to high school, and thereafter moved to Alva, Oklahoma, where she attended Northwestern State Normal School, graduating in 1910. After a stint of teaching, probably at Billings, she attended the College of Arts and Sciences at the University of Oklahoma in Norman, graduating with a bachelor's degree in 1915. The college's yearbook, the *Sooner Nineteen-Fifteen*, depicts a short, plump young woman of average good looks, with upswept, light brown hair, light eyes, a somewhat prominent lower jaw, and a slightly downturned mouth. Her activities during her university years appear to have been confined to the YWCA and Teutonia, "an organization for the study of German topics for people studying German." Perhaps she did not care for teaching at Eufala or Nowata, her next two posts; or perhaps as a good daughter of that time she just wanted or needed to be closer to her parents, especially her mother, who was wheelchair bound. Brown's parents were now in Bartlesville, where her father worked for a lumber yard. Whatever her reason for leaving teaching, Brown moved to Bartlesville in 1919 in anticipation that the Carnegie Library director's position would be available and that she could get it. In November, at age twenty-eight, she began the job she soon discovered was exactly suited to her. Like many other professional women of her time, Brown felt a calling to her chosen life's work. Although at one time she was engaged to be married, she decided that "she was doing it because everybody else was doing it" and that she was not a person who should get married. Instead, the library was "like a marriage to her."[37]

It was a marriage with children. Although, despite her somewhat abrupt manner, Brown enjoyed warm relationships with many adults, especially women, from the beginning, it was the children she courted. She provided a stereopticon and slides for their amusement, and, unlike some librarians of her generation who disdained a mechanistic approach to the production of literature, she willingly purchased series, such as the Oliver Optic and Little Colonel books. Although she seemed "ferocious" to children at first—she whispered and insisted that they do so, too—her kindness and concern gradually came through. She allowed one youngster with an overdue book fine on her card, for example, to check out books on her grandfather's card. She used story times, charts, games, and contests to encourage reading among the children. One Bartian recalled, "She knew us all by name."[38]

Brown also cultivated promising young people by giving them employment in the library. Thomas Finney (son of an early pioneer family), Naomi Stocker, Lester Smith, and Reba Norris were among her employees. She also helped a number of young people—Alline Huffman, Elmo Olson, and James Henderson—go on to college. Some followed Brown into the library profession. Smith, who worked at the Carnegie Library sometime in the 1920s, ultimately retired from the Library of Congress; James Henderson, who worked in the library as a student in the 1930s and as Brown's assistant in 1941–42, eventually became the head of the Research Libraries of the New York Public Library, of which Brown was extremely proud. Henderson's relationship with Brown was somewhat difficult, he said, because she wanted him to "toot his own horn" more than he was willing to. Brown herself was both shy and "formidable—not a sweet old lady type of librarian." She read "everything" and tried to convert her protégé to her passion for bird-watching. She kept in touch with a number of her young employees long after they left the library, and several of them went to bat for her in 1950 when she was fired. Elmo Olson wrote in 1939 from the University of Chicago to thank her for money she had sent and to comment both on readings she had recommended and on her "analysis of religion" in a previous letter. It disturbed him somewhat because she had indicated that she felt no need "of subscribing to a system of theology" even though she seemed to believe in prayer. He commented wryly on a visit to a Unitarian church where the minister urged a change in whites' attitude toward other races: "Not immediately, of course—nor need his good bourgeois parishioners do any personal thing that might cause them to contact another, admittedly inferior race, but they should think equalitarian [*sic*] thoughts."[39] Olson clearly felt that Brown would sympathize with his opinion of the preacher's message.

Two young people in whom Brown was especially interested were Mildred "Holly" and Ellen Holliday. Brown had attempted to adopt them in 1937 when they were left orphaned by the death of their mother, but the welfare agency was unwilling to place them with an unmarried woman. In 1942 Holly, then nearly eighteen, ran away from her abusive foster home, and Brown finally was able to take her in. Safe with Brown, Holly encouraged her younger sister to run away, too, so that she could also live with Brown. She did. Brown adopted the twelve-year-old Ellen officially but remained foster mother to the older Holly. When the girls moved in with her, Brown left her room at Edna McFann's rooming house and bought a small four-room white house with a garden next door, just half a block from the library. She had always lived close—at her parents' home, in a room at Judge and Mrs. Clarence Kahle's, and at McFann's—as she did not drive. The tiny house, nestled among trees and squeezed between larger structures on each side, was simply furnished, reflecting Brown's detachment "from material things," with pictures on its light green walls ("She loved green"), "really ordinary furniture," lots of books, and a piano that had been her mother's (Brown herself did not play, but a group of her

Mildred "Holly" Holliday (far left), Ruth Brown (third from left), and Ellen Brown Ericksen (fourth from left) at the time of Ellen's marriage to Chris Ericksen (next to Ellen), 1946. Courtesy Ellen Brown Ericksen.

women friends formed a small chamber group that practiced at her home). Holly said, "At first I was struck with how her voice boomed—I would start to shake. She *whispered* in the library. I was shocked." Ellen remembers Brown's constant need to be busy; when she was not reading or bird-watching, she loved playing Scrabble or cards or doing needlework—badly. Holly and Ellen remember Brown as "so clean she squeeked," with her nails always manicured, not polished, and hair always "beautiful, curly, perfect," but in a net, like she was "afraid to let it loose." That seemed to symbolize her, a person who was "very bold in some ways, very reticent in others." It seemed she was always "trying to hold herself in." Others of Brown's young friends confirm the sisters' recollections; some attribute her bluntness to her need to build up momentum before speaking in order to overcome her shyness.[40]

Brown's interest in religion—even if not in a "system of theology"—manifested itself in her membership in Bartlesville's St. Luke's Episcopal Church, where she joined her parents as a member in 1919, immediately after her arrival in the community. It also resulted in her teaching a series of classes on comparative religions for young adults in a program called the University of Life. Co-sponsored by the Christian (Disciples of Christ), Methodist, and Presbyterian churches, the YMCA, and the YWCA, the University of Life ran two courses concurrently in the spring of 1946, Brown's and one on "Minority Problems" taught by Douglass principal Roosevelt Gracey. Brown's talk on books about religion for the Oklahoma Library Association also suggests that she considered religion an area of special interest or expertise.[41]

Brown was elected secretary of the OLA in 1920, less than a year after she became Bartlesville librarian. After a stint as treasurer in 1926, she was elected president for 1931. In November 1931, in the deepening days of the depression, Brown delivered a presidential address to her colleagues at their annual conference in the southwestern Oklahoma city of Weatherford. She commented that in Bartlesville, as in all Oklahoma, library use surged in the depression as unemployed people sought means to learn new job skills, recreational reading to fill idle hours, or simply a place to keep out of the weather. In the year in which she spoke, for example, Brown reported that the library's collection of 25,062 volumes enjoyed a circulation of 193,765, or 13.19 items for every one of the 14,763 people in her service area. Brown urged librarians to "reduce to a minimum worry about lost books" and "other red tape" so as to encourage the many who did not "make use of their right to library service." Rather than simply be "bureaus of information," libraries should also provide "recreational culture suited to all needs," she said.[42]

In that regard Brown practiced what she preached. She announced the acquisition of John Steinbeck's controversial *Grapes of Wrath* soon after its 1939 publication. During the depression she kept the library open and functioning, even when its income sank to just over $3,700 for the year. She prided herself on providing useful materials for unemployed men as well as for housewives and children. Said one former Bartlesville resident who became an academic librarian, "She was never a mere 'keeper of the books,' but rather one always interested in 'having books worn out in use.'" Not only was her library "a public service institution," he said, but Brown was a "moulder of public opinion." In a 1932 newspaper article Brown described the library's users and uses on a typical day: 240 adults and 116 children checked out a total of 792 books. Some of the eighty-two readers who sat at the library's oak tables sampled everything from newspapers and magazines to poetry and mysteries. A "Negro boy" read *Luck, Your Silent Partner*; two girls wanted the Damon and Pythias story "to be used in church work"; a club woman wanted a "humorous literary introduction"; a "Negro girl wanted Robert Frost's poems." What Brown chose to report supported her vision of the library as both a repository of information and a source of wholesome recreation.[43]

It also reveals an early and unusual commitment to allowing African Americans to use the Bartlesville Public Library, an apparently growing commitment to racial equality on which Brown eventually felt compelled to act even outside the library. Perhaps in another time and another place this commitment would have raised eyebrows, caused comment, or even garnered praise. But in the charged postwar Bartlesville world, with changes impinging on and appearing to threaten the social order that ensured so many white Bartians a comfortable life supported by the manual labor of black residents, it was a commitment that would lead to charges of subversion and of exposing the young people she cherished to harmful ideas.

It is hard to explain why Brown, who had spent most of her adult life in Bartlesville, developed a commitment to racial justice that would not only lead her to end segregation in the library but also take her out of the library and into controversy. Those who worked for her, like James Henderson, attributed it to her voracious reading habits, which exposed her to liberal ideas. Brown herself, in a letter to the *Library Journal* in 1961, while the American Library Association was considering what actions it should take to help end library segregation, attributed her commitment to her reading of Richard Wright's 1945 *Black Boy*. Referring to the passage in which Wright recounts having to pretend to get books for a white man in order to use the library, Brown wrote, "How can a librarian read it and not be influenced, and how can anyone fail to see that freedom to read must include all who have that desire?"[44]

But Brown's growing activism on behalf of civil rights—beginnings of which we see evidence as early as the 1932 news clipping and Elmo Olson's 1939 letter—no doubt had other roots as well.

THE COMMITTEE ON THE PRACTICE OF DEMOCRACY

Among the roots of Brown's activism may have been the School of Library Service of Columbia University, which she attended one or more summers during the 1930s. While there, she was probably exposed to Helen E. Haines, author of the highly acclaimed text on book selection, *Living with Books*, and a fierce advocate of intellectual freedom, who taught summer school at Columbia for nearly a decade beginning in 1937. Also on the faculty for several summers beginning in 1935 was Ernestine Rose, an expert on library services to African Americans. Another of the roots of Brown's interest in civil rights most certainly was the influence of Don Sheridan, the young, liberal minister of the First Christian Church who was a member of Bartlesville's library board and often engaged Brown in lively discussions about current events. Sheridan's First Christian Church was a chief sponsor of the University of Life series for which Brown and Gracey were teachers. During and just after World War II Sheridan and his wife, Ida Helen, formed a group with Fred and Betty Frey, Odie and Leo McReynolds, and George and Katrina Cade—all associated with Phillips Petroleum's research and development—who were inspired by their friendship with refugee scientist Gerhardt Gerson and his wife, Tove, to pack and send CARE packages to war-ravaged Europe. As the circle of liberal friends, sometimes including Brown, worked together on the CARE packages, they talked about the war against Nazi Germany, the horrible death camps, and the evil of race hatred. In 1946, spurred by the contradiction of denying basic rights on account of race to men who had fought in a war to end racism, Sheridan and others in the group joined with Brown and members of the African-American community to found the Committee on the Practice of Democracy (COPD) in an effort to improve "relations among people of all races; more particularly, to foster improvement of conditions arising out of discrimination based on race, creed, or color."[45]

An article in the February 1946 *Survey Graphic* describing the Congress of Racial Equality convinced Brown that a connection with CORE would benefit the COPD. Brown was attracted by CORE's philosophy of nonviolent direct action to confront racism. The rest of the group agreed. Thus the COPD became the only CORE affiliate south of the Mason-Dixon line. Sheridan was president, Gracey vice president, and Brown secretary. The lineup of officers reflected the group's understanding of the social order in which it operated: a white man was chairman; neither a black man nor a woman ever filled that role for the COPD. The group was well aware of the difficulties it faced in working to end discrimination, both those based in law and those based in custom. In a letter to CORE executive secretary George Houser, Brown outlined major problems of the African-American community that the group hoped to address: lack of employment for men, the inability of African Americans to get mortgages, inferior medical care, and exclusion from most recreational facilities. The twenty members' first major projects were a survey to determine the "complete economic and social status" of the African-American community, a cleanup campaign, and a health clinic.[46]

By the time of the COPD's first annual report, Leo McReynolds, a Phillips chemist, had replaced Sheridan as president. Apparently, in a foreshadowing of events to come, the Sheridans had left the community in 1947 after dissension erupted in their church when they entertained an African-American musician who had performed in the city. The other COPD officers remained the same. T. P. Scott, superintendent of the Taft School for Negro Deaf, Blind, and Orphans, was joined by Jan Nelson, the wife of a Phillips researcher, on the executive committee. Now numbering twenty-eight, the group met once a month in the summer and twice a month during the rest of the year. In September 1947 Brown told Houser that the group had been meeting socially at the homes of white members without the neighbors being "unduly shocked." The "community at large" was "cooperating very favorably," with less negative reaction than expected, she claimed.[47]

In fact, there was impressive cooperation on several projects. Frey, a Phillips research and development manager, bought paint to be used in the cleanup of the ramshackle houses in which many African Americans lived. He aided another project to secure a doctor for the community by quietly helping to purchase a building that the new doctor, J. B. Dixon, and his family could use as both home and office. Dixon arrived in the community in March 1948.[48]

Volunteers from the Bartlesville YWCA also joined in the cleanup and in setting up a health clinic. At Brown's invitation the YWCA co-sponsored with the COPD and the American Association of University Women a February 1948 interracial conference that "provided stimulating lectures by Negro and white university professors"—among them Melvin Tolson of Langston—and provoked discussion of the problems of segregated education, stimulated by the recent Supreme Court decision in the *Sipuel* case. The YWCA's cooperation with the COPD as well as its other efforts at interracial activity were encouraged by national leadership. In 1946 the national YWCA adopted an Interracial Charter that pledged members to work for racial justice. Its 1949 book, *Toward Better Race Relations*, drew from the experience of representative chapters to develop guidelines other groups could follow. The Bartlesville YWCA board, however, was committed only to a very limited interracial program. They had sponsored a Y-Teen group for

Douglass School girls since 1932; its officers and leaders had participated in the intergroup council since that same year.[49]

In addition to YWCA members, some members of the AAUW provided "nurse aide, clerical, and taxi assistance" for the 1947 health clinic and, working with African-American women, made draperies and surgical gowns for Dixon's office. The same group took a leading role in the interracial conference on segregated education. Their willingness to help grew out of the Racial Problems Study Group formed in the Bartlesville AAUW branch in 1945 by Lois Ogilvie, wife of a Phillips engineer. Study group members shared a belief that segregation—"basically undemocratic and impractical"—was a nationwide problem that educated women could help to address. Unlike the YWCA, the Bartlesville study group was ahead of its national organization, which postponed coming to grips with racial discrimination, and its state organization, which declined to adopt the Bartlesville group's proposal for a statewide study of racial problems following their successful model. A presentation by two African-American women had convinced the group that "with the proper education and a reasonable opportunity for self-expression, the Negro has much to offer." Motivated by their exposure, Ogilvie and several others joined the COPD.[50]

Ogilvie became very active with Brown and COPD president McReynolds's wife, Odie, in the months following the interracial meeting on segregated education. As Gov. Roy J. Turner rapped "agitators" who, he charged, jeopardized gains made by Oklahoma's "minorities," Ogilvie and Brown attended a Norman conference featuring CORE's Houser and field worker, Bayard Rustin. The gathering was designed to assess and encourage campus and state support for the desegregation of the University of Oklahoma. On their return home they began a new project. As Brown explained to Houser, she had been conducting a story hour for children at Douglass School with the help of "a Negro woman" since the previous fall. Now she and some of her COPD colleagues had decided to try an interracial story hour at the library. "Having been librarian here for so many years," she said, "I seldom ask permission to do anything." However, "this seemed so controversial" that Gracey insisted on getting the city manager's approval. When one city official after another declined to make a decision, Ogilvie and Odie McReynolds approached the city commissioners and "met with violent rebuffs." The project was abandoned. City officials objected to integrating the story hour because, they said, it would break the school law that mandated the separation of the races in education.[51]

The doctrine of "separate but equal" facilities for African Americans and whites complicated and exacerbated the South's—and Oklahoma's—rural nature and poverty, with the result that it retarded the development of schools and other cultural institutions such as libraries. The region's meager resources were spread thin in attempting to provide dual educational systems and numbers of other duplicates—water fountains, rest rooms, railroad waiting rooms, parks, and the like. While the majority white educational system fared poorly under Jim Crow, the minority African-American educational system suffered abysmally. Without education, and the felt need to continue that education as adults or to share it with children, citizens usually did not put libraries high on their list of desired civic improvements, or if they did, they found little tax base ready to support libraries. When southern communities did begin to provide funding for libraries in about 1895, those libraries were strictly segregated. Like the rest of Oklahoma's libraries, and indeed, like other southern libraries, the Bartlesville Public Library was originally intended for use by whites only.[52]

SOUTHERN LIBRARIES

As Eliza Atkins Gleason reported in *The Southern Negro and the Public Library*, in 1939 only 99 of 774 southern public library units provided service for African Americans. And although library services for whites were far from adequate, those for African Americans were marked by cast-off books, short hours, poor locations, and uncertain and minuscule budgets.[53] In 1946–47, when the Southeastern Library Association completed its cooperative survey of library services in nine southeastern states, two-thirds of African Americans in those states were still without any access to library services.[54] Frequently the public library served whites for many years before any kind of library service was available for African Americans, in spite of the fact that they, too, paid the taxes that supported the library. In Jackson, Mississippi, for example, although one librarian, Pearl Sneed, sometimes allowed an African American to use books from the public library in her office, there was no general access to library services for African Americans until 1951, nearly forty years after the 1914 founding of the Jackson Public Library. Jackson's main library was not desegregated until college students staged a "read-in" ten years later. The Mississippi city's situation was not unique.[55]

When publicly funded library service to African Americans did occur, it took one of several forms: an independent library; a separate, segregated branch of a city library; a book deposit station; or service (usually limited) at the main library.[56] Each of these forms was present among the fifteen Oklahoma public library units reported as offering services to African Americans in 1948.[57]

Guthrie's independent, tax-supported Excelsior Library, founded in 1906, the year before statehood, was the state's oldest library serving African Americans. In 1948 it reported a circulation of 25,378 items, with a book stock of only 2,810 volumes and an income of $1,720.[58] Muskogee's active Wheatley branch began in 1914 as an independent library, but in 1929, after a fire, Cora Case Porter, the white librarian, persuaded the city to support the library as a separate branch.[59] Aside from branches in Oklahoma's two largest cities, Oklahoma City and Tulsa, no other libraries—except the Women's Industrial Club Library in the all-black town of Boley—were reported to serve African Americans by the end of World War I, and Tulsa's Greenwood Library burned in the wanton destruction visited on the thriving African-American district in the race riots in 1921. The Greenwood Library was reestablished, however, and by 1948 boasted a collection of 4,700 volumes and a circulation of 58,702.[60]

Okmulgee built the first branch library building specifically for African Americans, investing the princely sum of $18,000 in 1923. Although Muskogee's Wheatley Library gave up its independent status to become a branch of the city's Carnegie Library in 1929, the decade following the Stock Market crash saw no new African-American branches develop.[61] WPA funds, which made possible several community libraries in Oklahoma during the depression, enhanced African-American access to library services chiefly through the "village reading room" or library service projects. These delivered small collections of books—by bookmobile, pack horse, and even rowboat—to groups of readers in communities throughout the state. According to the project's last state supervisor, Mary T. Asfahl, "Negro civic and federated clubs were eager to accept the opportunity" to establish some sort of library service.[62] The *Oklahoma Library Commission Report* for 1938 listed eleven "branches" in as many counties, serving two thousand African Americans. The historically black towns of Boley and Taft were among those served, as were Ardmore, which had 175 "registered readers," and Dewey, the second town founded by Jacob Bartles, just five miles northeast of Bartlesville. The next year twenty-five "colored service units" were reported. In 1940, under WPA auspices, Ponca City's African-American Lit-Phy-So Club and white librarian Gertrude Sterba established the Community Branch of the Ponca City library to serve the African-American community of Bartlesville's neighbor to the west. When the library service projects ended in 1942, several of the branches launched through WPA efforts continued.[63] By 1948 African-American branches had been added in Ardmore, Cushing, Pawhuska, Sapulpa (started earlier in a school), Stillwater, Shawnee, and Wewoka.[64]

In the 1920s the third type of library service to African Americans, book deposit stations, were established in the separate schools in Enid (1922), Sapulpa (1923), and Chickasha (1926). Like most such deposit stations, they had little support and were open only when school was in session, making them minimally useful. In 1935–36, in fact, the sum of only $10.50 was expended on the Sapulpa station.[65] Fortunately, by 1948 Sapulpa African Americans had a branch library, which reported a circulation of more than 17,000 to a user population of just 1,609. The same year, however, Chickasha and Enid still served mostly schoolchildren and had tiny collections. Chickasha, however, did provide a salary for the teacher-librarian to keep the library open four hours daily in the summer.[66]

The fourth form of service, at the main town or city library, is difficult to measure, because it may well have been unofficial and unrecorded. Both Tulsa and Oklahoma City probably gave some service to African Americans at the main library by 1948; in 1954 they and Norman's main branch provided full service, according to Anna Holden's "The Color Line in Southern Libraries."[67] Even the term "full service," however, would have been open to interpretation. According to Gleason, some main libraries in the South allowed African Americans access to their collections under "special circumstances." A teacher, for example, might be allowed to do research if there was a place separate from the main reading room where she could sit. Or a reader might be allowed to check books out with special permission but could not sit in the library and read.[68] In 1941, however, Gleason reported only Ponca City, where the University of Wisconsin Library School graduate Gertrude Sterba was librarian, as giving any kind of service at the main library.[69]

Nevertheless, evidence points to some kind of service to African Americans at the Bartlesville Public Library at least since the 1920s. Brown recorded borrowers' names in a register; she identified the small number of African-American borrowers as "colored" (in red typewriter ribbon) following their addresses. She may not have been impartial in her service, however. Although she apparently cooperated to a certain extent with Douglass School teachers to provide supplementary reading material for classes, one member of the African-American community, Bernice Brown, has negative memories of Ruth Brown from the time she was a schoolgirl in the late 1920s and early 1930s. "When we'd go to the library," she recalled, "she acted always like—you had the card, but she didn't want you to get the book." She described a common practice:

African Americans using the main public library were not allowed to sit down and read but had to get their books promptly and leave. Another graduate of Douglass School, Marie Littles, was paid by the National Youth Corps in 1936 to work at the Douglass School library under its first librarian. She recalls selecting books from the Bartlesville Public Library to be used at the school. On at least one occasion, however, when another student went to pick up the books Littles had selected, they could not be found. Although there was no way to confirm her natural suspicions that they were purposely misplaced, Littles recalls that the majority of the books that the Douglass School library used came from Booker T. Washington School in Tulsa. Rose Bean Hicks, a Douglass graduate of 1956, on the contrary, remembers a very different picture of Ruth Brown's service to African Americans. "When we were coming up," she recalled, "the library was the only public facility that was integrated." Although she could not go to the movies or "do anything else," she had used the library "all through [her] schooling."[70] While it is difficult to draw conclusions from the memories of three individuals, it appears that Brown provided increasing levels of service at the Bartlesville Public Library over three decades. In addition, she appears to have made a significant shift in her attitude toward African-American users by the mid-1940s. By 1950 the library's periodical holdings included *Negro Digest* and *Ebony*, titles not found in any of the surrounding small city libraries, and Brown was actively fighting Jim Crow in the library and out.[71]

Although the shift in her racial attitude and actions was far more dramatic and complete than that of most librarians, Brown seems to reflect gradually changing attitudes among librarians throughout the South. In 1948 Emily Miller Danton of the Birmingham Public Library surveyed twenty-one public libraries to determine the level of service provided to African Americans as well as the attitude toward African-American staff members. She reported the results in an article liberally illustrated with pictures of ardent African-American library users in Birmingham and Atlanta. Danton found that nineteen of the twenty-one libraries surveyed did provide service to African Americans and that the same number employed African Americans, for the most part at separate branches. Although most allowed limited use of the main library by African Americans, one placed no restrictions and one allowed no use at all. Librarians as a group clearly were not prepared to throw over local law or custom, but a number of those surveyed seemed to reveal a growing awareness of the need for change. Said one, for example, "I have about come to the conclusion that it would be much better for all concerned if we removed segregation laws in libraries, universities, and other cultural institutions." In that same year Clarence Graham, director, announced that the Louisville, Kentucky, Free Public Library would open its main library without restriction to African Americans, thus becoming, according to him, the first southern library to "open its doors to Negroes." Graham, who was the president of the ALA when Brown lost her job, pushed for an investigation of the circumstances.[72]

The literature of the library profession also hinted at other events that were affecting librarians, including Brown, nationwide. In 1947 Alice G. Higgins, then chairman of the ALA's Intellectual Freedom Committee, reported in the *American Library Association Bulletin* that the ALA had been asked to inform President Truman's Civil Rights Committee what it was doing in the area of civil liberties. Higgins urged her librarian colleagues to study the committee's report, *To Secure These Rights*, when it was published. If she read library publications, and there is evidence that she did, Brown also would have found an increasing interest in materials, especially children's books, that gave positive and realistic views of minority people and fostered intergroup understanding. She would also have found many warnings regarding growing attacks on books and libraries, the most notable of which was the New York City Schools' ban of the *Nation* from school libraries.[73]

Although she seemed aware of the local and national danger signals, Brown was prepared to integrate story times in defiance of the city commission, but Gracey dissuaded her. He said that Bartlesville was "too far South, and too small a town," for the direct action advocated by CORE to be feasible, Brown reported to Houser. "What difference should that make?" she queried plaintively. Both

Holly and Ellen were grown and gone. "Just now I have no family to consider. I know as your material points out, what the consequences might be but I know too that as long as we have segregation and worse life isn't good." "It might mean," she concluded, "that I would no longer be Bartlesville librarian, but I've had that fun for thirty years anyway."[74] Gracey's caution prevailed at this time, but Brown's willingness to risk the consequences of a confrontation over segregation would ultimately split the city and draw national attention to the imperfections of "America's ideal family center."

CHAPTER TWO

HASTENING THE DAY

There are many who find it difficult to live in such a city. But this should hasten the day.

—ELIZABETH DAVIS,
YWCA Executive Director, in the 1950 *Annual Report*

"I must talk to Mr. Gracey again and again, for as he said today, 'I have been in this thing all my life and you are still only on the edge,'" Ruth Brown wrote to George Houser as the summer of 1948 turned the corner toward autumn. Her urge to action dueled with her respect for Douglass School principal Roosevelt T. Gracey's years of suffering and striving. He appealed to her to stay the long course of educating the Bartlesville community rather than become a martyr to the cause of direct action on behalf of racial justice. "He has promised to find some really big task for me," Brown concluded.[1]

Ruth Brown was not the only one in turmoil that summer; it seemed as if everyone was aware that the times demanded the performance of really big tasks. In July Southern Democrats, angered over their party's civil rights campaign plank, walked out of its convention and nominated South Carolina's Strom Thurmond to carry the standard for the newly formed States' Rights, or Dixiecrat, party. A few days later another group of Democrats, dissatisfied by the slow pace of change, formed the Progressive party and nominated former Vice President Henry Wallace for the presidency. Less than two weeks after the divisive convention that nominated him for his first full term as president, Harry Truman ordered an end to segregation in the military and unsuccessfully pressed Congress to pass civil rights legislation. When the former communist Whittaker Chambers named Alger Hiss, who had served in the Roosevelt administration, as a onetime party member, the summer's simmering fear of internal communism began to boil. CORE, meeting in convention, found it necessary to adopt a resolution opposing "any degree of Communist influence" in its affiliates. As Houser pointed out, in resisting "jimcrowism" CORE members were sometimes unjustly labeled communists because they were "bucking the main currents of our culture."[2]

The ALA also had a convention that summer, also felt the heat, and also bucked the main currents of the culture. The ALA centered its conference on the theme of intellectual freedom and resistance to censorship. In addition, it adopted a strengthened Library Bill of Rights, the profession's pledge to develop collections that reflect a diversity of views on controversial topics and to fight censorship; established state committees on intellectual freedom; and adopted a resolution opposing the use of loyalty programs in libraries. And its Intellectual Freedom Committee immediately joined the battle to restore the *Nation* to the shelves of the New York Public School libraries from which it had been removed because a series of articles by Paul Blanshard were said to be hostile to Catholicism.[3]

The Bartlesville COPD, meanwhile—successful in attracting an African-American doctor, J. B. Dixon, and unsuccessful in integrating the library story hour—caught its breath. The composition of the group clearly revealed the changes that had been taking place in the Bartlesville community and in the role of women in challenging Bartlesville's status quo. The forty-five members listed in the 1948 Membership Directory (of course the membership varied from time to time) were almost evenly divided between whites and African Americans. Among the twenty-two African-

Faculty of Douglass School, 1951. Front row, left to right: Roosevelt T. Gracey, Alpha Pierce, Nasira Ledbetter, Geraldine Luck, Luvenia Brown, Clara Cooke, Ira O. Garcia. Back row, left to right: Harry McClasky, Mary Ellen Street, Nellie Gracey, Frances Madison, Alice McCreary, Velma Brown, Horace W. Johnson. Courtesy Bartlesville Public Library.

American members, Douglass School teachers were conspicuous by their presence, making up nearly one-third. Led by relative newcomers Roosevelt and Nellie Gracey, the group also included longtime teachers Luvenia Brown, Ira O. Garcia, Alpha Pierce, and George H. Johnson and newcomers Mary Ellen Street and Clara Cooke. All but Street and Cooke had also been members of the NAACP during its earlier efforts to secure better jobs for African Americans. In addition to the new doctor, domestics, laborers, small business persons, and ministers made up the remainder of the African Americans. W. H. Jones was the proprietor of the Golden Pumpkin Café on Santa Fe; William James was a grocer; member Birdie Harris's husband, Joe, was the bellman at the Burlingame Hotel; and Ada Bean's husband, William, was a teamster.

Birdie Harris and Ada Bean probably worked as domestics. Henry Moore may have been a carpenter; D. C. Green was a laborer for Lair Plumbing; Lucille Black and Betty Jackson were maids. Both Clifford Gibbs, janitor at Douglass School, and his wife, Sadie, were members. The Reverend Allen Martin worked part-time as a farmer. The Reverend H. Scott, of the Greater First Baptist Church, and his wife belonged. Ten of the twenty-two appear to have arrived in Bartlesville in the 1940s; half were women.[4]

Among the twenty-three white members, eighteen (most of the white and two-fifths of the total membership) were Phillips employees or their spouses; ten of the eighteen had arrived in Bartlesville since 1940 (others had arrived in the late 1930s). There were four couples: Fred and Betty Frey were the old-timers; Leo and Odie McReynolds, who had arrived in 1939 and 1941, respectively, George and Katrina Cade, and George and Janet Fairley were among the newcomers. Both Fred Frey and Leo McReynolds were managers in sections of the research and development arm of Phillips in which COPD members Francis E. "Frank" Condon, George Cade, George Fairley, and Henry L. McMurray worked. Meta Jones's husband, John Paul, was a patent attorney and George Cade's immediate supervisor. All the other women were connected through their husbands with Phillips's research and development effort. Among the other Phillips spouses were Lois Ogilvie, founder of the AAUW Racial Problems Study Group, and four AAUW (and probably study group) members: Janet Fairley, Imogene Mahoney, Helen Neidert, and Priscilla Bearer. Margaret Varvel, along with Katrina Cade, was part of the chamber group that practiced at Brown's home; both taught music as volunteers at Douglass School. Emeline Hays and Argye Briggs completed the list of women whose husbands were attached to Phillips.[5]

Ruth Brown and four other white women were not connected with Phillips. According to what can be gleaned from city directories, Dorothy Harvey was a student whose father worked for the other oil company, Cities Service. Esther Carlton was an English teacher in the Bartlesville School System. Mrs. Esther Brigham, executive secretary of the American Red Cross, and Elizabeth

"Betty" Davis, executive director of the YWCA, rounded out the white membership. Both Brigham and Davis had come into the community within the decade.[6]

Thus of the forty-five members, eighteen, or two-fifths, were connected with Phillips research and development in some way; and twenty-eight, or almost two-thirds, were women. Most of the white women were motivated, at least in part, both by religious beliefs that stressed "acceptance of people who were different from [them]" and by their experience fighting discrimination against women through women's groups, according to Lois Ogilvie. Twelve of the women, almost one-fourth of the group, were Phillips employees' wives. Twenty of the members, or a little less than half, had moved to Bartlesville since 1940, with several coming not long before. Some members, such as Fred and Betty Frey, were not active participants but supported projects such as the cleanup campaign and Dixon's recruitment. The group's leadership was drawn mostly from among the newcomers. The president was always a white man, at Gracey's insistence. "They have never liked the idea of a woman president," chafed Brown, chosen corresponding secretary in 1949. That year Frank Condon was president, Gracey remained vice president, and Douglass teachers Clara Cooke and Mary Ellen Street were recording secretary and treasurer, respectively. Lois Ogilvie, Sadie Gibbs, Henry McMurray, and Robert Davis constituted the 1949–50 board.[7]

After their defeat on the story hour, Brown and the other active members apparently contented themselves with a less controversial agenda for the remainder of the year. Early in 1949 Brown asked Houser for help gathering materials for an educational exhibit on "Negro culture from Africa to today" and informed him that a visit by CORE field worker Manuel Talley had given the group a badly needed boost. In June Brown found herself the eldest of those at the CORE national conference, attended by forty representatives of groups from Cincinnati, Cleveland, and Yellow Springs, Ohio; Chicago and Evanston, Illinois; Minneapolis, Minnesota; St. Louis, Missouri; and various New York locations. As she prepared her report to the July meeting of the COPD, which was to be held in her backyard, she reflected that although she arrived at the conference discouraged, she left feeling that they "must do more, but . . . had made a good beginning."[8]

THE UNRAVELING

In the summer of 1949 the fabric of the good beginning began to fray a bit, as some differences over philosophy and level and kind of activity began to surface within the COPD's membership. Brown asked Houser to "answer a question which is tearing our Group": Should the group fight the establishment of a segregated park or, as Brown put it, "sanction the half loaf that so many whites seem to think is enough"? A newspaper article suggesting that land had been purchased for an African-American park had sparked a meeting that exposed differences not only between whites and African Americans but also between the more conservative and the more activist members of the group. One faction wanted to get what it could from the white establishment while the other did not want to accept another segregated facility. Such conflicts were not unusual for interracial social action groups, and Gracey acknowledged that fact on one occasion when he compared Brown to "the old abolitionists." Brown, apparently oblivious to the implied criticism that she was imposing her vision on others without their consent, embraced the comparison, responding, "They didn't sit still and fold their hands, nor do I intend to." Although Houser tried to address the pros and cons of compromise on the park issue, he clearly did not want to tell the group what to do. He did, however, urge the COPD not to invest most of its energy in securing a new segregated facility but in "the kind of activity that will lead ultimately to the ending of segregation."[9]

Ruth Brown took his words to heart, as she always did, and acted on them without consulting the group as a whole. Several times in 1949 or early 1950 she took Jean Jones, a recent arrival in the African-American community, to worship with her at St. Luke's Episcopal Church, which Brown attended irregularly. Jones was an Episcopalian, and there was no other Episcopal church for her to attend, but some of the parishioners were very displeased. Elizabeth Chamberlin, the city's public health physician and a leading church member, objected "violently." Chamberlin thought Jones "should be allowed to worship," Brown said some time later, "but must sit by herself." Bringing Jones to church with her was part of Brown's "pushy" integrationist attitude, which church members disliked, according to the Episcopal pastor Richard Rodgers. Chamberlin and others were so incensed at Jones's presence that they wrote to the bishop of the diocese of Rochester, New York, from which Jones had come, to verify her claim to Episcopal church membership. Although it was confirmed, they also spread a rumor, which Jones heard from some of her friends who worked as maids for white women, that Jones was "a communist come down from New York" to create trouble.[10]

Similar rumors about Dr. Dixon were beginning to circulate. It did not go without notice—especially by Preston Gaddis, the Nash automobile dealer and Americanism leader in the local James H. Teel Post 105 of the American Legion—that Brown herself, with her "accelerated" ideas about race relations, was Dixon's patient and that she had taken her daughter, "a very beautiful white girl," to him on one occasion. Lois Ogilvie's neighbors certainly noticed when Dixon's daughter attended her son Johnny's birthday party.[11]

It was a time ripe for rumors, as fears of domestic communism reached new intensity. A U.S. Justice Department employee, Judith Coplon, had been arrested in March for spying for the Soviet Union, and Alger Hiss was in the midst of his trials for perjury regarding accusations that he had passed State Department documents to the Soviets. In September 1949 President Truman announced that the Soviets had exploded a nuclear device, intensifying concerns about spies within the defense industry. In the same month a Peekskill, New York, concert featuring the famous African-American singer Paul Robeson—for many the embodiment of the conflation of integrationists and communists—ended in an American Legion–led riot in which more than one hundred fifty concertgoers, mostly Jews and African Americans, were injured.

The Peekskill riots, as they were called, seemed proof positive to many in Bartlesville that Robeson was a communist and that those who, like Robeson, favored integration were also communists. There were rumors that pictures of Robeson were on display in the library and in Douglass School. The trials of the eleven leaders of the U.S. Communist party at Foley Square in New York City dragged on for nine months, with the prosecution spinning tales to a large newspaper audience, as well as to the jury, of communist subterfuge, conspiracy to commit industrial sabotage, and deliberate playing on the grievances of minority groups.[12]

As 1949 turned into 1950, conversation in Bartlesville dwelled on these national events but also on the changes evident in the community. In early 1949 Frank Phillips had left any active management of the company he founded; since his wife had died the year before, he had spent a good part of the time at Woolaroc supervising the building of a mausoleum (complete with telephone) where the two would be buried. His absence had not kept Phillips Petroleum from advancing, however. In 1950 it moved into the nuclear age when the U.S. government chose Phillips to operate its reactor in Idaho. The Presbyterian church was preparing to break ground for a new building. YWCA executive director and COPD member Betty Davis looked forward to the January dedication of the YWCA's new building, just two blocks from the library; many of Bartlesville's most established residents had contributed to the building fund. All these things boded well for the wealthy city, despite national tensions.[13]

On January 15, 1950, the YWCA invited the entire community to an open house to see its new building. Among the more than twenty-five hundred people attending were about thirty-five members of the Douglass Y-Teen groups, operated by the YWCA since 1927. The YWCA's extensive weekly calendar for the building, published in the following Sunday's paper, included the meetings of the two African-American Y-Teen groups. Davis later reported, "A storm of protest was quickly whipped up by a few individuals"—apparently a loosely knit coalition of members of

The YMCA and the new YWCA, Johnstone Avenue, Bartlesville, Oklahoma, early 1950s. Courtesy Archives, Phillips Petroleum Company.

the DAR, the UDC, the conservative Republican women's group Pro-America, and superpatriots within the American Legion. At a hastily called meeting the YWCA board of directors affirmed its decision to allow the Douglass girls to meet in the new building, although it disallowed any social events including boys. At a subsequent meeting a few days later the board approved a statement to be presented at the annual meeting on January 30 that emphasized the long-standing nature of the interracial program and stated that "the only change is in the scheduled place of meeting for all Y-Teens." Despite the attendance of some of the YWCA's most vocal critics, the annual meeting went smoothly.[14]

BROTHERHOOD MONTH

Just two days later the COPD launched its February 1950 observance of Brotherhood Month. Much to the COPD's surprise, president Frank Condon had succeeded in placing CORE's "Call to Action for Brotherhood Month" in the February 1 evening *Examiner-Enterprise*. The advertisement urged "those who believe in interracial brotherhood to accept responsibility for their convictions" and refuse to use segregated facilities during the month. The ad's appearance disturbed some COPD members, who were already "pretty afraid" for their positions at Phillips. Brown, however, exulted that "the real CORE members" had been thrilled "that at last people [would] really see what we stand for."[15]

In fact, the very next day, "without much encouragement" from the COPD, Brown and two young African-American teachers, Mary Ellen Street and Clara Cooke, "decided they were ready for another step." That evening Brown recounted their "step" to Houser in a detached third person. At about 5:00 P.M. "the three" went downtown to Hull's, "the largest drugstore that serve[d] food," seated themselves in one of the red leather booths near the back, and waited. The employees and the customers stared at them, but they "they were perfectly nonchalant." For about ten minutes it seemed they would be ignored, but after some "frantic telephoning" on the part of the cashier, the headwaiter approached. "Sorry," he said, "but we have called the owner and he says we cannot serve you." The trio had planned their response according to CORE guidelines, Brown reported. "So the white person said, 'Why?'" The waiter, now "slightly belligerent," answered that he "didn't ask why[,] for he owns the store." Brown, Street, and Cooke left, resolved to repeat the action at other drugstores if "repercussions from this . . . [weren't] too violent."[16]

Almost as an afterthought, Brown told Houser that the COPD had scheduled a public appearance by Bayard Rustin (who later would become one of A. Philip Randolph's lieutenants during the 1963 March on Washington) on February 13 at Jefferson School auditorium. However, an "Anti group" that had been screening speakers in the community's Town Hall series opposed Rustin's appearance on the grounds that he had refused to fight in World War II because of segregation. Their protest would probably just prove to be good advertising, Brown guessed. She was optimistic: "You can see people are thinking and that makes some act."[17]

Act they did. On the day of Rustin's scheduled speech, the school board, polled by telephone, voted five to two against allowing a school auditorium to be used for "this particular speaker" and canceled the COPD's contract. The public event dwindled to a gathering of COPD stalwarts at the home of George and Katrina Cade, members of the Phillips "family." There Rustin told the group that a CORE chapter was probably not possible in Bartlesville, confirming both Condon's and Gracey's feelings that Bartlesville was too far South and too small a town for direct action to work. Although Brown had already commented to Houser that the white members "were becoming afraid of their shadows" and thus the number of active whites had shrunk to five, for Brown the group's demise was not welcome.[18]

Nor did she welcome the attention she received a few days later, in spite of her earlier realization that direct action on behalf of integration might have repercussions. On February 16—little more than a week after Sen. Joseph R. McCarthy burst onto the national scene with his accusations that some indefinite number of State Department employees were "card-carrying" communists— a group of about forty citizens appeared before the Bartlesville City Commission to charge Brown with supplying "subversive" materials at the public library. "To illustrate the extent of sub- version believed to be in Library affairs," they introduced Burton Hull to describe Brown asking for service at Hull's lunch counter with the "two young Negro teachers," Cooke and Street. When the mayor reminded the group that Brown's interracial activities were conducted on her own time and thus were her private concern, the group's leader, Mrs. Charles (Mae) Warren, wife of a Cities Service officer, brandished the *Nation* as further evidence of the subversive materials "filtering" unchecked from the Bartlesville Public Library. Warren apparently was firmly fixed in her belief that African Americans' struggle for civil rights was a "communist plot." At about this time she espoused and ostensibly proved her position in a pamphlet, "Documented Facts of the Growth of Communism in the United States," which she published with the sponsorship of the American Legion post. In it she also warned against communist infiltration in libraries. Without Brown in attendance, the startled library board president, Russell Davis, a junior officer in a savings and loan, promised to check on the charges. Despite his promise, Mayor R. H. Hudson agreed to allow Warren to name a group to examine the library independently. At least three of the group—Warren, Mrs. Bessie Smysor, and Mrs. Frank (Anne) Sissons—were simultaneously opposing the YWCA's interracial program.[19]

Others in the self-designated citizens' committee were Mrs. J. M. (Audrey) Ribble, Mrs. G. F. (Henryetta) Wills, Mrs. M. J. (Odonah) Kirwan, and W. D. McGinley. Warren's and Kirwan's husbands were both Cities Service officers; Ribble's and Sissons's husbands were Phillips engineers. Smysor was president of the Memorial Park Association, and Henryetta Wills's husband was a district superintendent of a local plant. McGinley, the only man on the committee, was the public utility manager and a member of both the American Legion and the Chamber of Commerce. Perhaps not coincidentally, three members of the group were members of the Episcopal church.[20]

The library board that met with the citizens' committee was a mixture of old and new Bartians. Davis's family had lived in the city since shortly after the turn of the century, as had the family of Richard Kane, a young attorney whose father was Phillips's corporate counsel. Mrs. Effie Freiburger's long-standing family business was insurance. Olga Beecher's husband was a Cities Service manager. The two newcomers were Phillips scientist George Cade, at whose home Rustin had been a guest, and Darlene Anderson Essary, the first woman attorney employed by Phillips. Essary had joined the board just the previous month, replacing Mrs. H. R. Straight, wife of the former head of Cities Service. Her daughter, Lois, the first woman attorney at Cities Service, and indeed in

Bartlesville, and a YWCA board member, had foreseen the controversy and advised her mother to resign.[21]

The meeting was quite civil. It began with a formal statement
by the citizens' committee outlining suggestions for an "appraisal"
of the library's purchases and a study of the city's library ordinance.
The committee suggested that the library board, which had
apparently been meeting at least annually to approve the budget,
meet more regularly and requested that Brown supply a list of all
titles purchased in the preceding year so that the committee could
evaluate them. "We are seeking only the most friendly relations
with the board members," the group insisted, and asked that
"feelings of antagonism" be forgotten. Nevertheless, the committee
urged that the basis for "personal criticisms" against Brown be
investigated by the board. The library board seemed anxious to
cooperate while affirming their view that the library should "effect
a reasonable balance between conflicting views on controversial
subjects."[22]

The two groups' next encounter, before the city commission on
March 6, was anything but civil. More than two hundred attended
the "stormy" session, which "overflowed" the commissioners' room
and had to be moved to the Civic Center ballroom. The citizens'
committee expressed dissatisfaction with the library board's alleged
"whitewash." It accused Brown of exposing Bartlesville's children
to subversive literature, literature that "created in the minds of the
reader doubts and mistrust of the form of government established
by the constitution of the United States of America," and of refusing
to remove *Soviet Russia Today* from the library. A number of heated
exchanges followed. When Robert Manuel, a Phillips engineer,
questioned the committee's qualifications to judge the library's
contents—they did not even have library cards—some of the crowd
yelled epithets and called for his removal. When he persisted Mayor
Hudson interrupted with what the newspaper called a "scathing
denunciation": "Who are you? What right have you to challenge
this group of respected citizens? Are you a Commie?" A "stunned
silence" followed—a reaction to Manuel's dreadful questions, said
the newspaper; a reaction to the mayor's "undemocratic means"

of stifling criticism, said a letter to the editor by Charles Varvel, another Phillips scientist in attendance. Two other Phillips researchers supporting the library, Anthony Andrews and Daniel Jones, also were verbally accosted. The mayor finally ordered the library board to conduct a thorough investigation of the library's collections and operations and authorized the citizens' committee to conduct a parallel investigation. E. S. Dunaway, the vice-mayor, ended the meeting with a brief oration on the dangers of communism. The library, he read, "should be a place where our youth will be thoroughly indoctrinated with the principles of Americanism, and where they will be protected from the teachings of subversive doctrines." All efforts at civility had ended. A campaign to purge the city of Brown and her sympathizers had begun. The weapon of choice was McCarthyist rhetoric; the ostensible aim was to defend the "impressionable mind of formative years" from "subversive propaganda," but, Brown wrote Houser, "everyone knows what they are really fighting and there has been one real battle."[23]

That night the battle had its moment of terror for Robert Manuel. The ugliness of the crowd was like nothing he had seen before. When he left the city commission meeting he ran all the way home to Choctaw Street, "afraid for his life," recalled the Reverend James Spivey of the First Presbyterian Church. Manuel called Spivey as soon as he got home and asked Spivey to stay with him and his family until he was sure there was no danger. Daniel Jones found the meeting extremely unsettling as well; people who he thought knew and liked him suddenly were calling him "Commie." According to his close friend William Nelson, Jones decided then and there to leave Bartlesville and soon accepted a teaching position at the University of Utah. Philip Lorenz of the Bureau of Mines Research Station in Bartlesville remembers the meeting as "the worst experience of [his] life."[24]

The library board attempted to circle its wagons and recruit reinforcements. Still trying to deflect attack, they removed the *Nation*, the *New Republic*, and *Soviet Russia Today* to locked storage. In so doing they anticipated the advice of Lucy Ann Babcock, assistant to Mrs. J. R. Dale of the Oklahoma Library Commission. "When the matter of censorship arises," Babcock responded to Davis's request for help, "we usually recommend that the questionable material be withdrawn from the shelves and either withheld from public use entirely or restricted to specific requests from responsible borrowers for a period sufficient to quiet the alarm." But the board's attempt to calm the situation while they prepared for their next report was for nought. On Thursday, March 9, the *Examiner-Enterprise* pictured the sequestered magazines on the front page. On top of the pile of *Nations* and *New Republics* were two books, one in its dust jacket and without apparent library markings. The title of one, *The Russians,* was clearly visible; its subtitle, *The Land, the People, and Why They Fight,* which placed the 1943 book within the period when the Soviet Union was a U.S. ally, was not. No one on the board had authorized either the picture or the removal of the books, which thereafter could not be located, as Russell Davis explained to the city manager. Some board members believed that the Civic Center custodian, unfriendly to Brown, had given the photographer access. No one ventured any guesses about the books.[25]

The incident of the photograph was symptomatic of the events and emotions of the next few months: the city was gripped by a "grim underground struggle." The attack on Brown and the library "split [the city] down the middle with strong feeling and mounting tension on both sides." Brown was philosophical as she brought Houser up to date on events. "Of course this isn't fun," she said, "but it can't compare with what the Negro has to take all the time. I did go into it knowing this might happen, which makes it much easier to take." Although Preston Gaddis, an apparent ringleader of her opposition, blasted Brown for "interfering with God's plan" through her efforts at integration, the board stood by her and examined the collection "for subversive literature which they and everyone else" knew was not there. The situation was "extremely serious," as Davis told ALA's Intellectual Freedom Committee chairman, David K. Berninghausen, to whom he turned for advice.[26]

Magazines removed from the Bartlesville Public Library. This photograph appeared in the March 9, 1950, *Bartlesville Examiner-Enterprise*. Courtesy Western History Collections, University of Oklahoma Library.

"BEHIND THE LACE CURTAINS"

The situation certainly was serious for the YWCA. During February and March the "Opposition," as Betty Davis called them—the same group attacking Brown and the library—"besieged" the board with letters and late-night telephone calls to change its long-standing interracial program. It also pressured the United Community Fund, which financed the YWCA, with threats to withhold pledges if the YWCA's policies did not change. Bombarded with rumors that there were interracial dances at the YWCA and that Betty Davis was sent from up north to implement "dire national policies," the fund, in turn, pressured the YWCA board to retreat, as the Girl Scouts had already done.[27]

Late in March the Opposition, armed with propagandist Joseph Kamp's *Behind the Lace Curtains of the Y.W.C.A.*, a veritable catalog of alleged communist influences in the YWCA, announced they were going to bring a thousand "disgruntled citizens" to the next board meeting. Mary Jane Willett, a national YWCA worker, attended a special meeting to help the board prepare. She provided them with information on Kamp, an antilabor, antidemocratic propagandist whose Constitutional Educational League was praised by Hitler. Willett reassured them, in addition, that all the recommendations of the YWCA's Interracial Charter did not apply to all YWCAs. As it turned out only one hundred thirty people actually accompanied spokeswoman Mrs. Don (Grace) Anderson to the board. They presented ten charges in writing and demanded the ouster of Betty Davis. Meeting in executive session following the brief meeting, the YWCA board decided to call a membership vote on the Douglass Y-Teen's use of the new building, with an informational meeting ahead of time to prepare for the ballot. The women also decided, "in order to forestall any sudden influx of either proponents or opponents of [their] long-standing policy," that only those already enrolled as members on April 3 would be allowed to participate. The meeting and the vote were announced in the papers. In addition, the board sent Davis and one of their number to explain what was happening to the Douglass Y-Teen groups.[28]

When the Opposition mounted a membership campaign, those who were sympathetic to the YWCA's position did so as well. Their combined efforts swelled the YWCA's ranks from 385 to almost 600. Davis commented that the new members were apparently three to one in favor of the YWCA's position. "Interesting, too," she said, "is the fact that those who rallied to the YWCA's assistance were, by and large, the young matrons and business people of town; those opposed were more often 40, 50, and 60 year olds." The community's newcomers and young people were making themselves felt.[29]

The YWCA's executive committee met frequently during the next two weeks in preparation for the April 18 meeting. They choreographed every move of the agenda for the 301 women who attended. Despite several interruptions early in the meeting, the YWCA board followed its script. They addressed the various rumors swirling around the YWCA, assured the audience that its subscription to the *Nation* had been canceled, and debunked *Behind the Lace Curtains of the Y.W.C.A.* When the planned agenda ended, YWCA president Marie D. Chaney, a beauty consultant, opened the meeting to discussion. After a contentious debate about who would be allowed to participate in the April 20 vote, the discussion turned to the use of the building by the Douglass girls and the whole question of the YWCA's stand on racial integration. Grace Anderson read a prepared statement attacking the YWCA's Race Relations Committee and Betty Davis's "accelerated race relations ideas." To support moving the program out of the building, Mrs. Lloyd (Lois) Lynd, a Pro-America member whose husband was a Cities Service vice president, indicated that her maid had told her "she believed the Negroes were opposed to using facilities designed for whites." In spite of a plea by Mrs. F. E. (Ida) Rice, whose husband was a Phillips vice president, to think of "the white girl harmed by our prejudices," several of the protestors commented that "prominent Bartians" had donated to the new building without knowing that it would be used by Negroes. Mrs. Preston (Gladys) Gaddis added that "the 'best' people" were opposed to the program, so "it must be changed."[30]

The "best" people notwithstanding, two days later the membership upheld the policy of allowing the Douglass Y-Teens to meet in the new building by a vote of 164 to 92. The Interclub Council, an interracial planning group of adults and officers, was supported even more strongly—189 to 66. But the controversy refused to die. Twenty-seven members who contested the constitutionality of the vote were invited to meet with the board. Prominent among the protestors were Mae Warren, Bessie Smysor, and Anne Sissons, of the group investigating the library; Gladys Gaddis and Grace Anderson, who had spearheaded the earlier protest meeting; and Mrs. Burton (Kathleen) Hull, whose husband had refused service to Brown, Cooke, and Street at the drugstore. They reiterated much of the debate from the previous meeting, including threats that the YWCA's stance would hurt the Community Chest drive and prevent the development of a community center for the African-American neighborhood. They demanded an answer in writing to their complaints.[31]

The YWCA board issued a written statement of support for the rumored westside community center, agreeing to have the Douglass Y-Teens meet there when it was completed. The statement, and the end of the school year program, freed the YWCA from "the pressure of the Opposition, but not from the dread of it." The YWCA board, despite its members' many different points of view, had managed to present a united front to its opponents. Thus it gained for itself a summer's reprieve. Although the focus of the controversy once again shifted to the library, the Anti group was also using divisive tactics on a more vulnerable and less visible group.[32]

When the YWCA board said that inferior facilities for African-American youth activities made use of their new building necessary for the meetings of the Douglass Y-Teen groups, the Anti group said they were "eager to help the Negro" and could quickly raise $60,000 for an African-American community center. W. D. McGinley and several other whites met with a contingent of the African-American community, including Roosevelt Gracey; J. B. Dixon; T. P. Scott, an electrician (formerly head of the School for Negro Deaf, Blind, and Orphans and at one time a member of the COPD board);

and the Reverend R. D. Drew, now minister of Greater First Baptist Church. According to the Oklahoma City *Black Dispatch*, which combined in one article the only coverage of this meeting and Rustin's canceled appearance and comments on the library and YWCA controversies, the March meeting grew out of discussions between African-American Bartians and their white employers, who "wanted to get behind any project desired" by the "neglected" African-American community. Drew, Kabby Mitchell (a teacher at a neighboring community), Joe Harris (a porter at the Burlingame Hotel whose wife Bessie was or had been a COPD member), and Douglass teacher Ira O. Garcia (also a present or former COPD member) said they wanted no involvement in "white activities or projects" and asked for a park and youth center. When Dixon spoke against "all forms of total segregation" and Gracey said that better jobs were the community's first need, Drew intimated that either he or Gracey "must go, because the building must be delivered now or never." Rumors that Gracey was a communist and would be "gotten" began to circulate to parents of school-children. The "prevailing opinion," the *Black Dispatch* reported, was that the African-American community should avoid allowing a fight among whites to fracture their unity. The center's white promoters repeatedly told the YWCA board that it would not be built if the board maintained its policies. Anxious not to be an obstacle, yet equally anxious that the center not be "built in hate," the board announced that the Douglass Y-Teens would meet in the center when it opened. Their action relieved some of the pressure on the YWCA.[33]

"ONE REAL BATTLE"

The pressure against the library continued to mount, however. The March 13, 1950, city commissioners' meeting heard no fewer than four letters or resolutions of support for the citizens' committee and its investigation of the library. They came from Grace Anderson (with Gladys Gaddis a leader in the group fighting the YWCA's policy), the Past Matrons Club of the Order of the Eastern Star (a Masonic group), the UDC, and the DAR. The DAR chapter, in fact, announced its intention to monitor books and periodicals that circulated not only from the public library but from school libraries as well, reflecting a national DAR policy.[34]

Ordered to examine the collection and the operation of the library and report in April, the library board worked long hours, with Richard Kane doing much of the evaluation of the collection in the "Political, Economic, and Social sections of the Library's catalog." He found that "there was a little leaning toward the left" but no evidence in the collection that Brown was a "Communist sympathizer," as the rumors purported. "That was a coverup . . . because people were unwilling to express the real reason," Kane recalled. In fact, the real reason for the challenge to the library was one of those open secrets that characterize close-knit communities. None of the local newspaper articles about the library controversy, with the exception of the report of the February 16 commission meeting at which Burton Hull had described Brown, Cooke, and Street's attempt to be served at the drugstore, had ever mentioned the issue of race. Nor had the divisions revealed in the meeting with the African-American community or Rustin's speech or its cancellation appeared in any Bartlesville paper. The library board, however, was well aware that Brown was under suspicion, not because of her allegedly subversive library collection practices, but because of her interracial activities—including bringing African-American children into the library for story hours, an activity they had supported. Nevertheless, they still had to respond to the charges of subversive materials in the library, as the Anti group sought to shift attention away from their real concerns.[35]

Russell Davis and the board sought information on the *Nation* and *New Republic* from neighboring libraries and from the ALA. Tulsa, Oklahoma City, and other nearby libraries had subscribed to the two titles for some years.[36] The ALA had been fighting censorship of the *Nation* since 1948, when the New York City Public Schools banned it from the libraries. The ALA joined the Ad Hoc Committee to Lift the Ban on the *Nation* and continued to recommend the respected liberal magazine for use in school as well as public libraries. Berninghausen described the ALA's actions and argued the importance of diverse opinions on controversial topics, even for high school students, in an article he sent Davis in response to his request for help. Davis and the library board cited the annotations of all the library's periodical holdings, including the *Nation* and the *New Republic*, from the ALA's *Periodicals for Small and Medium Sized Libraries* (8th ed., 1948) in their report to the commission.[37]

The report the library board delivered to the commissioners in April also included portions of the Library Bill of Rights, the ALA's official statement opposing censorship and upholding the freedom of inquiry in a democracy. While insisting, with the ALA, that publications should not be restricted or removed "because of partisan or doctrinal disapproval," the board was also quick to point out that its members did not necessarily agree with the views expressed in all library material. It asserted that the periodicals collection was appropriately balanced and defended the *Nation* and the *New Republic*. The board had gone so far as to get from both the U.S. attorney general and the Federal Bureau of Investigation statements that there was "no list of communistic or subversive periodicals." It agreed, however, that *Soviet Russia Today* should not be retained.[38]

The board spoke directly to the issue of race: the library was open to all citizens; story hours for "both white and Negro children . . . are now, and have always been, conducted on a segregated basis." The board denied Brown had promoted the reading of subversive materials by giving people marked passages to read, adding (somewhat facetiously?) that the library did its best to prevent people from marking in books. It rejected the suggestion to create an "adult research section," a euphemism for restricting books on controversial subjects to use by selected people under the careful eye of the librarian. Not only was it impossible to establish criteria for including materials in such a collection, but it "might well invite constant pressure" to segregate and restrict books or periodicals on controversial topics such as politics, race, religion, and morals. In addition, segregating material would "tend to exaggerate . . . the attractiveness of unorthodox viewpoints" in the thinking of youth, the board said. Finally, the board set up mechanisms of communication with citizens, such as keeping lists of new book purchases at the circulation desk and establishing a bulletin board for patron comments and book reviews.[39]

The city manager's office acknowledged the report's receipt on April 25 and made it a matter of public record in the city clerk's office on May 5, 1950. Three days later board member George Cade, also a member of the COPD, resigned; he was being transferred. He was the first, but not the last, of Brown's friends to be abruptly transferred by Phillips.[40]

"No Fireworks at Library Meeting," the *Bartlesville Record* reported after the May 25 meeting at which the city commission finally heard the board's report. The newspaper failed to note, however, that the library board "had not been officially notified" that the report was on the agenda and was not informed at all until shortly before the meeting. Dunaway, mayor following the sudden death of Hudson, minimized the importance of the oversight, saying all the library board needed was a single representative to present the report; Russell Davis was that single person. An audience of seventy-five people at the meeting suggests, however, that even though the library board had not been notified, the citizens' committee had been.[41]

Using HUAC documents provided by the American Legion, the citizens' committee analyzed the Bartlesville Public Library's periodicals list. "There is ample evidence," their report said, that the *Nation* not only peddled "the prattle of the Communists" but also advertised "such subjects as sexology and homosexuality." They offered an article by Carey McWilliams, "against whom there are literally scores of citations" by un-American committees, as proof of its subversive character. McWilliams, active in the American Civil Liberties Union (ACLU), frequently wrote about violations of the civil rights of minority groups. The *New Republic* was similarly scored for "offering the views of the pro-Communist press, along with erotic literature and atheist books." *Soviet Russia*

Today, the free subscription to which the library board had agreed should not be kept, was charged with being a communist front.[42]

But the committee added another magazine—or two—to its list of suspect periodicals. It had found, not surprisingly, that none of six nearby libraries owned *Negro Digest*. This magazine was "so strongly influenced" by communists, according to the group's citation to a document of the California Tenney Committee, "as to be in the Stalin solar system." Last, *Consumer Reports* was decried as "subversive and un-American." "Counterfeit literature, designed to defame and destroy the heritage of American freedom, should be exposed instead of tolerated," they insisted.[43]

Following the citizens' committee report, Preston Gaddis—dubbed the "Chief Hater" by Brown—presented an American Legion petition, approved in substance by the Legion's executive committee in February, that put the Legion "on record as being concerned" about the possibility of communist literature emanating from the public library. "[Is such literature] distributed to the youth of our community with advise [*sic*] to read certain marked articles?" the resolution asked. Although it did not directly accuse Brown of promoting communist literature, the resolution's repeated questions about and references to such literature left little doubt as to the Legion's belief that Brown was guilty. The American Legion commended the citizens' committee and asked that their report "be given full consideration." Davis was not questioned concerning the library board's report or given an opportunity to respond to the citizens' committee charges.[44]

The interval between the airing of the two sets of reports—the months between March 6 and May 25, 1950—had been "one vast confusion," Brown wrote Houser. In addition to the YWCA meetings and election and the fight within the African-American community over the advisability of accepting a community center for the west side, the churches were sometimes scenes of conflict. For the most part, these conflicts did not spill into the open. One exception was the Easter sunrise service jointly sponsored by the Methodist, Presbyterian, and one of the African-American (probably the African Methodist Episcopal or Colored Methodist Episcopal) churches in 1950. According to Presbyterian minister James Spivey, the traditional service in Johnstone Park featured an interracial choir, and young people from each of the churches led the service. Although he did not normally do so, Gaddis, who was a trustee of the Presbyterian church, attended. "When the sun came up and he saw that the choir was mixed, he exploded," Spivey recalled. Gaddis proceeded to the three Easter morning services at the church, stood on the sidewalk out front, and "buttonholed people about what a disgrace" the interracial service was to the church. He "demanded a public apology" from Spivey and threatened that without such an apology, the building of the new church would not progress beyond the excavation that had already been completed. Spivey did not apologize.[45]

Brown was not apologetic about the city's confusion. "The Negro has more friends than he ever had here and in the long run it will, I am sure, prove to be a good thing," she mused. The COPD made people see "that they can no longer be neutral on the question" of race, she asserted. If they could have another interracial group by fall, however, it could not be associated with CORE: "It frightens people just as a real practice of Christianity would frighten them." Brown commented that people had been "amazed" at how little she worried about her job, but, she concluded, "if you know what you did was right I cannot see why you should worry." She ended her philosophical letter with words of comfort for Houser: "Don't be discouraged for the South is changing very rapidly." But there would have to be "throes and agonies" in the process of change.[46]

There were more agonies to come in Bartlesville. On June 14, without warning to the library board, the city commission adopted "An Ordinance Pertaining to the Control and Operation of the Bartlesville Public Library." The new ordinance, effective July 1, repealed the existing library ordinance and allowed the commission to dismiss board members without cause, to hire and fire the librarian, and to approve all materials selections. In a letter to Lee Erhard, editor of the *Tulsa Daily World*, Russell Davis reacted angrily to the ordinance: "The present Library Board has no wish to be put under either protective custody or surveillance, which-ever this is."[47]

Davis need not have worried. On July 10, with "sincere appre-ciation" to its members for their years of service, the city commis-sion replaced the library board with an entirely new one, made up of members and sympathizers of the Anti group. The commis-sioners unanimously selected postmaster E. R. Christopher as chairman, a position he accepted at the urging of the presidents of both Phillips and Cities Service. Christopher was a former Amer-ican Legion post commander and a former member of the national organization's Americanism Commission who in 1951 would be named to the national Un-American Activities Committee. Those who joined him were Dr. Elizabeth Chamberlin, who had strongly disapproved when Brown had taken her African-American friend with her to the Episcopal church; Lois Lynd, wife of a Cities Service officer, who was active in Pro-America and had been one of the YWCA's vocal critics; George Cohrs, office manager at National Zinc; Russell Blachly, a Phillips clerk; and young Donald T. Koppel, his father's partner in a women's clothing store. Koppel was surprised to be appointed because he had been a poor student and had never used the library.[48]

Ruth Brown wrote to Houser despondently about the ouster of her "wonderful" library board, the "sole object" of which was to get rid of her. Another of her COPD friends, Frank Condon, had also become a casualty of the battle, she told Houser; he had been forced to transfer to Borger, Texas—Phillips's version of Siberia, according to Bartians. When Condon's boss, the head of research and development, had first spoken to him about his transfer, "there was much reference to CORE," Brown related, but when he was finally transferred another reason had been given. Because Condon wanted to stay with Phillips, at least until a couple of research articles were published, he did not want to press the issue. Although Brown felt like resigning—"that would be so simple"—her friends urged her to stay on. National progress toward inte-gration gave her hope. "Can't some people see that Bartlesville can't hold back the world?" she asked.[49]

Brown could not hold back the forces working for her removal. On July 25, she was summoned to an executive session of the city commissioners. As no one was present to record the interrogation and she was concerned that her answers to the commissioners' questions would be misrepresented, Brown agreed to answer questions pertaining to her personal life only in writing and only if submitted to her in writing. The stipulation itself was presented in written form; the mayor read it to the commissioners at Brown's request. Her condensed record of the one-and-one-half-hour session, written a few days later, reads like a movie script.[50]

Brown faced Mayor Dunaway, commissioners Milo Margenau, William A. Forrest, and Joe Henton, city attorney Alton Rowland, and city manager E. E. Jones in the city manager's office. E. F. Kindsvater was absent. The first and a number of subsequent questions dealt with her interracial activities.

Mayor Dunaway asked the first question: "Miss Brown, did you take two young colored women with you to a drug store where you knew they weren't supposed to be?"

Brown replied, "Personal question to be answered only in writing." She made the same reply to other similar questions that followed.

> *Dunaway:* "Have you ever signed the Loyalty Oath?"
>
> *Brown:* "I have never seen a copy but would be willing to sign one." (The city manager scrambled through the papers on his desk but could not find a copy, even though he had asked the city clerk to have one there.)
>
> *Margenau:* "You agree to the old board's decision as to the *Nation* and *New Republic*?"
>
> *Brown:* "I do."
>
> *Margenau:* "Who was responsible for those magazines being ordered?"
>
> *Brown:* "I was."
>
> *Margenau:* "How many years has the Library taken them?"
>
> *Brown:* "I do not remember, fifteen or twenty years."

Margenau: "What do you think of buying such trash from your very inadequate book fund?"

Brown: "Considering that they were our only two liberal magazines and we subscribed to about seventy-five other magazines I felt perfectly justified. As to our inadequate book fund, that merely meant a more careful spending, and mine was careful." (According to some reports, Brown agreed to remove the offending magazines if ordered to do so.)

Margenau: "What about the advertising in the *New Republic*? Didn't you know there were some very bad things advertised there?"

Brown: "Mr. Margenau, I don't know what you're talking about."

Margenau: "Did you read *Soviet Russia Today*?"

Brown: "Very little, for I found it boring."

Margenau: "How many free publications did you receive?"

Brown: "I do not remember, although they were listed in our report."

Margenau: "And you did not read all of them? Wasn't it your duty?"

Brown: "I did not so consider it but considered my public capable of deciding what they wanted to read."

Margenau: "But weren't they accessible to our young people?"

Brown: "They had never heard of them until this controversy began."

Margenau: "Did you ever have a picture of Paul Robeson hanging in your library?"

Brown: "Not to my knowledge."

Margenau: "Would you be willing to put that in writing?"

Brown: "Mr. Margenau, I would, for I am not lying."

Margenau: "Don't you know Paul Robeson is a Communist?"

Brown: "I do not."

Margenau: "You, a librarian, and do not know that?"

Brown: "I do not know he has ever said he is a Communist."

Margenau: "Don't you ever listen to the radio?"

Brown: "Not often, for I prefer to read."

Margenau talked of "the great harm" Brown had done to the city.

Brown: "I do not consider I have done any harm."

Margenau: "I understand you to say you are not a Communist."

Brown: "I certainly am not."

Forrest (entering the questioning): "Of course we will agree that what Miss Brown is advocating is according to the Bible and the Constitution[,] but it is not according to the majority in Bartlesville."

Brown: "Are you sure? I would like to see a poll taken of that." (Forrest and Margenau responded vehemently that they were absolutely sure.)

Margenau (jumping back in to the questioning): "Miss Brown, if you remain here as librarian would you agree to do nothing more that would harm Bartlesville?"

Brown: "Mr. Margenau, I have said that I have done nothing to harm Bartlesville but, if the young man who interviewed me last week should send this story to a national magazine as he is thinking of doing[,] that would not be very good for Bartlesville."

Margenau (angry): "Miss Brown, did that happen?"

Brown: "It did."

Margenau: "Who is this young man[?]"

Brown: "I am not saying."

Margenau (voice rising): "Do you mean that you talked to him without saying anything to us?"

Brown (at least outwardly calm): "I do. It was my private life."

Margenau (very angry): "Mr. Mayor, we can't have this! They might make her out a martyr."

Brown (placating): "Oh no, they don't want my biography."

Margenau: "Mr. Mayor, write this resolution: Miss Brown is not to interview this young man again and if he writes this he must show it to the commissioners!"

>*Rowland* (the attorney): "But you can't stop a reporter."
>
>*Margenau:* "You still refuse to answer personal questions except in writing?"
>
>*Brown:* "I do, my attorney so advised."

With that the commissioners abruptly ended the questioning. "She hadn't reached the bottom of the stairs before she was out of a job," the mayor said later. Within an hour, during which the commissioners discussed and voted in open session, the city manager delivered the statement of dismissal to Brown over the telephone.[51]

"City Library Chief Fired Tuesday Night," blared the morning *Examiner-Enterprise*; "City Librarian Is Relieved of Duty by Commissioners," proclaimed the *Record*. The following day, Brown's fifty-ninth birthday, all editions of Bartlesville's papers carried the news. By noon Brown's assistant, Alta R. Riggs, had resigned "in sympathy." The new library board, which had met only briefly once before, convened that evening in the city manager's office to appoint an acting librarian. A note the new board president had sent to the other members the week before—saying they would not meet until the city commission had met—suggests that he knew in advance that Brown was to be dismissed. Virginia Lasley, a retired teacher, accepted the post of temporary librarian.[52]

Brown's statement regarding her dismissal, issued Wednesday night, July 26, hit the Thursday morning papers. Brown asserted that "certain of her personal opinions and outside activities" the commissioners had found "distasteful" had led to her firing. She reaffirmed her belief "that discrimination on account of race, creed, or color is contrary to democratic and Christian principles." The commissioners disapproved, she said, not of her performance as librarian—which neither they nor the city manager had ever told her was unsatisfactory—but of her attempt to "live as a Christian in a democracy."[53]

If the city commission thought that firing Brown would end the controversy, they were sorely mistaken. Brown's long service had won allegiance even from people who did not share her activism; they were stunned by her summary dismissal. Her treatment attracted defenders who had little interest in interracial activities. As Russell Davis wrote to the Oklahoma Library Commission, Brown's reward for more than thirty years of service was to be one month's salary. He hoped the community would "be sufficiently aroused to practical and constructive behavior."[54]

CHAPTER THREE

The Many Friends
of Miss Brown

We do not need to be conquered in a war by a totalitarian power to lose our liberty. Whenever any person in any community is denied the rights guaranteed to him under the Constitution, whenever the local authorities assume power which violates the principles of justice which are the very foundations of our American democracy, then all the people of that community have lost a portion of their liberty.

—MRS. F. E. (IDA) RICE,
letter to the editor, *Bartlesville Examiner-Enterprise,*
July 28, 1950

Someone said to me, "Haven't you found out how many enemies you have?" I said, "Quite the contrary. I have found out how many friends."

—RUTH W. BROWN
to George Houser, November 6, 1950

"Gentlemen," wrote Mrs. Lee Still to the Bartlesville City Commissioners on July 28, 1950, "I would like to suggest you consult your Public Library on the subject of the Salem Witch hunts." Mrs. Still was one person among many willing to engage in "practical and constructive behavior" to protest Brown's treatment. If hopes of quieting controversy that would detract from the image of "America's ideal family center" had motivated city officials to oust Brown, their actions instead propelled the controversy onto a regional, even national, stage. Within days of her firing a group calling itself the Friends of Miss Brown had begun a publicity and fund-raising campaign; they planned to challenge the library's takeover and Brown's dismissal through the courts. In the weeks that followed their publicity and the earlier contacts of the ousted library board, as well as CORE, would add the ACLU and the Oklahoma and American library associations to the roster of Brown's friends.[1]

The Friends, representing about two hundred supporters, numbered a dozen old Bartians and newcomers. Their reasons for supporting Brown were varied. Some truly were "just friends" who felt she had been wronged; others were concerned for their own—and the community's—freedom to read and the effects of "witch-hunting." Still others embraced Brown's desire for what her opponents called "racial equalization," and some seemed to avoid too close a connection with her desire for integration. Only one had been on the ousted library board; the other board members, although sympathetic to Brown, no doubt felt they could not participate. Russell Davis, for example, believed he had to have a "neutral" stance in his position with the savings and loan; he simply did not talk about the conflict with those he met during the day. Some people, however, pointedly avoided exchanging the traditional greetings with him when they met him on the street. Board member Olga Beecher, for another example, was a good friend of Mae Warren's, one of the leaders of the Anti group; she did not take a role in the Friends of Miss Brown. All five of the male members of the Friends were Phillips employees. Robert Manuel and Anthony Andrews had spoken at the stormy commissioners' meeting. John Widdowson, like John D. Upham, was a Phillips patent attorney; M. L. Studebaker was a chemist. Jean Barker, a secretary at National Zinc, was president of the Business and Professional Women and served on the YWCA board; her niece, Friends member Hannah Parry, also worked at National Zinc. Mrs.

F. J. (Gladys) Spies was an established Bartian and Episcopalian whose husband was self-employed in real estate loans and insurance. Edith Jones, an elderly widow, was a former neighbor of Lois Ogilvie's (Ogilvie's husband had been transferred). Mrs. Alberta Bradstreet, a popular piano teacher, dissociated herself from the group shortly after the first newspaper publicity; apparently she was threatened with loss of students if she persisted in openly siding with Brown. Mrs. Gordon (Dorothy) Allen, wife of a Phillips engineer, replaced her. Ida Rice, a regal, white-haired woman whose husband was a top Phillips vice president, took a leadership role in the group. A devout Presbyterian and an AAUW member with a history of interest in race relations, Rice had spoken during the heated YWCA open meeting about the "white girl harmed by our prejudices" and asked for a Christian approach to the racial controversy. She served as treasurer of the Friends and contributed liberally of her own funds. Darlene Anderson Essary, a Phillips attorney, was more than a Friend. A member of the ousted board, she joined Brown in her suit against the Bartlesville City Commission, the new library board, and the temporary librarian.[2]

Essary was also the anonymous author of a letter to Freda Kirchwey, editor of the *Nation*. (The new library board chairman, E. R. Christopher, was unsuccessful, despite the best efforts of his national American Legion contacts, in identifying who the letter writer was—other than that it was a woman.) In the letter, entitled "Patriotism in Bartlesville," the first description of the Bartlesville situation to appear in the national press, Essary implicated the leadership of Phillips Petroleum. She claimed that employees "vocal" in the library board's support had been "instructed to be silent," and two who "had been active in interracial activities" had been transferred. Essary and the Friends also wrote letters to the *New Republic*, the *Saturday Review*, other national publications, and the Bartlesville newspapers, as well as press releases to newspapers such as the *Kansas City Star* and the *Saint Louis Post-Dispatch*.[3]

Perhaps the most dramatic action in the local publicity campaign was the striking, large advertisement the Friends placed in the *Examiner-Enterprise* on July 30, just five days after Brown's

Mrs. F. E. (Ida) Rice and family. Courtesy Archives, Phillips Petroleum Company.

dismissal. In large bold type it questioned, "U.S.A. or U.S.S.R?" It called the treatment of Brown a "subversive attack on American liberties" and compared the commissioners' methods to those used in the Soviet Union, where "the Government tells each citizen what opinions to hold, and gets rid of those who refuse to conform."[4]

Members of the Friends were among the large crowd of citizens who showed up on August 7 to hear the city commission explain Brown's firing. A substantial number of people, starting with Charles Varvel of Phillips (whose wife, Margaret, was a COPD member and Brown's close friend), asked why Brown had been dismissed. Those inquiring had already called him to ask that same question, the mayor indicated with apparent irritation, and they

Darlene Anderson (Essary). Courtesy Archives, Phillips Petroleum Company.

Reproduction of an advertisement placed by Friends of Miss Brown, July 30, 1950. Courtesy *Bartlesville Examiner-Enterprise*.

all knew the answer, as did Brown. M. P. Matuszak, another Phillips scientist, recounting the meeting to Friends member Upham about a month later, said that "in spite of all the pleading, the mayor continued not to give a direct answer to the questions." Someone in the audience finally stood and proclaimed that Brown had been fired because she kept "a closet full of communistic literature" in the library. Another chimed in that "Communism was a satisfactory reason for dismissal." However, the mayor announced that neither communism nor Brown's interracial activities had led to her firing. In their interview with her on July 25, he reported, "Miss Brown displayed a high-handed and arrogant attitude . . . and at no time even indicated that she would be willing to co-operate with the Commissioners" regarding the operations of the library. She was insubordinate. But when asked for specific instances of Brown's insubordination, neither the mayor nor any of the other commissioners could substantiate the charge. "The Commissioners maintain that race or Communism had nothing to do with my dismissal. I was 'insubordinate,' but they cannot remember just how," Brown wrote Houser after the meeting. Later Dunaway told the *Christian Science Monitor* that Brown's insubordination consisted of her refusal to answer "the commissioners' questions unless they were in writing." In addition, she had given an interview to a writer from a national magazine who would give Bartlesville "derogatory publicity" by airing the civil rights issue.[5]

Although Brown welcomed the Friends' support, their continued monitoring of the new library board, and their "strenuous effort to place the facts of the situation before the public"—to generate "derogatory publicity" for the commissioners' actions—she was a reluctant participant in the planned lawsuit. "I am definitely not fighting for my job," she told Houser. Instead she sought to preserve small gains in integration and to forestall further attacks on the YWCA. They would fight the court case, she said, even if it took two years. Many of her friends said that going to the drugstore seemed to have been the last straw for the commissioners and called it "indiscreet." When the first questions the commissioners asked Brown in secret session had to do with her visit to the drugstore, however, she knew it was "a good CORE project" that had confronted the power structure. "It worked better than we could have dreamed," she said wryly.[6]

The same could not be said for the search for an attorney to handle the suit. Nevertheless, by mid-September Upham and Essary had retained retired Oklahoma Supreme Court justice Thurman S. Hurst of Tulsa to represent Brown and Essary against the City of Bartlesville. Their court petition charged that the new library ordinance adopted by the city commission in June violated the state law in several of its provisions, such as allowing board members to be dismissed without cause, and that the state law should prevail. They asked that the actions of the commissioners and the new library board be declared null and void and that Brown be restored to her position.[7] District Judge James T. Shipman of Bartlesville, scheduled to hear Brown's suit on October 2, 1950, disqualified himself because the case had divided the community sharply and, as a member of the community, he considered himself "interested." The Oklahoma Supreme Court assigned Jess Miracle of Okemah to hear the case, reset for November 9.[8]

CORE's George Houser wished the suit well, but beset by the difficulties of keeping itself together, CORE could only help to publicize the case through its newsletter, the *CORE-lator*. CORE's inability to help financially or in any other substantive way was just as well, Brown confessed to Houser. Rumors of support from outside groups, especially CORE and the NAACP, had elicited a "bitter feeling" in the community and forced Essary and Brown to issue a denial of support from "any organization." However, Brown and Essary told the press, the ALA and the OLA, although not planning to join the suit, did intend to investigate the censorship of library materials.[9]

FORMER EMPLOYEES AND THEIR FRIENDS

As the Friends awaited the court hearing, Naomi Stocker Gordon, who as a young person in the mid-1930s had loved working for

Ruth Brown, approached Abbott Gould, a New York attorney with ties to the ACLU, with Brown's plight. Gould encouraged the ACLU to take an interest in the case and communicated with the Friends of Miss Brown as well. Speaking for the Friends, Upham reiterated the group's desire to continue the suit "at the community level" and rejected "direct legal action" on the part of the ACLU. Upham suggested, however, that the ACLU could help Hurst to identify other cases that would be pertinent to the suit and that "merely publicizing the facts would be constructive." The ACLU's associate staff counsel, George Soll, sounded grateful that the Friends did not want outside participation in the suit. He wrote Gould that it would be "one of the difficult ones" for the ACLU "to tackle." Although he had "rarely seen a more outrageous and stupid violation of a person's rights than that perpetrated on Miss Brown," there seemed to be "no legal remedy at all." He was in communication with Berninghausen, chairman of the ALA's Intellectual Freedom Committee, who had some publicity ready, but Berninghausen felt he had to await the results of an ALA Personnel Board investigation before going further. Aside from publicity, "the only solution" seemed to be "the hope that either the hysteria will die of its own accord or that sufficient people with courage will stand up to the forces which caused the dismissal of Miss Brown."[10]

The ACLU contributed to the publicity on the case with an article in the October 1950 *Civil Liberties*. In addition, its 1950 Bill of Rights Day radio broadcast featured Brown's ouster. Aired nationwide on NBC on Wednesday, December 13, from 10:30 to 11:00 P.M. EST, "Friday Is a Great Day" included three minutes about Brown and the Bartlesville Public Library. The broadcast elicited vitriolic responses from some of Brown's opponents. One excoriated the "big rubber tears" shed for Brown by the "civil liberties outfit," and another called the broadcast an attempt to bias the Oklahoma Supreme Court, to which her case—defeated at the district court level in November—had been appealed on December 11. But Brown was delighted that the ACLU broadcast "made it so clear that what we are fighting for is the right of a man to believe and think as his conscience dictates."[11]

Brown was delighted, too, with the support and publicity from the October 15, 1950, *Library Journal*. It carried the news of her dismissal as the context of a letter from James Henderson, another one of her former young employees. Writing from the New York Public Library, where he was on the staff of the reference library, Henderson described the physical and cultural geography of the conservative but "enlightened" town and the role the library played in it. Brown was a "familiar figure" in the community, he wrote. A "zealous civil servant," she had kept the poorly supported library "an important channel of communication" even during the "difficult depression years." It was "to her credit," he said, "that she took seriously her responsibilities as a Christian and a democrat." He told of her interest in and assistance to numerous young people. "Being in constant contact with ideas," he explained, "she developed a liberal philosophy consistent with her religion and her innate sense of what was right and just." Henderson referred to the events of the past year as recounted in the Nation letter written by Essary, and he reported that the commissioners' action was being contested in court. He was "confident" that Bartians would demand Brown's reinstatement. He wrote to the *Library Journal*, he concluded, because, "remembering this town, I realize with a sudden shock that if such a thing could happen there, it could happen almost anywhere. I wonder if those who love liberty and justice should not be on guard to recognize the symptoms of hysteria before it does such harm."[12]

THE LIBRARY PROFESSION

The ALA and the OLA certainly counted themselves among those who loved liberty and justice and agreed with Henderson's warning. Since 1939 the ALA had maintained through its Library Bill of Rights librarians' prerogative—indeed, their professional responsibility in the service of freedom and democracy—to collect and make available library materials on all sides of controversial issues, so that citizens could make the informed decisions needed to govern themselves. In 1948, just two years before Brown's ouster, the ALA Council had strengthened the Library Bill of Rights. It now not only asserted that libraries should collect materials representing diverse viewpoints but also specifically stated that "censorship of books, urged or practiced by volunteer arbiters of morals or political opinion or by organizations that would establish a coercive concept of Americanism, must be challenged by libraries in maintenance of their responsibility to provide public information and enlightenment through the printed word." Because Ruth Brown had lost her position in the course of such a challenge, the ALA and its Oklahoma chapter, of which Brown had long been a member, had an obligation to provide whatever support they could.[13]

That was David Berninghausen's position. When he had first heard from board chairman Russell Davis, however, he was still struggling with an internal conflict within the ALA over the association's appropriate response to loyalty programs that affected libraries. For two years the ALA had been debating whether to have a resolution opposing loyalty programs in libraries, and if so, what such a resolution should say. The ALA Council finally came to agreement at the annual conference in summer 1950, at about the time Brown lost her job. Berninghausen thus was unable to devote as much time as he would have liked to his response to the board's and Brown's dilemma, although he did send the Library Bill of Rights and other materials and advice to the library board. Executive Secretary John Mackenzie Cory counted that aspect of the ALA's response a success, because the board "upheld the librarian's contention that she should retain controversial materials in the collection." Of course, the board had shown no inclination not to support Brown, so the importance of the response may have been exaggerated. The board did, however, appeal to the authority of the Library Bill of Rights and the ALA in its report to the city commission. Although the ALA's statement did not alter the actions of the commissioners, it gave the board a sense that they stood on firm ground.[14]

The repercussions from the internal ALA struggle made the ground on which Berninghausen stood a bit rocky, however. The

ALA Executive Board apparently was somewhat irritated at the persistence of Berninghausen and Edward B. Stanford of the Board on Personnel Administration, who had together pushed the association to adopt a strong stance against loyalty programs over the protests of some prominent ALA members. Thus they had limited both the personnel board and the Intellectual Freedom Committee to "observ[ing], investigat[ing], and calling attention to the pertinent policy statement," including the Library Bill of Rights. Any action beyond these required executive board approval. The limitations on the Intellectual Freedom Committee's authority made meaningful action very difficult, Berninghausen protested. He received almost simultaneously both Davis's announcement that the library board had been replaced and a note from Freda Kirchwey, editor of the *Nation*, inquiring if Brown's case was not "one which is of direct interest to the American Library Association and should be fought in her behalf by the Association." Berninghausen felt hamstrung in his response. He complained that the committee could not even protest Brown's treatment publicly or send a copy of the Library Bill of Rights to the mayor.[15]

But Berninghausen could, and did, offer Brown help in publicizing her case as well as in finding a new job. Both Berninghausen and ALA president Clarence Graham, who had apparently met Brown before her dismissal when he attended the OLA conference in early May 1950, pushed for an investigation of the case. Graham asked Oklahoma state librarian Ralph Hudson for a "full and accurate account of the case" to which there seemed to be more "than appears on the surface." Berninghausen urged the OLA to establish an intellectual freedom committee to conduct an on-site probe of the situation, the first such investigation ever undertaken by the ALA or one of its state chapters. The ALA specifically directed the OLA to limit its investigation to the case's censorship aspects, however. The racial issues precipitating the incident were carefully omitted as beyond its scope and jurisdiction, as they appeared not to come within the interpretation of the Library Bill of Rights, the policy under which the Intellectual Freedom Committee could act.[16]

OKLAHOMA LIBRARIANS

In September 1950 the OLA Executive Board met specifically "to consider the situation in which [its] colleague, Miss Brown of Bartlesville, has found herself since her dismissal on July 25, due to a purported mixup with communistic literature." Headed by its president, Esther Mann McRuer, director of the Ardmore Public Library in southeastern Oklahoma (the area known as "Little Dixie"), the OLA appointed a Select Committee on Intellectual Freedom to investigate the censorship aspects of Ruth Brown's dismissal. The committee would serve until the next OLA meeting the following March. Oklahoma City University Library Director Frances Kennedy was named chairperson, and Ralph Hudson was named a member. Mary Hayes Marable, a teacher in the University of Oklahoma Library School, and Clarence Paine, director of the Oklahoma City Libraries, were asked to serve as well. Marable responded immediately that although she was much too busy, she felt "so strongly on this matter of Bartlesville's treatment of Miss Brown" that she would indeed serve on the committee. She added that two of her former students had been assistants of Brown's and had told her "much of the inside story."[17]

Paine declined to serve, however, citing personal and professional responsibilities that had claims on his time, as well as concerns that the committee would be too weighted with Oklahoma City people to be acceptable. Furthermore, he questioned "the advisability of intercession at either the state or the national level in the affairs of any community unless such intercession has been specifically requested."[18]

McRuer then turned to Gertrude B. Davis, director of the Muskogee Public Library—much closer to Bartlesville—to be the public librarian on the committee. "We are sorry this action has been necessary," McRuer told Davis, "but after long discussion, we decided that undoubtedly the time has come to be alerted in this grave matter." Davis also declined, however. Not only was she, like Paine, "personally against such an investigation," but the Muskogee Public Library had received both the *Nation* and the

New Republic for years, and she believed that being on such a committee "would only serve to stir up trouble for us here."[19]

Kennedy responded to Paine's and Davis's refusals with amaze-
ment and concern. She wrote to McRuer, "There must be some
hidden danger in serving on such a committee of which I am not
aware. It does seem rather strange that two people whom I have
always thought rather courageous and out spoken [*sic*] have refused
to serve." The committee was "hampered," she believed, without a
public librarian who was not "afraid to serve." McRuer responded
that she had begun "to sense a sub-current of extreme caution" even
before the meeting naming the committee was over. As OLA president, she would be on the committee ex officio; she authorized
Kennedy to use her name as the public librarian. "I am not afraid,"
she said.[20]

In spite of being unable to find a public librarian other than
McRuer who was willing to serve, the committee began work.
Hudson and Elizabeth Cooper of the Oklahoma Library Commission collected news clippings about the incident, and on October
2, the date Brown's case was scheduled for district court, Frances
Kennedy visited Bartlesville on a fact-finding mission. When the
judge disqualified himself, she spent the day fact gathering,
including talking to two Phillips librarians and visiting the Bartlesville Public Library. There she asked for the *Nation* and the *New
Republic*. They were produced from under the circulation desk by
the replacement librarian, Virginia Lasley. *Soviet Russia Today* was
no longer available. It was "the consensus of opinion in Bartlesville," she said, "that Miss Brown's active defense of negroes was
the cause of her dismissal, and not the so-called communistic
literature." The committee reconvened, and Hudson, "eager" to
report to Graham, agreed to write the report. A month later the
report was still not finished, a frustrated Kennedy told McRuer.
She had hoped to have their work completed "while the question
was still under discussion." Now the case had already been
decided in district court on November 9, although Kennedy did
not yet know the outcome—a rejection of Brown and Essary's suit.
The report had still not arrived by December 4, and Kennedy

advised McRuer that Hudson had refused her offer to finish the work on the report herself. Finally, on January 22, 1951, McRuer sent the report—a "masterful job"—to the OLA Executive Board and to ALA president Graham, just in time for consideration at the ALA's Midwinter Meeting that would start the following week. It had also been released on that date to the press, McRuer reported, "in keeping with the charge" to the committee. At the same time she congratulated Kennedy on "an excellent job." "Now, probably the fireworks will begin," she said. "But we could do no other."[21]

Kennedy and Hudson experienced at least a sparkler's worth of fireworks when they appeared the Thursday before the report's official release at a public discussion of the case at the Frederick Eliot Forum of the Oklahoma City Unitarian Church. Kennedy and Hudson declared that Brown had been discharged because of her private beliefs and that the integrity of the library had been violated. Harold C. Price, Jr.—son of Bartlesville's H. C. Price of oil pipeline fame, a student at the University of Oklahoma School of Law, an ACLU member, and an active supporter of Brown's cause—revealed that Brown's antisegregation activity had been the true cause of her firing. The explosion came, however, when Robert Porta, Americanism officer for the Oklahoma Department of the American Legion, attending the meeting at the behest of E. R. Christopher, defended Bartlesville city officials and then stalked out of the meeting, followed by a half dozen others. "You are communists!" yelled a departing woman. (Such epithets were also directed against Price and his wife in Bartlesville.)[22]

The public discussion definitely created interest in the report. With her letter of transmittal to the OLA Executive Board, McRuer included an inquiry as to the wisdom of allowing the report to be reproduced and distributed by groups outside the OLA, such as the Frederick Eliot Forum, which had asked to do so. McRuer also posed the question to Jesse L. Rader, director of the University of Oklahoma Library. Although McRuer considered the report "a discreet and fearless statement of our convictions" and was "willing to stand by it," she was concerned that "some communist-front group might take it and harm the very thing we want to accomplish." Rader's response to her inquiry was brief: the report should not be distributed because "it looks like a slap at Bartlesville." McRuer's other correspondents were neither so prompt in their response nor so succinctly negative. By the time she had heard from everyone, she had a request to reprint from a group she strongly wanted to oblige, the Friends of Miss Brown, who wanted to send the report to contributors to Brown's cause. Although the vote was not unanimous, the executive board allowed reproduction of the report. They filled additional requests for the report from Frances Lander Spain of the Library School of the University of California at Los Angeles and from Christopher, chairman of the replacement library board of the Bartlesville Public Library, among others.[23]

The "Report of the Intellectual Freedom Committee of the Oklahoma Library Association on the Bartlesville Public Library" was summarized or excerpted in many state newspapers.[24] After briefly recounting events that had transpired in Bartlesville in 1950, the report set out the intellectual freedom tenets that undergirded its conclusions: "Our nation's public libraries are a safeguard of its freedoms. The maintenance and strengthening of this bulwark requires that libraries have freedom—freedom of acquisition, freedom of access by all people, and freedom to give complete information." These things are required to assure a "fully informed citizenry" and a nation that can achieve great things. Librarians must always be vigilant to preserve freedom of expression against those who would deny it "else [they] fail the ideals of [their] profession and of scholarship." Totalitarian systems such as communism do not allow free public libraries containing a diversity of views, the report continued.

> We realize that such a political creed means our extinction and we oppose it completely. We know this because we were born and live in a nation of free public libraries. We have seen the clash of ideas, we have had access to free inquiry. We are well aware that we have the opportunity to discover who is our enemy, to know his beliefs and his tactics in order to

oppose him successfully. The Citizens Committee would deny this to the citizens of Bartlesville. It would require them to read only that which it considered proper. It would leave them in ignorance.

We can only infer, in view of the published record, that Miss Brown was unjustly and cavalierly discharged because of her private beliefs and her professional belief in free libraries. Had she been professionally unfit to be the librarian then Bartlesville is somewhat tardy in discovering it only after thirty years. We feel that the Public Library of Bartlesville was made a scapegoat for a misguided group, that the reading matter in the library was not the primary cause of the complaint, and that censorship of the Library was used as a weapon against Miss Brown. She has suffered the loss of her position, but the City of Bartlesville has suffered more. It has transgressed against the freedom of its Library and thereby transgressed upon its distinction as an institution for free public information. It has denied its patrons free access to reading matter and the free acquisition of these materials by the Library.[25]

The committee acknowledged it could do nothing to "remedy the situation"; Bartlesville must do that for itself. Nevertheless, it stated its "objections to censorship of libraries clearly and straightforwardly" and held strongly to its belief in the importance of free expression.[26]

The OLA's report drew praise from a number of sources. It apparently also gave support and courage to the handful of African-American librarians in the state. In February 1951 McRuer asked Gaston Litton, archivist at the University of Oklahoma in Norman, what arrangements were being made to house African-American librarians who planned to attend the OLA annual conference scheduled to be held there in March. The response to Litton's inquiry to John Freeman, director of the Extension Division, who was handling the details, suggests that housing African-American attendees for a conference was not an issue that had previously been confronted and solved—at least on the University of Oklahoma campus. Freeman agreed that "it would be possible to house negro people," if the men were to stay in the dormitory set aside for African-American men and the women in prefab units in another area of campus. It would be difficult to get these facilities ready to use, however, so he needed to know how many African Americans would be attending. He recognized the difficulty of that requirement: "It does not seem to be in good taste to ask people to state whether they are negro or white on the application or reservation for housing. Do you have any suggestions?" The OLA and the venues that hosted its conference would from this date forward have to consider how to accommodate all librarians. Oklahoma's African-American librarians were prepared to test the Oklahoma Intellectual Freedom Committee's statement of belief in access to libraries for all. Those who attended would hear Frances Kennedy present the report on the Bartlesville Public Library at the March 16 business meeting and participate in the vote to continue the Intellectual Freedom Committee, "looking to the time when it may be made a Standing Committee if the need continues."[27]

THE ALA BREAKS ITS SILENCE

While Frances Kennedy had been trying to accelerate Ralph Hudson's report writing, Brown and Essary's case had been argued in the district court. Judge Miracle did not find convincing the legal arguments in favor of the state's interest in library services over that of the local community. On November 9, 1950, he rejected the argument that the state had a sovereign interest in libraries and that state library law thus should prevail over the municipal charter. Hurst quickly appealed the decision to the state supreme court. Berninghausen apparently asked the members of his committee if they thought the ALA should enter a friend of the court brief on Brown's behalf when the case went to the Oklahoma Supreme Court. At least two members, Miriam Matthews of the Los Angeles Public Library (who was African American) and

Marion Hawes of Baltimore's Enoch Pratt Free Library, responded. Both agreed that the ALA should make a statement regarding both the censorship and the tenure aspects of the Bartlesville case and that a statement or brief should be entered with the court. Hawes cautioned, however, that action should come from the association, not from the committee, and that "it would be wise to get the reaction from someone on the spot before sending a letter to the commissioners," lest such an action simply arouse further antagonism. Despite the discussion no obvious and immediate action was discernible by the ALA membership.[28]

One concerned public librarian asked executive secretary Cory to explain the ALA's "silence" on the Bartlesville case. Indeed, the ALA had responded slowly, Cory said, but because of the complicated nature of the case, not from lack of interest or committee machinery. He outlined the three aspects of concern to the ALA: censorship, "one of the original charges directed" at Brown; tenure, "arising from the method in which Miss Brown was fired"; and the legal question, "concerning state vs. local responsibility for library service." In addition, Cory said, the ALA lacked funds for an investigation by the personnel board, something needed for a delicate tenure matter. And if the ALA were to enter the court case along the way, that would require extensive research—and a good deal of money. Notably missing from his analysis of the important aspects of the case was any mention of race. Despite its inclusion in the OLA report as a necessary aspect of the freedom of libraries so important to an informed citizenry, the ALA had yet to include "freedom of access [to libraries] by all people" in its intellectual freedom tenet.[29]

Cory's answer did not satisfy Berninghausen (now acting as secretary of the committee), who was still frustrated by the restrictions on Intellectual Freedom Committee action. He appealed to Cory to ask the executive board to remove the restrictions. Meanwhile, he and the new chairman, Rutherford D. Rogers, did "compromise" and send to the mayor of Bartlesville a "letter of inquiry" that presented the association's position on intellectual freedom, especially the need for libraries to make available materials on all sides of controversial issues. On January 29, as the Midwinter Meeting got under way, the executive board revised the statement defining the powers of the Intellectual Freedom Committee (and the personnel board) by adding "protesting as a board or a committee any actions which appear to violate the [previously approved] policy statements if so authorized by the President and the Executive Secretary." It was not a big step, but it was something. The Intellectual Freedom Committee would not have to poll the executive board by mail or wait for a meeting before it could take any kind of action. Such requirements had made the committee's assistance to Ruth Brown too little too late. The ALA's inability to provide worthy support for its professional credo had finally been obvious even to the executive board, which relinquished a tiny bit of authority to the Intellectual Freedom Committee.[30]

On February 3, 1951, in response to the OLA report, the ALA Council unanimously adopted a resolution condemning Brown's firing. However, the executive board decided it would not "at this time . . . undertake a full-scale tenure investigation." In addition, the ALA declined to enter an amicus brief with the Oklahoma Supreme Court. Helen Ridgway, the ALA's chief public library specialist, explained to Darlene Essary in more detail the association's reasons. "The continuing difficulties in keeping A.L.A.'s budget balanced, and the nebulous policies concerning state-local relations throughout the country" had led the executive board to decide not to venture into court in this case, Ridgway said. The ALA had broken its silence with a whisper, but it was a stage whisper that raised the profession's level of awareness of the dangers of volunteer censors and of the need for a united, effective response. The whisper "Remember Bartlesville" would echo in librarians' memories for years to come.[31]

In all fairness, however, the ACLU had made the same decision with regard to the court case. Because the case was being argued on what appeared to be the only available grounds—the state-local conflict—and not on any constitutional or civil rights grounds, it did not appear to be either the right vehicle or a winnable case from the ACLU's vantage point. As late as May 1951, however, both the ACLU and the ALA were still considering some sort of action, perhaps in concert with the American Book Publishers Council—a frequent ALA ally against censorship—and other book trade organizations. Such action apparently never occurred.[32]

"BLACK EYES AND BARTLESVILLE"

From late 1950 through early 1951 the Friends of Miss Brown continued their campaign to keep Brown's case before the public. Their efforts were aided by the timing of the report of the OLA's Select Committee on Intellectual Freedom and the resolution condemning Brown's firing passed by the ALA. When the case was appealed to the Oklahoma Supreme Court in 1951 and again when the Court dismissed Brown and Essary's claims against the city on September 16, 1952, the details were aired, much to the dismay of the city commissioners.[33]

While the Friends kept the case in the public eye, the lack of a viable constitutional ground on which to argue the suit, raising either the issue of segregation or that of censorship, or for that matter of Brown's right to some sort of procedural safeguards before being dismissed, limited the resources on which they could draw for help. Civil rights groups such as the NAACP (CORE had neither money nor infrastructure at this time), civil liberties groups such as the ACLU, and professional associations such as the ALA and the American Book Publishers Council were unlikely to expend scarce resources on a case without constitutional implications. Since Brown and Essary's suit, apparently of necessity, was cast as a matter of state interest versus local jurisdiction, the ACLU, the ALA, and their allies opted out of joining the court case. In addition, by determining to keep the funding of the case local, but especially by moving the focus of the case away from segregation to censorship and finally, by virtue of the court case, even away from censorship, they moved away from their natural allies.

Of course, many of the Bartlesville citizens who fought on Brown's behalf also wanted to remain in the community. They had no desire to use tactics, such as bringing in outside support or emphasizing the most divisive of the issues underlying the case, that they viewed as ultimately harmful to the community, or to their continued participation in it. Regardless, the publicity that they sought was perceived as very harmful to the city. As Bob Snair, quoting the "city dads" in a byline article in the *Bartlesville Record* said, "If these plaintiffs felt the strong sense of civic pride they claim, they would not have split the community by bringing such a large amount of unfavorable publicity upon Bartlesville." *St. Louis Post-Dispatch* writer F. A. Behmyer characterized the captains of the powerful Cities Service and Phillips Petroleum companies as "allergic to publicity as something that might hurt the town." "There are indications," Behmyer added, "that . . . [they] deplore the fuss that has been made over such a little issue as control of the public library."[34] From their perspective, Bartlesville's "black eyes" were caused by those who protested Brown's firing and drew attention to the less than ideal qualities of "America's ideal family center." The Friends of Miss Brown, however, attributed the shiners to blows the citizens' committee and the city commission had dealt to Brown's right to free expression and library users' freedom to read. In the contest for publicity, the Friends of Miss Brown and the outside organizations that supported her, however ineffectively, won. But the Bartlesville City Commission and the replacement library board won the contest in the courts.

When the contest shifted to the courts, most scrutiny from the outside world, the OLA, the ALA, and the ACLU shifted there as well. Those who kept their eyes fixed on Bartlesville witnessed both quiet drama and not-so-subtle retribution in the aftermath of the highly publicized battle over the public library and the actions and attitudes of its "indiscreet" librarian, Ruth Brown.

CHAPTER FOUR

The Cleanup

Bartlesville and Its Library after Brown

I need help! Here is what I am up against: I was recently appointed on the local library board and my duty appears to be to clean out the Library, and believe me, it is some job.

—E. R. CHRISTOPHER
to W. C. Sawyer, August 17, 1950

The frightening aspect of the present day in Bartlesville is that the young progressive leadership is leaving the community, in one or two [cases], "by request,"—and others "because we don't want our children brought up in this kind of atmosphere."

—ELIZABETH DAVIS,
YWCA *Annual Report*, September 1, 1950

The new board of the Bartlesville Public Library, headed by postmaster E. R. Christopher, was clearly anxious about its first regular meeting on August 1, 1950, just a few days after Ruth Brown was fired; they even arranged for a court reporter to record the entire affair. With the Friends of Miss Brown mounting an active publicity campaign and soliciting funds for a court challenge to the takeover of the library by the city commission, the board expected visitors at its meeting. It had met only twice before, the first time to elect officers and the second time, on the day after Brown's dismissal, to appoint Virginia Lasley, a retired school-teacher, as temporary librarian. And just as they had expected members of the Friends of Miss Brown and others came to the August meeting to try to discover what role the board had played in firing her.[1]

In a meeting characterized by barely disguised hostility, the Friends also questioned why the *Nation* and the *New Republic* were sequestered behind the circulation desk. Although Christopher said that the periodicals were being kept out of sight until the new board had time to evaluate them in order not to "wave a red flag in a bunch of women's faces" (referring to the citizens' committee), the list of periodicals submitted to the city commission for its approval for purchase less than a week later did not include the two magazines in question. A memo "for your information" from Chamberlin, the board's secretary, to the commissioners said that two additional titles, *Negro Digest* and *Consumer Reports*, were "cited on a subversive list published by the United States government" and thus would not be renewed. The *Nation*, the *New Republic*, and yet another title, *Survey Graphic* (in which the article that had interested Brown in CORE had appeared), would not be renewed pending "more time for study." The new board was accurate in asserting that technically it had nothing to do with Brown's firing, and could only recommend her replacement. But its actions in the ensuing months revealed that it was allied firmly with the citizens' committee and the commissioners. The board members shared their views both of Brown and of the role they believed the library should play to indoctrinate youth "with the principles of Americanism" and protect them from "the teaching of subversive doctrines."[2]

To help the library fulfill that role, the board's chairman enlisted the American Legion. Christopher was a past post commander and was active in Legion Americanism activities at local, state, and national levels. He had served as Americanism chairman for the Oklahoma Department of the American Legion for several terms in the late 1940s and had been a member of the national Americanism Commission from 1946 to 1948. In 1950 he would become a member of the National Commander's Special Committee on Un-American Activities, a membership he retained in 1951–52. Christopher had contacts throughout the country that he could tap for information and assistance. He had already made use of them to try to "dig up" information on Bayard Rustin and to acquire lists of speakers and entertainers "whose past activities [made] them unsuitable or inappropriate for Legion sponsorship." The Anti group apparently used this list to determine which of Bartlesville's Town Hall speakers to attack. Christopher made good use of his network as he set out to accomplish the task for which he had been recruited: purging the library of materials contrary to the "American Way of Life" and hiring a loyal American librarian.[3]

In August, less than a month after Brown's dismissal, Christopher wrote W. C. "Tom" Sawyer of the national American Legion's Americanism Division in Indianapolis asking for help in "clean[ing] out the Library." "They had it well stocked with all the Commie magazines and papers," he explained, "and we have probably missed half of them." What he needed were some lists. First he needed a "list of Communist writers, authors, etc." Then he needed "a list of Negro magazines published by *Americans.*" "All we have," he said, "have either been cited or the publishers have been, as being Communistic." And finally he needed both the list of citations issued by the attorney general and the list issued by the HUAC. "I have bought five or six the past year and given them away to womens [*sic*] organizations, mostly. Now when I need one, the Superintendent of Documents informs me they are out," he lamented.[4]

The American Legion and its lists guided selection of materials for the library throughout the year that Christopher served as chairman of the board. While various members of the Friends of Miss Brown attended library board meetings all through the fall and into the winter, lodging protests against the board's failure to renew subscriptions to *Negro Digest* and *Consumer Reports* and the segregation of the *Nation* and *New Republic* (to which subscriptions

E. R. Christopher. Courtesy Western History Collections, University of Oklahoma Library.

were, finally, renewed), Christopher compiled lists of materials for purchase from the titles recommended in the Americanism Division's monthly *Summary of Trends and Developments Exposing the Communist Conspiracy*. He prefaced one list of suggested purchases with the observation, "There appears to be quite a lot of interest locally in communistic literature and how to combat communism." He recommended that forty-two titles be added to the collection if they were not already available. In addition to such titles as Victor

Kravchenko's *I Chose Freedom* (also on the ALA's list of "50 Out-standing Books of 1946"), Benjamin Gitlow's *I Confess*, and David J. Dallin's *The Rise of Russia in Asia*, his suggestions included such materials as Joseph Kamp's crudely propagandistic *Behind the Lace Curtains of the Y.W.C.A.*, and *Red Channels*, the guilt-by-association pamphlet compiled and published by former FBI agents and used to create the blacklist of entertainers. He recommended the anti-communist pamphlets of the Chamber of Commerce, including *Communist Infiltration in the U.S.* (which devoted two pages to the subversive nature of the *Nation* and the *New Republic*) and *Program for Community Anti-Communist Action*, in addition to requesting all releases from HUAC. Finally he urged the board to thank Armais Arutunoff, head of Bartlesville's Reda Pump, for his gift subscription to the ultraconservative anticommunist *National Republic* magazine. The following month Christopher submitted a list of fifteen books related to farming and poultry production recommended by the county agent. But he could not resist adding to that list eight "new books off the press which should be added" to the anticommunist titles he had submitted the previous month. Among them were Frederick Barghoorn's *The Soviet Image of the United States* and Angela Calomiris's *Red Masquerade*. The American Legion's lists replaced the book selection aids of the American Library Association while Christopher was at the helm of the Bartlesville Public Library board.[5]

LIBRARIES AND THE AMERICAN LEGION

At its 1951 Midwinter Meeting—the same meeting at which it unanimously censured the Bartlesville City Commission's summary dismissal of Ruth Brown—the ALA Council warned librarians to prepare for possible "attacks" sparked by an article, "Why You Buy Books That Sell Communism," appearing in the January 1951 *American Legion Magazine*. The *Library Journal* even reported, apparently in error, that the council had adopted a resolution opposing American Legion attempts to "establish the principle that Legion posts are properly qualified" to determine library selections. Indeed, the contest between American Legionnaire and librarian over the selection of appropriate materials was not unique to Bartlesville. Unlike the DAR, which had a national policy to keep public libraries "free from false and insidious doctrine," the national Legion did not single out libraries for special attention. Nevertheless, the Legion kept a watchful eye out for subversive influences everywhere—in schools, libraries, unions, churches, and women's organizations. In 1948 the *American Library Association Bulletin* reported on a 1947 Illinois Legion resolution that called on its members to "purge all *libraries, schools,* and *book stores* of 'subversive' books" (emphasis in the original). The lists of writers with allegedly subversive connections that Christopher collected included a large number of well-known and highly regarded popular and scholarly writers, from mystery writer Dashiell Hammett to playwright Clifford Odets to novelist Pearl Buck. Because their works were very likely to be found in libraries, the "antisubversive" activism encouraged by the Legion put pressures— sometimes extreme ones—on librarians.[6]

While Brown struggled in Bartlesville, for example, in Peoria, Illinois, librarian Xenophon Smith was combating Legion objections to several films: *Brotherhood of Man* and the United Nations–sponsored *Boundary Lines*, which promoted "brotherhood," or improved race and intergroup relations, and *Peoples of the U.S.S.R.*, a travelogue that had earlier been used to train U.S. troops. The Legion later also challenged another UN film, *Of Human Rights*, designed to promote discussion of the UN's Universal Declaration of Human Rights. The episode followed the Legion's opposition to a 1947 Peoria concert by Paul Robeson, opposition that resulted in the closing of Peoria's Negro Legion Post and attacks on that post's vice-commander, an NAACP officer. The sequence of events gives rise to the suspicion that the objections to the films—like the objections to "subversive" materials in the Bartlesville library— were rooted not in the Legion's claimed concern about communist propaganda but in not so subtly veiled racism. Smith got support from his local ministerial alliance, the ALA, and even the Librarian of Congress, Luther Evans (U.S. representative to the UN Educational Scientific and Cultural Organization), who came to Peoria to explain the UN Declaration and to support Smith, a former employee of the Library of Congress. Nevertheless, Smith restricted the films to showings in the library screening room and allowed viewers' comments to be attached to the cans in which the films were contained. And while Smith, unlike Brown, did not get fired, he finally resigned his position—a casualty of tension and ill will. The Peoria episode led the ALA to adopt at the 1951 Midwinter Meeting a footnote to its Library Bill of Rights that explicitly included film and other media among materials that should not be proscribed or removed from libraries because of partisan or doctrinal disapproval.[7]

These were certainly not the only instances in which pressure from Legion posts—or individuals closely identified with the American Legion—was directed against librarians, library collections, or the ALA. A 1952 attack on the Boston Public Library was supported by two local Legion commanders, among others. In Fairmont, West Virginia, the college librarian, Harold Jones, lost his job because of his support for one of his colleagues in the art department, Louella Mundel; the American Legion was a major actor in the Fairmont conflict, one of the most dramatic instances in which anticommunism served the purposes of local politics. The *Shreveport Times* in January 1953 approvingly reported that *Firing Line*, a publication of the Un-American Activities Committee of the Legion's Americanism Commission had launched a "blistering attack" on the ALA's 1951 "Notable Books," not so much for what it contained, but for what it did not contain: titles about "Soviet Russia and its aggression against the West" or titles on the Korean War. The Punxsatawney, Pennsylvania, *Legion News* blasted the local library board for adopting the Library Bill of Rights and called the ALA a "Red Front Organization" in a 1955 challenge skillfully managed by librarian Mildred Harlan and her board with the help of the ALA.[8]

It would be unfair to say that the American Legion was responsible for all the attacks on libraries during this period. It is true, however, as James Rorty pointed out in a 1955 *Commentary* article, "The Libraries in a Time of Tension," that the publications of the Legion's Americanism Commission and later its Un-American Activities Committee (first *Summary of Trends and Developments* and then *Firing Line*), "by stimulating and coordinating" the activities of local anticommunist groups, were the source of a good deal of pressure. These publications, and many of the other publications they cross-fertilized, tended to "lump together indiscriminately books of widely differing merit and tendency," thus clearly demonstrating what Rorty called a lack of "fair-mindedness, not to speak of good sense."[9]

By 1952 apparently the national Legion's Un-American Activities Committee had decided that libraries, especially school and college libraries, needed focused attention. As part of its outline for action it intended to urge libraries to subscribe to *Firing Line, Counterattack,* and *Alert* (the latter two, publications of American Business Consultants, an enterprise devoted to blacklisting and then clearing authors and entertainers) and to use memorial donations of anticommunist books "to overcome the influences which keep anti-Communist books out of libraries." According to the July 11, 1952, *Counterattack,* these influences included the June 28 issue of the *Nation.* Not only did the *Nation's* special issue, "How Free Is Free?" include "an arsenal of misinformation for the Smear America bund" about dangers to freedom of thought and speech, but its "line of thinking greatly influence[d] U.S. librarians." The dangers of anticommunists were "fed" to librarians at their annual conference, *Counterattack* charged, while "little or nothing was said about the danger from the Communist fifth column and its shock troops in the publishing field." Because anticommunist books by writers like Ralph de Toledano (also a speaker at the ALA conference, a fact omitted by *Counterattack*) were not well reviewed in major organs, librarians would have to be pressured to buy them. The alleged communist tendencies of book reviewers for major reviewing organs, such as the *New York Times Book Review,* had earlier been painted vividly in the *American Legion Magazine* article "Why You Buy Books That Sell Communism." In the May

1952 issue of the same magazine the director of the Americanism Commission listed the ten books considered by commission "research specialists" to be the "most important and effective books combatting subversion currently published." He urged Legionnaires to see if their libraries carried the books, and if not, to find out why. "Remember," the article exhorted, "books are block-busters in the war against communism."[10]

Perhaps Christopher's experience as Bartlesville Public Library board chairman influenced the Un-American Activities Committee, of which he was concurrently a member, to elevate libraries to a position of importance in their campaign against subversion. It is clear that the American Legion, like other superpatriotic groups, saw texts (both print and film) as weapons and the libraries that selected them as contested arenas in a battle against foreign ideology. Librarians, although not directly accused of being communists, were, according to the Legion, being led astray—duped—by journals like the *Nation*, speakers at their own conferences, and reviewers, not to mention their own mistaken notions of freedom of speech and the press and their professional freedom of book selection.

A LOYAL LIBRARIAN

The new library board needed a "loyal American" librarian who would be amenable to its Legion-inspired book selection practices. Christopher's American Legion contacts were an important element in the selection process for a librarian to replace Ruth Brown as well. Immediately after Brown was fired—by the time of their August 1 meeting—the board received an application for the librarian position from Wilma Ingram, a member of the summer school faculty of the College of the Ozarks in Clarksville, Arkansas. Fred A. Walker, the college's president, responded to Elizabeth Chamberlin's inquiry about Ingram with assurances regarding not only her abilities as a librarian but her Americanism as well. Ingram herself, following an August 9 interview, wrote to Christopher that she was "not a reformer" and that it had "always been her policy to follow the regulations of the institution" for which she worked. The board appeared to be satisfied with her credentials. Brown and Essary's suit delayed the process of replacing Brown, however, and Ingram was not hired.[11]

It was not until the city had bested Brown at the district court level in November that the board renewed its search. Then, following the recommendation of Jesse Rader, librarian of the University of Oklahoma, Christopher solicited the application of Mary Mathis, the librarian at Camp Polk, Louisiana. Although Mathis seemed willing to discuss the Bartlesville position, she questioned the status of the suit and was apparently not persuaded by Christopher's assurances that Brown would not be able to return to reclaim her position. She remained at Camp Polk.[12]

In April 1951, with the suit still pending in the Oklahoma Supreme Court, city voters reelected incumbent city commissioners or their sympathetic successors in an election that was regarded—at least by Christopher and Brown—as a referendum on the issue of Brown and the library. (One could certainly not have detected that the library was the issue by reading the newspapers; there was very little mention of the library issue in the campaign coverage, and only one candidate's name had any obvious relation to members of the COPD or the Friends of Miss Brown.) Christopher and his colleagues felt comfortable searching yet again for a librarian. As Christopher wrote to Mathis, "The voters . . . settled the 'Library Question' at a city election." Not one of those supporting Brown was elected, he boasted, "and the library was our issue." He tried to answer Mathis's questions about what she had read concerning the Bartlesville case. "The only censorship that has ever been placed on the library was by Miss Ruth Brown and the former library board," he asserted. He sent her as evidence two pictures "taken by the *Examiner-Enterprise* photographer" of issues of the *Nation* and the *New Republic* stacked in the Civic Center basement while they awaited reconsideration. (One picture—the mysterious photograph that was not authorized by the former library board—had run in the paper.) He characterized the report of the OLA as "a smear campaign" and concluded by asking Mathis to help Bartlesville make the library one that could compete with that of neighboring Ponca City, an oil-rich city of comparable size just to the west of Bartlesville. It appears that Mathis was still not convinced, because within the month Christopher had contacted his American Legion connections to make sure that a different applicant met his standards.[13]

"Dear Commander," Christopher wrote to Edward Barron of the Athens, Texas, American Legion Post. "Wonder if you could do a little bird-dogging for me?" He established his credentials: he was not only "one of these useless Past Post Commanders" of the Bartlesville Legion Post, but he had been "Department Americanism Chairman 3 times" and "on the Department Americanism Commission for six years." He explained his status as library board chairman and continued, "We have had quite a bit of publicity, adverse and entirely unwarranted, I can assure you." A Miss Jon Gatlin of Athens had applied for the librarian position, and the board was considering her. But they first needed to verify her Americanism: "whether she believes in our Constitutional form of Government or that of Soviet Russia"; whether she was a member of any communist front organizations; and "whether she is a native Texaner[, or] whether she is a Northern [sic] that they have sent down south to get a job in a Southern Library, as we have found the Y.W.C.A. doing." They especially wanted to know, Christopher concluded, whether she belonged to CORE or the NAACP.[14]

Apparently the post commander's answers satisfied Christopher. On June 24, 1951, the *Bartlesville Examiner-Enterprise* announced Gatlin as the new head librarian. The library board apparently retained control over both book selection and budget, however. In March 1952, for example, board member Lois Lynd's offer of a year's subscription to Pro-America's *Freeman* magazine was accepted by her colleagues, apparently without any consultation with or comment from Gatlin. In addition, Lynd presided over the meeting "while Mr. Christopher moved that the board order the remainder of a list of books, recommended by the American Legion, dealing with findings on Communism." Finally, photographers from the local newspapers were present to record Ruth Brown's nemesis, Preston Gaddis, representing the local James H. Teel Legion Post, as he donated three copies each of Herbert Philbrick's *I Led Three Lives* and Clarence Manion's *The Key to Peace* to the library. The distribution of the Manion book was a part of the national Americanism Commission's program. In another instance the librarian was directed to provide the board with reviews of all books suggested for purchase; book committee members were to initial the titles they approved.[15]

In a little over a year Gatlin was ready to move on. Christopher responded to a July 1952 inquiry regarding Gatlin's qualifications by describing her not only as a sought-after book reviewer (144 public appearances in a year's time) but also as one who accomplished what the board wanted done. Christopher had been charged with "cleaning things up" and hiring a qualified librarian, and Gatlin had done an "excellent job here in all ways." He recounted, "We had no bon-fires but she has cleaned up the library, we are on our way to bringing the library into balance, we are stocking it with worth-while books and gradually eliminating the trash." Gatlin submitted her resignation, effective no later than December 1952, in August, before she found another job. She left in October.[16]

Her successor, Winnie Clayton, took up the position in November 1952. Clayton had recently spent more than a year as librarian at Bartlesville's Central Christian College, and was currently employed as assistant librarian for Continental Oil in neighboring Ponca City. By the time she was hired Christopher, Lynd, and Chamberlin had been replaced on the board by Mrs. Sam (Ruth) Harlan, the wife of a Cities Service vice president; Mrs. A. K. (Verna) Wilhelm, wife of a Cities Service geologist and a member of the YWCA board during the height of the controversy; and R. Kay Smith, a Phillips Petroleum personnel officer. Clayton was ready to leave by June 1953, less than a year later. Before Herbert E. "Gene" Winn took over as librarian in September, the library board moved to tie up loose ends and expunge all traces of the library battle. Harlan "questioned the propriety" of retaining Francesca Matusak, a recently hired part-time employee, because her husband, a Phillips scientist, had "figured prominently in the Library controversy three years ago." (Remaining evidence reveals only that M. P. Matusak attended a public meeting and described it in writing for an absent John Upham.) The board agreed not to reemploy her when she returned from vacation. Two members abstained from voting, however, signaling a slight shift as board membership changed. The board also debated what to do about book selection in the future, as it was not possible "to arrive at any just decision regarding books of a controversial nature in the limited time of a Board meeting." They deferred a decision until after Winn's arrival. At that time the board asked if he wished to be assisted in the selection of books, especially controversial ones. He did not, and, possibly because he, too, was a member of the American Legion, he made his selections without interference—although not without a warning visit from Mae Warren.[17]

BROWN'S RENTAL LIBRARY

By early September 1950 Brown was "getting bluer and bluer" as she destroyed her CORE papers. She had at first thought to stay in Bartlesville but, unable to return to her beloved library, had begun applying for other positions. Cincinnati, where her daughter Mildred lived with her husband and children, was attractive to her, largely because it had a CORE group. She would rent her house out and plan to return, but if she did not return, it was all right. The "Chief Hater" would "probably be here forever and always prejudiced," she said. "I'm sorry for him," she added. For the first time she also appeared to feel a little sorry for herself.[18]

Shortly thereafter, however, when Brown and Essary's suit against the commissioners and the replacement library board was filed, Brown's spirits improved. She decided to stay in Bartlesville, where she said, "I seem to be needed." Because there was no librarian at the library, there were no new books—"no one to order or catalogue"—so she decided to open a rental library in her home. Previous efforts at such a business had not succeeded, she admitted, but no "bookish person" had previously attempted it. Her location on Johnstone between downtown and the library, close to the YWCA and YMCA, should prove good for such a business. Staying in town would allow her also to continue some kind of interracial activities. She still talked to Gracey frequently and saw Dixon weekly.[19]

By the end of September Brown's Rental Library advertised new fiction and nonfiction books and "Morning Story Hours For Pre-School Children." But community pressures made establishing her business difficult. One Bartian, for example, recounted that while walking with a friend one day near Brown's home and seeing her shelf of books on the porch, his friend commented "I wouldn't be caught reading a book in Bartlesville, I don't care where it came from." Someone might think he had gotten the book from Brown. Nevertheless, the rental library provided Brown with reading material and brought her into contact with "people who really love books"—two things she found very important. Although she had done well selling books at Christmas time, in January Brown reported that her business was not "too profitable." Her friends prevailed on her to stay in Bartlesville, but she sometimes thought she would like to try working in a library serving African Americans. Her "chief interest" was still "the race question," she said. "Just yesterday," she told CORE's Houser, "I was able to tell our chief oily words hand rubbing *anti* that when color is forgotten all over the world we will have no more wars." Brown may have been defeated, but she was anything but repentant.[20]

Preoccupied though she might have been with "the race question," Brown did not give up on her book business. It was growing "better and better and I love it," she reported to her daughter Ellen on Washington's birthday, 1951, a day so bright and "thrilling" that she was moved to pen a poem about the golden crocus blooming in her yard. She was having a small display case made to put next to her walk, where she could advertise new titles, but because someone had run off with her last sign, this one would have to be brought in nightly. Again she returned to "the race question." A former CORE member, the dean of Bacone College, an Indian school several hours away, had come to visit her "to hear about what had happened here."[21]

In April, however, with the city election over and her supporters defeated, Brown decided to close the bookstore. Another opportunity—"the very work I want to do and can do"—had come her way. She had been invited to become the librarian at Piney Woods Country Life School, a school for African-American young people from kindergarten through junior college located about fifteen miles south of Jackson, Mississippi. She told everyone that she was going for the summer but that she would probably just stay. "The word communism is in everyone's mouth and four months away from it will be wonderful," she said. No doubt the fate of her friend, Roosevelt Gracey, principal of Douglass School, helped to seal Brown's decision to move on.[22]

"PROBLEMS OF A COMMUNITY NATURE"

Gracey's firing was the final scene of a show that began with the March 1950 offer of an African-American community center by the Anti group and R. D. Drew's threats against Gracey. In April 1950 the school board—composed of three longtime Cities Service employees, a building contractor, two Phillips employees, and the wife of a Phillips personnel manager—heard a committee of three African Americans present "several grievances" against Gracey. Nevertheless, School Superintendent George Roberts, to whom the matter was referred, apparently did not find cause for dismissal; Gracey's contract was renewed for the 1950–51 school year. In June 1950 Gracey's wife, Nellie, was added to the Douglass School staff. Early in January 1951, however, the board postponed contract discussions with Gracey because of apparent "opposition from local sources" to his "continued employment." In a subsequent meeting, the board—with its lone woman, Mrs. L. A. (Margaret) Whitehair (a Phillips employee spouse and a YWCA member), abstaining— voted to inform Gracey of the existing opposition so he "might feel free to exercise his option of . . . accepting another position."[23]

Gracey declined to take the hint. In a conference with the board president and the superintendent, Gracey stated, according to reports, "that there were some problems peculiar to a colored community" but nothing else that he knew of that was "controversial over his personal status." The board voted—Margaret Whitehair alone voting "No"—to warn Gracey, "as a courtesy to a professional man," that his job might be in jeopardy. The convoluted wording of the motion, which included such statements as "there were some indications that some of the members of the Board were seriously enough concerned about the renewal of his contract that he should be advised that his contract may not be renewed" and "the number that might vote for or against was indefinite since no official vote had been taken by the Board," suggests that the board wanted Gracey to resign and relieve them of the responsibility of deciding to fire him. He still did not oblige them by resigning.[24]

Instead, in response to the threat to Gracey's job, on February 14, 1951, fifty-six Douglass School patrons came to hear the board explain that it had as yet taken no official action. Twenty-two members of the group spoke. While no specific statements were recorded, the consensus, according to board minutes, was that "Mr. Gracey was an asset to the colored community and the separate school and should be retained as Principal." Less than a month later, however, a committee of twelve, including Drew and Scott, was, unlike the earlier group, "invited in and introduced" to the school board to offer "direct rebuttal" to the previous group's testimony. The charges against Gracey, quoted directly in the minutes, were that he failed "to cooperate with the community or church groups on all occasions"; that "he [was] somewhat swayed by prejudice in the treatment of co-workers"; and that he had "caused some of the community confusion and discension [sic]." The tone and specificity of the minutes of the two meetings differ considerably, suggesting that the board needed, encouraged, and perhaps even sought the rebuttal testimony in support of action they had decided to take against an "uppity" black man. A few days later the school board took up the matter of Gracey's contract. When asked directly Superintendent Roberts declined to give any recommendations, saying that Gracey's problems were "of a community nature rather than an academic nature." The majority—Margaret Whitehair again opposed—voted not to renew Gracey's contract.[25]

Whitehair's lone dissenting voice might have been joined by another, that of Paul J. Parker, secretary of Phillips Petroleum, except for the negative feedback he had received from a previous, related vote. In the telephone poll of the school board in February 1950, Parker had voted to allow Bayard Rustin to speak in a school auditorium. "I thought, 'Sure, let the fella come. Let him talk. And as long as the public wants to come and listen to him, fine,'" Parker remembered. But this expression of willingness to allow Rustin a voice and a venue apparently cast Parker as a "confrere" of Brown's. Word of his vote got to his employer, K. S. Adams, president of Phillips, by way of the wife of a co-worker, who apparently asked Adams if "he'd allowed a liberal person into the hierarchy of Phillips." Or rather, Parker suggested, perhaps she asked Adams if he had let a *communist* into the hierarchy. Adams did not keep this "loose talk" to himself, apparently, but relayed the gossip to Parker. "And so I had this stigma to live down," Parker said. In the final analysis Whitehair was the only voice of dissent on the school board. The white power structure had succeeded in dividing the African-American community and ridding it of its most powerful voice for integration.[26]

"ALLEY PINKS"

Gracey was not the only one of Brown's friends and colleagues to feel the effects of the power structure's wrath. George Cade and Frank Condon had already been transferred in connection with their activity in the COPD. Cade, who was protected by his superior, J. Paul Jones, went to Washington, D.C.; there Phillips sent him to law school to become a patent attorney. Although it was a move he ultimately wanted, he and his wife, Katrina, did not want to go at that particular time. Condon was sent to Phillips

Petroleum's "Siberia," a move he did not want. He left the company about two years later, after getting some articles published, and went into academic life.[27]

Some other COPD activists or Brown supporters connected with Phillips Petroleum had also left Bartlesville by the end of 1951 or shortly thereafter. Because transfers among Phillips's several facilities were not unusual, it is difficult to determine how many people left unwillingly, how many by choice. As Katrina Cade recounted it, those that Phillips learned "were being active in this cause were called upon the carpet and told to quiet down—to either leave the effort or they would take them somewhere else." Some, like former COPD president Leo McReynolds and researcher Charles Varvel, complied when told to "shut up or else be fired." They wanted to keep their jobs.[28]

John Upham, who with his wife, Marion, had played an active role in the Friends of Miss Brown, writing press releases and communicating with the ACLU and other organizations, was also instructed to "leave it alone." Although he and chief process engineer George Allen felt they were well received when they spoke about their involvement to Bill Keeler, vice president for refining, Upham suddenly began to receive job offers from around the country from people who were in some way connected to Phillips. A telephone call from Ida Rice of the Friends, whose husband was a Phillips vice president, confirmed his suspicions that the company wanted him out of town. She reported that a recent conversation among a group of traveling executives had turned to "how they were going to get rid of Upham." In 1952 Upham obliged Phillips. He took advantage of a good job offer from Monsanto to leave the community.[29]

Anthony Andrews, a Phillips researcher active in the Friends of Miss Brown ignored the message to be quiet. Instead of "shutting up," he wrote both the U.S. attorney's office and the postmaster general questioning the propriety of postmaster E. R. Christopher's membership on the controversial library board. When the U.S. attorney informed Christopher of the letter, his response was vitriolic: "I knew those alley Pink's [sic] were trying to get something to use on me. They don't like it because we have stopped using the tax-payers money to buy Commie magazines and books for the library."[30]

Christopher's response to the assistant postmaster general revealed his perspective in more detail. The new library board was not controversial, he said. It had the backing of "the Business Men, Chamber of Commerce, all the Civic Groups (Lion's, Kiwanis, Rotary Club) and Federated Women's Club, P.T.A., American Legion, D.A.R., U.D.C, V.F.W, and Public School System and all the other clubs and organizations that have taken action on the matter." Andrews was among the "fifteen or twenty people who call themselves liberals" who opposed the ouster of Brown and the old board. The library, which had been "at a low ebb . . . for several years," was "full of Communistic literature," he said, and had "nothing favorable to the American Way of Life." Following an investigation in which the library board "turned in a white-wash of the Library and the Librarian," Christopher explained, the commissioners fired the librarian when she "refused to talk or cooperate" with them. The new board had not renewed subscriptions to magazines with "citations," he conceded, and others were held at the desk "to ascertain if there was any demand" other than from Andrews, who asked for them weekly. Finally he listed as references the presidents of Phillips, Cities Service, and National Zinc.[31]

Attached to Christopher's letter was a separate "CONFIDENTIAL REPORT" describing Phillips's efforts to contain the controversy surrounding Brown and the library. "All of these liberals," Christopher wrote, "work for Phillips Petroleum Company and in their Research Laboratory." The company realized "that they let things get out of hand. They were hiring Scientists without checking their loyalty to the United States of America." In a comment revealing the undercurrent of anti-intellectualism that ran through the anticommunist movement, he continued, "If the man or woman had four or five degrees, they put them to work." Apparently Phillips researchers were subject to federal loyalty investigations because of their involvement with federally funded research. When the FBI checked some employees, Christopher said, the company "began a check of their own; [they] have been doing a lot of transferring around and in some cases, outright firing. . . . [A]t the rate they are going, in another six months all the so-called 'liberals' will be gone." Christopher explicitly linked intimations of disloyalty with Phillips employees' "liberal" activism. He suggested also that although Brown herself probably was not a communist, "these folks were playing up to her and advising her, entertaining her, and as she was getting old she fell for their line." A letter supporting Christopher had been sent just days before from Phillips president K. S. Adams, also president of the Chamber of Commerce and an American Legionnaire.[32]

Anthony Andrews paid for his letter writing and his persistence in monitoring the library board. According to several participants, he was cautioned to be quiet and then fired outright. Others suggest he was offered a transfer to the nuclear facility that Phillips had begun to operate for the federal government in Idaho but refused the transfer and was fired. Although the circumstances are unclear, it is clear that Andrews left Phillips "by request," and left Bartlesville as well.[33]

In April 1951 Adams responded to charges from Adolph Dryer, husband of Ruth Brown's elder daughter, Mildred, that Phillips management "helped to persecute" Brown. Dryer had returned unsigned a proxy for a stockholders' vote with a statement that he "lacked confidence in the management of the Company" because it helped to persecute the librarian. Adams denied "categorically and emphatically" that Phillips was at any time "involved in the matter." He asserted that Phillips employees had "the greatest freedom in their personal and social affairs" and that many were active in civic life.[34]

Of course, in one sense he was right. There is no evidence that Adams, or any other member of Phillips management, directly urged the firing of Ruth Brown. There is evidence, however, that the company intensely disapproved of the controversy generated by the Committee on the Practice of Democracy's activities, as well as the subsequent defense of Brown by the Friends. The oil companies wanted to protect their amicable and profitable relationship with the city's long-established residents, who wanted no change in the status quo. While virtually no one connected with Cities Service was active in promoting racial equality or in defending Brown, Phillips employees were numerous and active in both causes. To avoid accusations of having brought in outsiders who disrupted "America's ideal family center," Phillips made every effort to quiet the controversy by transferring, whenever feasible, those active on the side of integration or retaining Brown. Those who contributed to the controversy on the other side—by urging Brown's ouster or Gracey's nonrenewal, for example—were apparently not cautioned or transferred. Thus while Phillips protected their human capital—their engineers, scientists, and lawyers—it was "involved in the matter" by virtue of transferring supporters rather than opponents of racial integration and Brown. They did not choose to punish involvement in the controversy but to punish involvement on the side of Brown and integration.[35]

Might Adams have chosen to use his power to quiet the controversy? Adams's use of power is legendary in Bartlesville. Brooks Spies, a lifelong Bartian and longtime Phillips employee whose father had come to Bartlesville initially to work with Frank Phillips and whose mother was a member of the Friends of Miss Brown, indicated, for example, that Adams had used his power and Phillips's wealth to force Cities Service to leave Bartlesville. Whenever Cities Service tried to buy a property to establish its headquarters, Adams bought the property or otherwise made sure it would be removed from the market. "He didn't want them here, another frog in his puddle," Spies said. But would Adams have involved himself in matters less closely related to the business? Spies told one especially revealing story of which he had firsthand knowledge. According to Spies, a young Phillips employee, a member of the 66ers basketball team, was transferred out of Bartlesville because his wife publicly encouraged other parents not to enroll their fourth-grade children in Adams's wife's "Cotillion"—an etiquette and dance class. If a wife's activism regarding such a minor matter merited a transfer for a husband, one's own or a family member's activism on behalf of a more serious social issue certainly merited a transfer. Spies said, "I'm sure if they [Phillips employees] had been doing that [being active in race relations] they would have been 'taken care of.' Phillips in those days was just as prejudiced as anybody, and they had iron control. They could move a guy or fire him or anything. . . . You can't realize how much pressure can come."[36]

The women of the YWCA certainly felt the pressure. Elizabeth Davis commented in the annual report on the "many blows" the board had withstood during the year of controversy, including "feelings of intimidation when the husband's boss showed a different viewpoint." Perhaps Adams used this implicit pressure in 1951 when, as membership chairman of the Bartlesville American Legion Post, he nearly doubled the post's membership quota of eight hundred, earning himself the title Oklahoma's Outstanding Legionnaire. Bartlesville's American Legion membership thus outnumbered its entire African-American population. If the Legion's position upholding the traditional class and caste system of the South needed reinforcing within the community, both the 1951 membership drive led by the community's most powerful figure and the August 1952 celebration honoring him no doubt accomplished that task.[37]

It was enforced conformity and seemingly unmovable support for segregation that drove some of the young professionals away. Daniel and Alice Jones and Robert and Elva Manuel were among those who left of their own volition; the two men had been called "commies" at the March meeting. Jones took a position at the University of Utah; according to Nelson, "He never recovered from this incident." John Widdowson went to a new position. Lois Ogilvie, one of the most active members of the COPD, moved into a new house in Bartlesville in March 1950, according to the local AAUW newsletter. In September the newsletter noted the Ogilvies' new address as Dumas, Texas. During the summer Robert Ogilvie had gotten an advantageous transfer with a promotion. The Ogilvies discussed its timing. Lois Ogilvie, apparently suspicious,

told her husband that if the transfer was to get her out of Bartlesville, they should refuse it. He believed that the timing was
coincidental, and they left Bartlesville not long after Brown was
fired.[38]

Darlene Anderson Essary was not forced to leave, but after
several years, during which her marriage to Paul Essary ended,
she took a leave of absence, remarried, and left Phillips and
Bartlesville. In 1954, identified by Anderson, her birth name, the
elegant attorney was captured by a Phillips photographer for a
Philnews article, "Women in Oil." In 1956 she sent Vera and
Anthony Andrews, now living in Illinois, a copy of an article that
was, she said, "a singularly accurate account of my subjective
experience in the library fuss." The article was a first-person
account by Sarah Patton Boyle, a white southerner who had
worked for desegregation in Charlottesville, Virginia, and who
had a cross burned on her lawn. Boyle described the community's treatment of one of its own who dared to transgress its
carefully drawn racial lines. Although she expected to be disapproved of, threatened, even hated, she said, she was unprepared
for the "contemptuous jeers and obscene insults" she received.
She was even less prepared to have her motives misinterpreted.
She reported, "[There were] accusations that I am a paid agent of
the Communists, that I am bribed by the NAACP to tell lies, that
I oppose the status quo because of a perverted passion for
publicity and—hardly least—that I long for integration because
of a psychopathic yearning for the special pornographic skills of
black men." To make matters worse, those who supported her
fell silent as they witnessed the repeated attacks on her. As silence
gathered about her she felt increasingly isolated and, lacking the
nourishment of normal human interaction, fatigued. There were
no social rules to guide those who wished to support people such
as herself, Boyle surmised. Nevertheless, she explained, "If your
friends are silent, you hear only evil." As time goes on, she added,
both you and your onetime supporters "are filled with the unfor-
mulated suspicion that you got what you somehow deserve."
Essary too felt the powerful effect of being isolated and frozen

out of a community in which she had lived and had expected to continue to live amicably with others. As Don Koppel, one of the library board members named as defendants in Brown and Essary's suit said, the community thought it was "outrageous" that a woman "was an attorney and involved in something like this [the suit]. Why she ought to go home and bake some cookies." Both the experience Essary shared with Boyle—the jeers, the accusations of being a communist, the sexual innuendo, and the silence—and the attitude described by Koppel seemed especially designed to punish women who challenged the accepted racial ideology. And Essary's challenge to the ideology came from a professional woman, a woman, like Brown, already outside her assigned domestic sphere. Essary decided she had had enough of Bartlesville.[39]

THE YWCA AND THE CENTER

Elizabeth Davis of the YWCA decided that Bartlesville had had enough of her. She had finished out the 1949–50 program year, in spite of the Opposition's calls for her removal. The divisions in the community, however, "strongly affected" the 1950 United Community Fund drive. The fund's board decided to inaugurate a complicated allocation card to allow individuals to pledge to, or withhold pledges from, organizations of their choice, a move many perceived as a "direct attack" on the YWCA. Just before the fund drive began, a "concerted, though almost secret effort" to remove Davis met with, as she said, "practically no success." A few days before the fund drive began, however, the YWCA announced that Davis had introduced several new adult programs so as to have them established for her successor at the end of her contract year, September 1951. The YWCA met its funding goal.[40]

The YWCA did not manage to withstand the pressure to move the Douglass Y-Teen meetings out of its new building, however. When the 1950 school year began the Douglass girls met "in their own building," apparently with Gracey's approval. The Interclub Council meetings continued.[41]

As she prepared to leave for Evanston, Illinois, and her next YWCA post, Davis commented on the progress of the center proposed for the African-American community by those opposed to integration. Phillips Petroleum had donated construction "shanties" used by contractors of its new office building. Davis remarked, "The self-appointed joint committee of whites and Negroes" had made public the floor plans and was "going ahead without regard or consultation of the existing agencies in the community, drawing up fine plans of a Center that includes an area marked 'Y-Teen and Girl Scout room!' This sponsoring committee is all-male, and definitely pro-segregation." As preparations went ahead for the center, there were a bevy of farewell parties for Davis, who left Bartlesville in July 1951.[42]

"The tensions over the race question and the search for subversive influence in the churches, YWCA, and in individuals have eased during the last year," wrote Davis's successor in the September 1952 annual report. Despite the efforts of the American Legion's Americanism chairman to "inject prejudice and hatred into his program," only a small group of "believers" continued to follow his lead. Members of the Opposition fruitlessly attempted to have some of their number elected to YWCA leadership positions to "continue their scrutiny of YWCA policies and promote the anti-negro movement." The new Westside Community Center was nearing completion. Because the bids for its construction had been too high, the committee had awarded the contract to T. P. Scott, one of the center's early proponents and a member of the group who had appeared with Drew at the school board meeting to attack Gracey. Scott became the first president of the center's board of directors, composed entirely of African Americans, and has since been regarded as the "father" of the Westside Community Center. While not all members of the African-American community were uniformly pleased with its program, a year after it opened the YWCA believed it was serving a "great need."[43]

A WHIMPER

By the end of 1953 the United Community Fund drive was back to full funding. Although the American Legion remained "alert to possible 'dangerous' ideology" and the Pro-America group continued to urge the YWCA to sever its ties with the national organization, the "'racial-communist scare' disturbance of 1950 and 1951" had dwindled. Gene Winn had become librarian, and would remain so for many years, exercising his professional jurisdiction over book selection without interference.[44]

Of course, the community had changed. Ruth Brown and Roosevelt Gracey were gone. Dr. J. B. Dixon completed a five-year obligation to Bartlesville in 1953 and was called up with his reserve unit to serve in the Korean War. Rumors persist—but cannot be substantiated—that his active duty was encouraged or instigated by the Bartlesville draft board and the American Legion. Elizabeth Davis had moved to her next YWCA assignment. George and Katrina Cade, Francis Condon, Anthony Andrews, and a number of other young Phillips employees—the Ogilvies, Uphams, Joneses, Manuels, and Widdowsons—had left. Everything in Bartlesville, Oklahoma, was back to normal.

But even Bartlesville could not hold back the world. Just a year later the Supreme Court decision in *Brown v. Board of Education* ended the legal sanction for the segregation against which Ruth Brown, Roosevelt Gracey and the COPD, the women of the YWCA and of the AAUW's Racial Problems Study Group, and their cohorts had fought. In addition, in 1954 the U.S. Senate censured Joseph McCarthy, who inspired many extreme anticommunists, reducing his influence and giving courage to those who fought his brand of accusation, insinuation, and fear.

POSTSCRIPT

And what of Ruth Brown? The publicity accorded her firing drew her to the attention of the administration of the Piney Woods

Country Life School. Dr. Zilpha E. E. Chandler, the school's assistant administrator, invited Brown to become the school's librarian. She did so, joining a group of four or five white retirees or young volunteers from the upper Midwest who, along with a number of African-American teachers, worked at the school. The white teachers lived together in a house built for them; board was also provided, though they were required to eat at separate tables in the school's dining room, probably in an effort to avoid scandalizing the school's white neighbors.[45]

Brown later described how she came to the school: "I had lost my 30 years' position as Public Librarian in a Border Town because I became most actively interested in the Negroes of this town and, unlibrarian like [sic] couldn't 'keep my mouth shut' or my actions from showing. The last straw was probably asking to be served, with two lovely Negro high school teachers, at a drugstore." The three years at Piney Woods, she said, "became the wonderful experience of my life." Her experience in Bartlesville had taught her "to forget color," so she "fitted in" well.[46]

At least she fitted in with the students and her teaching colleagues. The administrators were another matter. Brown soon was bothered by the school's policies and rigid notions of education. Not only was it "all work and almost no play," she said, but the "Sub-Tyrant," as Brown in her blunt way dubbed one administrator, believed that the students' "natures" must be "sternly controlled." This resulted in very strict rules that could lead to the expulsion of junior college students found holding hands or to the corporal punishment of small children. Brown delighted in taking older students on astronomy walks at night or helping to chaperone long country walks on Sunday even if—or perhaps because—they provided opportunities for the students to "practice hand holding and an occasional kiss." She was "thrilled" to have the opportunity to teach the ninth graders "Religion for Living" and, later, to teach comparative religions to the junior college students at Sunday School time. But she lambasted a seminary student who was practicing his preaching at Piney Woods for his use of clichés and "so frightened him that he never returned." She was pleased to be

given the opportunity to work with elementary age children—
until she was told she would have to carry a switch because it was
the only form of discipline they knew. She refused and worked
with preschool children instead—"pure joy." She especially delighted
in teaching them poetry. "Oh, I hope some of these children love
it," she said.[47]

While it is certain that Brown loved many of the young people
with whom she worked at Piney Woods, it is equally certain that
the administration, especially "the Tyrant" (Dr. Chandler) did not
feel so well disposed toward the outspoken Brown. "So three years
of me and speaking my mind were all they could stand of me or I
of them," Brown recounted. "I filed my resignation to be produced
when necessary." That occasion came when a couple was expelled
"for little more than smiling at each other." Brown knew that
Chandler would be told what her reaction to the expulsion had
been. She was right. The next day, as she later told the story, she
was ordered off the campus immediately. Her departure actually
may not have been not quite so sudden, or at least it must have
been obvious that it was coming. In a letter written right after her
departure from the school, to Evelyn Barkdoll, a young white
volunteer teacher with whom she had formed a friendship, Brown
reported an emotional leave taking from three young women who
were "planning to be teacher-librarians," Mildred, Ollie, and Annie
Mae. They had come to see her "often those last few days" and
became "sort of choky and went away fast" when she "hugged
and kissed each one." She "needed to be alone for a few minutes
too," Brown wrote her friend, adding, "I suppose I am still referred
to as 'that Miss Brown.'"[48]

"That Miss Brown," jobless again after less than three years at
Piney Woods, stayed with her daughter Ellen in Collinsville,
Oklahoma, until in 1955 or 1956 she landed a job as librarian at the
Sterling, Colorado, Public Library with the help of some old
Bartlesville friends, the Espachs (Mrs. Espach was the daughter of
Judge and Mrs. Kahle, with whom Brown had roomed in her early
years in Bartlesville). The Sterling city manager, Marvin McElwain,
knew of her history but was "delighted to find a lady of her caliber

who was willing to do the job." Brown was regarded as "no-nonsense, very service-oriented," but she made little effort to become a part of the community, preferring apparently to concentrate on the library. Brown never discussed her Bartlesville dismissal.[49]

She was "very close-mouthed, . . . so stern," the children's librarian Bernia Barrows recalls. And she accumulated little or nothing during her Sterling sojourn, perhaps because she had been relatively nomadic over several years and had had no real source of income, but also because she had no real interest in "things." Barrows's most vivid memory of Brown is having lunch at Brown's home on the occasion of her job interview in 1959. Brown had only one place setting—one plate, one cup and saucer, one glass, one knife, fork, and spoon—which she divided between the two women. Their small sandwich and piece of fruit were typical of Brown's frugality. "She didn't have anything in her house," Barrows recalled. The walls were bare.[50]

The Sterling position was fortunate not only in that McElwain "liked the way she ran the library and she liked the way Marvin let her run the library" but also in that, for the first time in her life, at age sixty-four, she was in the Social Security system. Although she could have stayed "as long as she wanted," Brown retired from Sterling in 1961, at seventy. She was on the verge of retirement from Sterling when she wrote her letter to the *Library Journal* congratulating the American Library Association for finally dealing with the issue of racial segregation in libraries and wondering why it had failed to deal with the issue when it arose in Bartlesville in 1950.[51]

When Brown retired she moved to Cincinnati, where her foster daughter, Holly, lived with her family. She had a small apartment built on the side of their house, and she kept busy. She attended at least several meetings of CORE and volunteered to provide support services for the Freedom Riders and other civil rights activities. She walked to the senior citizens' center and played Scrabble and dominoes. Although her relations with Holly were sometimes strained, she enjoyed a before-dinner drink with Holly's husband, Adolph, and read and talked with Holly's children, especially Ellen and Nina, who did not appear to find her as stern as Bernia Barrows did. As she aged, her health, never robust, weakened. She was unable to travel and required hired help. When Holly decided to put her in a nursing home, Ellen dissented and came to take her to live with her family in Collinsville. Brown had lived there only a few months when she fell and fractured her pelvis. Complications of the fracture and diabetes led to a stroke. Brown died on September 10, 1975, at the age of eighty-four. At her request her body was donated to the University of Oklahoma Medical Center. She remained detached from "things" to the end.[52]

CHAPTER FIVE

"FIGHTING MCCARTHYISM THROUGH FILM"

The Ruth Brown Episode According to Hollywood

*We're telling Russia we can read a book designed to be
inimical to democracy and yet not be damaged by it, because
we are stronger than Russia.*

—DANIEL TARADASH,
Variety, July 6, 1955

In the waning days of the tense Oklahoma summer of 1950, with
news from the Korean War solidifying fears of international communism and McCarthy's attacks heightening concerns about
internal subversion, Darlene Anderson Essary, friend of librarian
Ruth Brown and member of the ousted board of the Bartlesville
Public Library, wrote a letter to the editor of *Saturday Review*. In it
she described the events surrounding Brown's firing by the city
commissioners. She could not have guessed that the screenwriter
Elick Moll would read her effort to draw the nation's attention to
Brown and the library. Nor could she have imagined that he would
suggest her September 30, letter to his friend and fellow screenwriter Daniel Taradash as the inspiration for a screenplay that they
would write "to fight McCarthyism through film." Had she known,
she might have predicted the squalls and flurries that would occur
from the conception of the script Taradash and Moll called *The
Library* ("as dull a title as we could think of") to the reception of

the film that Taradash ultimately called *Storm Center*. The controversy that swirled around the film and the events on which it commented echoed the one that swept over Bartlesville.[1]

Hollywood had reason to fight the brand of anticommunism dubbed McCarthyism. In 1947 the House Committee on Un-American Activities under J. Parnell Thomas launched hearings to uncover communist influence in the film industry. With great fanfare HUAC marched a group of producers, actors, directors, but mostly scriptwriters into the hearing room and asked them to testify as to their present or former memberships in the Communist party or organizations labeled communist fronts and, if they hoped to be forgiven their past associations and activities, to "name names." Friendly witnesses cooperated with HUAC. Among them were Roy Brewer, anticommunist leader of the International Alliance of Theatrical Stage Employees, who had long opposed the efforts of Hollywood's communists and liberals to organize for fairer treatment from the studios; and Lela Rogers, Ginger Rogers's mother, who claimed the line "Share and share alike" proved the communist influence in film scripts. Some "unfriendly witnesses" from among Hollywood's most politically active screen artists—writers John Howard Lawson, Ring Lardner, Jr., and Dalton Trumbo and director Herbert Biberman and the rest of the so-called Hollywood Ten—refused to cooperate and were held in contempt of Congress. The last of the Ten exhausted their appeals and went to prison in September 1950, at about the time Moll read Essary's letter. But even before that, they and others were blacklisted—prevented from working—by the studios. By late 1947, according to Larry Ceplair and Steven Englund's *The Inquisition in Hollywood*, studios "could no longer afford, and would no longer tolerate, activism." Studios became very cautious about who they hired and the scripts they produced, and anticommunist films appeared as the industry tried to mend negative perceptions and fend off additional investigations.[2]

Despite the Hollywood producers' efforts to appease HUAC by blacklisting "unfriendly witnesses" from the 1947 hearings, in spring 1951, while Taradash and Moll worked on the script of *The*

Library, HUAC revisited the film industry. Quite possibly its decision to return to the scene of its earlier drama was related to a March 1951 meeting between film industry representatives and members of the newly established American Legion Un-American Activities Committee—of which Bartlesville's postmaster and library board member E. R. Christopher was a member—"to determine the steps that could be taken to eliminate the communist infiltration of that industry."[3]

Regardless of whether the Legion pressured HUAC to act again, events of the past several years had strengthened the hand of the new HUAC chairman, John S. Wood. Since HUAC's 1947 hearings, Klaus Fuchs had been arrested for spying, the Soviets had exploded an atomic bomb, and Alger Hiss had been convicted of lying when he denied he was a spy for the Soviets. Further, China had fallen to the communists, Joseph McCarthy had debuted his anticommunist crusade, and Ethel and Julius Rosenberg had been arrested. Young American men were dying in Korea. The passage of the McCarran Internal Security Act, which required the registration of all communists, established the Subversive Activities Control Board, and provided for the detention of "subversives," reflected the heightened tension in the nation and the extent to which Congress, at least, was willing to sacrifice civil liberties for a sense of security. In 1947 HUAC had aimed for the most dedicated of the Hollywood activists, many of them former or present communists. In 1951 it went after the remaining activists.[4]

By this time, however, many of those targeted by HUAC had left the country or voluntarily "confessed." Liberal actor Edward G. Robinson, for example, testified at his own request before the committee, trying to clear himself of any "pink" taint. Robinson's appearance before HUAC, while it benefited him, established a new hurdle for others who wished to keep their jobs. Anyone subpoenaed by the committee was assumed to be guilty; artists who wished to avoid the blacklist had to "clear" themselves by appearing before HUAC and giving the names of colleagues who were or had been communists or Popular Front activists. To do anything less was to become unemployable.[5]

By late 1951 anyone with the slightest hint of thirties or forties activism who wanted to work in film, television, or radio had to be "cleared." But by now HUAC was aided in both blacklisting and clearance not only by the immensely powerful American Legion but also by American Business Consultants (ABC), a private firm of three former FBI agents. These two organizations examined hearing transcripts of such groups as the California Tenney Committee and HUAC, the pages of the *Daily Worker*, and letterheads of former Popular Front organizations to identify anyone who could be accused of following the party line. Unlike HUAC, these groups were not constrained by legislative guidelines to limit themselves to either former communists or fellow travelers. Through their publications—the *American Legion Magazine* and its *Firing Line* and ABC's *Counterattack* and *Red Channels*—they connected liberal activism with "un-American activities" and created a "graylist" from which only the proper posture of public penitence, and sometimes a few hundred dollars, could redeem an entertainer's career. Vincent Hartnett's Aware, Inc., joined the "smear and clear" business in December 1953.[6]

The American Legion had exercised its vigilance over the entertainment media for several years. In 1948 it commended the contempt citations for the Hollywood Ten, and it congratulated the film industry for producing *I Married a Communist*, *The Red Menace*, and *Behind the Iron Curtain* when it met in 1949. At the same time it applauded General Foods and Pepsi-Cola of New York for removing "from their radio and television programs certain persons of known communistic sympathies." In May 1949 the *American Legion Magazine* published R. E. Combs's "How Communists Make Stooges out of Movie Stars," which described Hollywood's Popular Front activities—in which communists had admittedly been active—and ascribed to them a sinister purpose. By showing that many screen artists had belonged to the same groups, Combs purported to demonstrate that those who joined must have deliberately done so because the groups were a means of furthering communist objectives. By changing the meaning of "front" as used in Popular Front—a coalition to achieve a common purpose—to mean a facade or false appearance masking an illicit purpose, as in "communist front organization," Combs's article, like the discourse of many other right-wing anticommunists, helped to accomplish the purpose of linking Popular Front causes such as integration, opposition to fascism, and unionism, embraced by noncommunist liberals, with the party line.[7]

In spite of HUAC's return to Hollywood and the plethora of informants—and unemployed—it had generated, the *American Legion Magazine* nevertheless published J. B. Matthews's "Did the Movies Really Clean House?" in December 1951, precipitating another meeting in March 1952 with industry representatives fearful of threatened boycotts and the publication of lists of films that the Legion claimed were made with the help of un-American screen artists. By the following fall, when the Legion's Un-American Activities Committee had completed its first full year, its new publication *Firing Line* had become a watchdog of the entertainment industry. The committee's annual report boasted not only that the newsletter was a "primer on Communism" but also that each issue compiled "front activities of prominent 'Hollywood' and other entertainment stars." The same report protested that the Legion could not be used as a "whitewash" or "clearance" agency. While it could—and did—investigate individuals' suspect activities and associations "and present the facts to the proper individuals for their own action," the accused individuals alone could "clear" themselves, the report stated, "by future conduct, and their own assertions." Nevertheless, as a result of the meeting with producers, at which the Legion presented 300 names of people with tainted pasts, 298 of them not previously called by HUAC, the Legion *was* in the clearance business. It not only prescribed a formula for a letter of penance, but it published articles by the penitents, such as Edward G. Robinson's "How the Reds Made a Sucker out of Me," which appeared in the October 1952 *American Legion Magazine*. In one form or another the blacklist and its accompanying clearance procedures would last until the end of the decade, when a combination of award-winning pseudonymous scripts, lawsuits, and a change in the direction of the political winds emptied the blacklisters' sails.[8]

"THE LIBRARY"

This was the situation that not only made Taradash and Moll's story pertinent but also made a story about "book-burning and character assassination" so controversial that they feared it would not sell in "a town in fear." The screenwriters took several important elements from Essary's letter about Brown's firing, which emphasized the takeover of the library by the city commission, the removal of materials, and the firing of Brown amid implications of subversive activities that included her participation in interracial programs. The first, of course, was the figure of the librarian. Taradash and Moll's librarian, Alicia Hull, was fifty-seven and had been librarian in the town they called Kenport for twenty-five years. Although Essary's letter did not reveal Brown's age as fifty-nine, it did indicate she had been Bartlesville librarian for three decades. And, in fact, in one version of the script Hull served as librarian for thirty years. Thus, like Brown, the fictional librarian was middle-aged and with long service to the community. The second element was locating the film's conflict and some pivotal scenes between the city council and the librarian over the censorship of communist library materials, as the letter described the conflict in Bartlesville. It was this conflict of librarian with city council that captured his imagination, Taradash said later. The third element of the film that paralleled the letter on the Brown episode, the one that linked the film's theme to the situation in Hollywood, was the Kenport City Council's equating participation in Popular Front causes with communism and the use of guilt by association to attack the librarian's character and reputation. In just the same way the Bartlesville City Commission and the citizens' group had suggested that Brown's liberal views and actions on race relations were subversive and communist. Although in 1956 Columbia Pictures responded to an inquiry from Oklahoma City reporter Jack Heaney that the film did not "relate in any way to the woman in Bartlesville," Columbia vice president B. B. Kahane was concerned. He asked Taradash about his story's source. The files do not contain Taradash's answer, but Kahane cautioned him against revealing any relationship. "Innocent as it appears on the face, the letter may really be the forerunner of a legal claim or suit," he warned. Despite Kahane's denials, the three central elements of the film were all briefly sketched in Essary's letter.[9]

The story Taradash and Moll finally worked out was embellished with a subplot that Taradash called a love story, between Alicia Hull and Freddie Slater, a little boy with an overactive imagination who loves to read. The rising action is launched when the Kenport City Council, pressured by citizens, asks Hull to remove from the shelves of the Free Public Library a book called *The Communist Dream*. In exchange they promise to build her long-desired children's wing. Hull at first agrees but on reflection, informs the council that as a matter of principle she has returned the book to the shelves. Hull's assistant, Martha Lockridge, tells her suitor, an ambitious young politician named Paul Duncan, that she is not surprised at Hull's reaction, because Hull has very strong views on civil liberties. Duncan's curiosity is aroused.

Meanwhile, Hull has allowed Freddie Slater to take home a book from the Treasure Room, and in a fight with his father over Freddie reading at the dinner table, the book has been torn. A contrite Freddie comes to Hull's apartment to bring her the book; rather than scold, she gives it to him. Freddie's father, who disdains books and cultural activities, is angry because his son is different from the other boys. Hull admonishes George Slater that there is "too much conformity" and that he should value his son for who he is.

In a scene reminiscent of events in Bartlesville, the council summons Hull to meet with them regarding her refusal to remove *The Communist Dream*. In the film's central scene, Hull defends her action. She argues that the book actually exposes the truth about communism and that having it in the library is testimony to America's faith in its citizens' ability to make judgments for themselves. Rather than try to take the book off the shelves, Hull insists, the city council ought to be fighting to keep it there. Upset by her intransigence on the principle of freedom to read, Duncan pulls a sheaf of papers out of his briefcase—papers that could have come only from Hull's own files—and begins to question Hull regarding

her membership in a half-dozen Popular Front–type organizations.[10] He insists that if Hull belonged to any communist front
organizations, it must mean that she "believed in some of their
ideas." On the contrary, Hull asserts, in words that many a Hollywood liberal must have uttered, "They believed in some of mine."
Voice shaking, Hull addresses Duncan: "It's obvious that you and
I don't agree on many things—including censorship. But in case
you are in any doubt, I'm not a Communist. I never was a Communist. I despise the Communists."[11]

Hull's protests are fruitless. With the thunder rolling outside
city hall, Duncan claims that he is not calling Hull a communist
but "an easy prey for a lot of high-sounding slogans." "Forgive
me," he continues, "but you were a dupe once and you may be
again." Several council members are disturbed by Duncan's tactics,
but his ally, Stacey Martin, escalates the tensions and ups the
stakes. "You realize what could happen if this got out?" he asks.
Hull understands his threat completely. Her friend on the council,
Robert Ellerbe, asks Duncan if the issue can be forgotten if Hull
removes the book. Duncan agrees, provided all "questionable
material" will henceforth be "screened" by the council. Hull con-
cedes that the council has the power to remove the book from the
library as well as to fire her. And, she says, "If you do one, you'll
have to do both." Despite Ellerbe's pleas, Hull refuses to reconsider
and leaves the meeting. Martin moves quickly to press for her
dismissal. Ellerbe and one other council member weakly protest,
but Duncan and Martin carry the day, pressing for—and getting—
a unanimous vote to fire the librarian immediately.

Hull's firing has a devastating effect on Freddie Slater, who
cannot understand why she will not just pretend to remove the
book from the library. As news of her dismissal and rumors about
her spread, people cool toward her. A meeting called to gather
support on her behalf draws a fraction of the expected crowd, its
attendance hurt by a newspaper story on her "red affiliations."
Stunned by the ramifications of the attack, she declines to allow
her shrinking group of supporters to fight for her reinstatement;
she does not want her friends to suffer.

Freddie is suffering, however. He does not understand what a communist is, and his mother, Laura, is concerned about his state of mind. George Slater thinks that Freddie's sense of betrayal by Hull might be a good thing, and he feeds Freddie's confusion. Later, when Hull invites Freddie, along with some other children, to a movie, he refuses even to speak to her. Freddie's growing hostility and the rebuff of the children hurt Hull deeply. Away from the librarian, Freddie, anxious to gain the favor of the other children, combines things he has heard his father say with fragments of conversation he and Hull have had about books. He talks himself into an even greater frenzy of fear and bewilderment.

When Martha Lockridge, now librarian, discovers Freddie in the library after hours, she calls on Hull to ask her to do something about the boy. In an awkward confrontation Hull tells her that she has nothing to do with Freddie, that in fact her life has changed drastically, as she supposed Lockridge and Duncan "would have suspected." Lockridge, now engaged to Duncan, begins to see that she has helped him launch a crusade against Hull to advance his own political ambitions. Her discomfort increases when these ambitions—and Hull—become the prime topic of conversation at the country club. Although Mayor Levering's daughter, Hazel, and Ellerbe both jump in to defend Hull, Duncan will not let go of his issue.

Freddie cannot let go of his nightmares of snakes emerging from books. In a rare conversation with Freddie, George Slater tells his attentive and vulnerable son that Hull is the cause of all his bad dreams—Hull and her "poison" books with which she wants "to smash everything we've ever built up in this country!" Later, as winner of a contest to name the world's ten best books, Freddie is participating in the groundbreaking ceremonies for the children's wing when Hull appears, escorted by a contrite and insistent Ellerbe. As they approach Freddie becomes distraught and is barely able to finish his part of the program. When Ellerbe invites Hull to wield the shovel to break ground for the new wing, a hostile murmur is broken by the scattered applause of her few supporters. As Hull lifts the first shovelful of soil, she urges Freddie to help her. But the disturbed boy screams at her in response, finally yelling, "You're a Communist, Communist, Communist!" Hull's strained composure snaps. She shouts, "Stop it! Stop it!" and slaps him across the face. The ceremony disintegrates as Ellerbe escorts Hull away.

In the aftermath, with Freddie missing, Laura and George Slater speak the anger and resentment they have harbored, and George stalks out to find his son. As Lockridge walks with Duncan to a hastily called council session, she anguishes over what has happened to "nice, normal people." She holds Duncan responsible for destroying Hull under the guise of patriotism for his own political advantage. The council members argue over who is to blame for the situation in which they find themselves. Duncan shouts down the others. "Cold, hot or lukewarm, this country is at war," he insists. "When you're at war, there isn't time to investigate every little wrinkle on every problem and be kind to stubborn old ladies to boot." He continues, "In war innocent people sometimes get hurt, and that's too bad. But it's got to be that way unless we are all going to wind up in the soup." Ellerbe charges Duncan with behaving like a communist himself by being willing to sacrifice others to get where he wants to go, by using the ends to justify the means. "I'm not afraid of Communism," he says. "Neither am I afraid of a Communist book in the library." But he is afraid of Duncan's willingness to trample on the rights of the individual, "even a stubborn old lady."

The scene shifts, and smoke curls ominously from the window of the Kenport Free Public Library, as flames consume all its books. Spectators gather as the fire accelerates, and firemen enter the building to rescue Freddie Slater, whom they have discovered inside. Lockridge, greatly disturbed by what has happened, rejects Duncan's invitation for a drink and Duncan himself. "You just don't get it, do you?" she asks. When Hull arrives, her supporters come to her side, and the picture wraps up neatly. "We're all to blame," says one. The mayor begs Hull to remain in Kenport and help rebuild the library. She fiercely agrees: "I'm going to stay here and I'm going to help rebuild this library if I have to do it with my bare hands. And if anybody ever again tries to remove a book from it, he'll have to do it over my dead body!"

From the perspective of 1951, the picture Taradash and Moll envisioned was "a dangerous picture about dangerous ideas." Its themes of book-burning and character assassination, leavened with anti-intellectualism and "political ambition disguised as patriotism," were not themes that would endear a writer or producer to HUAC or its allies. One reader of the script scrawled in his notes, "story very good—hell of a hunk of property—only pitfall—too closely un-Am Committee." Although Taradash and Moll knew their screenplay was highly original—no one else was likely to tackle this subject— they did not know whether it would ever be produced.[12]

NEEDED: "ONE COURAGEOUS PRODUCER"

Taradash and Moll nevertheless felt the story gave them the opportunity to "say something [they] felt deeply about our country." Taradash decided to approach two producers he knew. The first, Twentieth Century–Fox producer Julian Blaustein, who had been a friend during Taradash's undergraduate days at Harvard, liked what he heard. "He went to the front office and raved about" the story idea, Taradash later recounted. "He was told he was raving" and was turned down. Apparently Twentieth Century–Fox was not going to risk the wrath of HUAC or its surrogates. The second was Stanley Kramer, with whom Taradash had become friends during their army service together in World War II. In 1951 the Stanley Kramer Company had a long-term contract with Columbia Pictures that gave Kramer control over the subject matter of his films. He thus had the freedom to undertake a film that might be risky. Taradash was confident that he and Moll "could shoot Kramer right through the heart with this subject matter." Apparently, he was right.[13]

In March 1951 Kramer purchased the story. Taradash and Moll received $5,000 for the story idea; they would receive another $10,000 when they delivered the story treatment at the end of May.

If Kramer then picked up the option and hired them to write the screenplay, their contract called for them to receive $30,000 and 5 percent of the film's net profits. Needless to say, they were pleased. Taradash wrote Kramer to express his gratification at "the rare pleasure of . . . doing the kind of picture one really wants to do" and the pleasure of working with his old army pal.[14]

Kramer, too, seemed enthusiastic, but he wanted the volatile subject matter of the picture kept under wraps. He told the screenwriters to "stop worrying" about the contract and "keep writing," but in a bit of wry humor asked, "Isn't there a part for John Wayne in the story someplace?" In 1951 Wayne headed the conservative anticommunist Motion Picture Alliance for the Preservation of American Ideals (MPAPAI), founded in 1944 to combat radical and liberal influence, especially union activity, in Hollywood. The MPAPAI had allied itself with groups such as the Knights of Columbus, the American Legion, California's Tenney Committee, and HUAC; as early as March 1944 it had invited HUAC to investigate communist influence in Hollywood. At the same 1951 convention at which the American Legion announced an "information" campaign against entertainers they identified as supporters of communist front organizations, Wayne accepted a citation on behalf of the film industry for its "humanitarianism and patriotic endeavors" during its first fifty years with a speech assuring the Legionnaires that the industry was "in the majority patriotic and decent citizens." Tongue-in- cheek, Taradash thanked Kramer for his casting suggestion: "We are writing in [a part for Wayne], an old Czech janitor in the library. Think it will be a wonderful change of pace for him."[15]

Just how conscious both Kramer and Taradash were of the dangers involved in their joint enterprise is evident in Kramer's next brief letter. "I have a great idea for a test run on 'The Library,'" he wrote in May 1951, less than two months after the new batch of HUAC subpoenas had begun to arrive at screen artists' doors. "I have turned both of your names over to you-know-who, and you may expect your subpoena by a week from Thursday. I suggest you tell the story of this picture in a forthright manner, and, pending reaction from the Committee, we shall fix a starting date."[16]

Although his tone was facetious, Kramer may indeed have been waiting to see if Taradash, Moll, or even Stanley Kramer turned up in the lists of names provided by the fifty-eight new witnesses who decided to cooperate with the committee. Carl Foreman, a scriptwriter and producer who was Kramer's partner on such well-received films as *Home of the Brave, Cyrano de Bergerac,* and *Young Man with a Horn,* had been named in April testimony by screenwriter Richard Collins and was subpoenaed in September 1951. Several others who worked with Kramer were also called. Kramer's socially conscious films such as *Home of the Brave,* written by Foreman, about the effects of prejudice on a black soldier, might have made him vulnerable, but neither he nor Moll nor Taradash had been political activists within the Hollywood community, and none of them was targeted by the committee. Before the committee, Foreman took the "diminished Fifth," in which he talked about himself but not others and managed to avoid both contempt charges and naming colleagues. However, when another of Kramer's partners, George Glass, cooperated with HUAC, Foreman's position became unacceptable to Columbia—and apparently to Kramer. Glass kept his job; Foreman joined the blacklist. Kramer bought out Foreman's share of the company. Foreman's last film with Kramer was the acclaimed 1952 Gary Cooper picture *High Noon,* which some consider a parable about facing HUAC.[17]

Despite the ongoing HUAC investigation, Taradash and Moll sent off their story treatment on schedule on May 26, 1951. Taradash wrote Kramer that they were "anxious" to know whether he liked it. Having received an affirmative answer and their $10,000, the pair headed for California to complete work on the screenplay. They delivered the first draft of *The Library,* as they called it, on September 15. Some drafts later, they took the script to actress Mary Pickford, who, at fifty-eight, had not been in a film for almost twenty years. If they could get Pickford to use their film as her comeback vehicle, they believed, "it would draw the fangs of the McCarthyites." In November 1951 Pickford agreed. With Irving

Reis named to direct, it looked as if *The Library* would soon be playing in neighborhood theaters.[18]

EXPERT ADVICE

As soon as the American Library Association president Clarence Graham read of Pickford's role in a film called *The Library*, he instructed the executive secretary, David H. Clift, to write Kramer and Pickford to offer the ALA's help. Although there is no specific evidence that Clift knew the subject of the film, he sent copies of the letters to David Berninghausen, chairman of the Intellectual Freedom Committee. Perhaps Clift read between the lines stating that Pickford's character led a group of young people "to the path of true Americanism" or that the picture stood "for everything we Americans hold dear." Kramer's response was polite but cool. When he later received a packet of material from Berninghausen concerning the ALA's position on intellectual freedom, however, he forwarded the material to Reis.[19]

Reis warmly thanked Berninghausen. The material had been "an inspirational assistance" as he prepared for the film. His hope was "to present the American library and the American librarian honestly, and . . . to make the audience aware of their great contribution to our democratic culture." In addition to the material Berninghausen had already sent, Reis requested other items listed in the Intellectual Freedom Committee pamphlet "Propaganda and Pressures," including the report of the Oklahoma Library Association on the Bartlesville Public Library. Soon after, Reis sent a copy of the Library Bill of Rights to Taradash and urged him to look it over so they could discuss it when Taradash returned to Hollywood.[20]

In addition, Reis informed Taradash that Pickford was coming to visit him. "Treat her gently, for these are our dreams you deal with," he cautioned. Kramer had other things besides Pickford to deal with. He was spending time, Reis said, on "'Wage Earners' committee biz," a warning sign of things to come. The Wage

Earners' Committee was one of the antiunion, blacklisting groups. Formed in October 1951, its publication, *National Wage Earner*, listed more than ninety so-called subversive films, among them Kramer's 1951 *Death of a Salesman*. Reis did not explain Kramer's "biz" with the group. While Reis was casting the remaining parts, however, the summer start date was postponed "'in order to get a color commitment.'" This, Taradash later said, was "a public relations way of saying that pressure and persuasion had forced a halt." By fall the film was back on the calendar for an October 1952 shooting date, in black and white, with Santa Rosa, California, and its public library as the setting. Dorothy Drake, president of the California Library Association (CLA), asked Reis to write a statement on the film—now called *Circle of Fire*—for the *California Librarian* and to join Pickford at the CLA meeting in October.[21]

But Pickford would make no CLA appearance. In fact, Pickford appeared for her first day of rehearsals in mid-September and never returned. She dropped out of the film because it was to be shot in black and white, she said, and she felt her return to the screen "should be in a Technicolor production." Her contract had said nothing about color, however. Taradash believed that Pickford was chastised "by 'friends' such as Hedda Hopper," a Hollywood gossip columnist allied with the MPAPAI, "for working for 'that red, Stanley Kramer.'" But Taradash also blamed Kramer. Kramer and Reis had changed the script and Pickford's role without consulting either the writers or Pickford. In addition, Kramer "didn't attend . . . [a] woman of this temperament and fame" as necessary and even allowed Pickford "to come to [the] studio . . . with no reception, no flowers, no fanfare." To add insult to injury, Taradash and Moll had to learn of Pickford's withdrawal from the newspapers.[22]

Regardless of setbacks, Kramer forged ahead on the film. He promptly signed Barbara Stanwyck for the lead and set a new starting date—after Stanwyck had completed a commitment to another studio. But before filming could begin Kramer had split with Foreman and a number of his other employees had resigned or been fired as a result of their encounter with HUAC. Columbia "put all its muscle on Kramer," Taradash said later, and the script of *The Library* "went into the icebox." All Kramer's projects except *The Caine Mutiny* were canceled. The sudden death of Irving Reis in the summer of 1953 added to the film's misfortunes. Whether Columbia found Kramer too liberal for comfort or simply not a big enough moneymaker, or Kramer found Columbia too restrictive, by 1954 the Stanley Kramer Company and Columbia had parted ways. *The Library* became a Columbia property in the breakup.[23]

"DON'T JOIN THE BOOK-BURNERS"

Another event of the summer of 1953, however, held a hint of promise for Taradash and Moll's project. Speaking to Dartmouth College's graduates in June, President Dwight D. Eisenhower surprised the crowd by exhorting, "Don't join the book-burners. Don't think you are going to conceal thoughts by concealing evidence that they ever existed. Don't be afraid to go into the library and read every book, so long as that document does not offend [y]our own ideas of decency—that should be the only censorship." The speech came in the midst of a months-long assault on the overseas libraries of the U.S. International Information Administration (forerunner of the U.S. Information Agency) by Sen. Joseph McCarthy's Permanent Subcommittee on Investigations of the Senate Committee on Government Operations. It was interpreted by many as an expression of disapproval of McCarthy's actions. The speech was widely publicized, and librarians capitalized on it to bolster their position supporting the freedom to read and opposing a rising tide of challenges to materials from groups such as the American Legion and the Daughters of the American Revolution.[24]

Taradash took note of the speech. He believed it meant that the "temperature of the times" was beginning to change and that the chances of getting *The Library* filmed might be improving. But he was busy completing the screenplay for *From Here to Eternity*, which won him the 1953 Academy Award and also increased his influence with Columbia Pictures. In the summer of 1954 he began to lobby Harry Cohn, Columbia's boss, to make the abandoned film. Although the blacklist continued, Taradash's lobbying effort was actually aided by McCarthy. Televised Senate hearings into a dispute between the U.S. Army and McCarthy over his investigation at Fort Monmouth, New Jersey, exposed McCarthy's unethical tactics. By September a Senate committee recommended his censure, and in a December vote McCarthy's colleagues put an end to his four-year assault on domestic communism. While McCarthy had not been the source of Hollywood's problems, his descent into obscurity signaled an ebbing of the anticommunist (and antiliberal) tide.[25]

Early in 1955 Taradash and his old friend Julian Blaustein, who had been enjoying some success as a producer at Twentieth Century–Fox, formed an independent production company they called Phoenix Corporation. They made a two-picture deal with Columbia: Blaustein would produce and Taradash would write and direct two properties they had lined up. They decided they would step up the lobbying efforts with Harry Cohn to try to make *The Library* their first joint effort.[26]

Cohn—"considered a monster and God's angry man"—did not prove easy to convince. Nevertheless, Blaustein and Taradash "badgered him, left quotations on his desk," and finally made him an offer he could not refuse. They lined up Bette Davis to play the part of Alicia Hull for far less than her usual salary, and Elick Moll agreed to return for small rewrites for just a fraction of the film's income. Taradash and Blaustein also agreed to work for no salary, "gambling on the possibility of profits." Finally the pleading paid off. Over Kahane's protest Cohn gave Phoenix $800,000 for the picture. Kahane was "aghast," Taradash recalled. He was sure the film would be a flop. "We've had flops before," Cohn replied, "but we've never had one made with such enthusiasm." In August 1955 filming of *The Library*, now called *Storm Center*, finally got under way. Featured with Davis were Paul Kelly as Robert Ellerbe, Brian Keith as Paul Duncan, and Kim Hunter (who just a year earlier had to clear herself with Vincent Hartnett's Aware, Inc.) as Martha Lockridge.[27]

STORMS OVER *STORM CENTER*

Even before *Storm Center*'s cast and crew began shooting in September in Santa Rosa, the same site that Reis had chosen, Taradash and Blaustein tried to forestall possible criticism. The story of the film was no longer secret, and Davis's presence ensured a certain amount of press attention. Speaking to the industry paper, *Variety*, Taradash asserted that the film would be "more of an anti-Communist picture than the usual variety of melodramas about spies and little men boring from within." "We're telling Russia we can read a book designed to be inimical to democracy," he said, "and yet not be damaged by it, because we are stronger than Russia."[28]

Their caution appears to have been warranted. First, Hedda Hopper wrote that the blacklisted Carl Foreman had written the *Storm Center* screenplay; Taradash and Moll cabled Hopper to request a correction. Next, Anne Smart, a crusading housewife from Marin County, California, wrote Bette Davis to try to persuade her, as a mother, to "re-evaluate" her decision to star in the film. Smart sent Davis a "report of the book controversy" she was causing in Marin County, a controversy of sufficient scope to be featured in an Edward R. Murrow "See It Now" television segment. Her report depicted in "vivid detail," Smart said, "the type of material being given our children in some schools." This "report," which made its way around the country for several years, contained the names of authors "all extremely well listed as to their communist and/or communist front affiliations by various government investigating committees." Included were historians Charles Beard and Merle Curti, novelists Pearl Buck and John Steinbeck, educator John Dewey, poets Carl Sandburg and William Carlos Williams, and former First Lady Eleanor Roosevelt. Smart charged that books by these authors in a school library would be proof that the library had "been tampered with." She suggested that Davis was "not fully aware of the implications of such a picture as 'The Library,' and the reasons why it is being made at this time." "It is possible," she warned, that "certain interests are using or misusing . . . your ability without your full knowledge of what is behind this picture." On the contrary. Bette Davis responded, "As an American I was extremely careful of my approach to this film, both as to its contents and to the people in charge of it. . . . I wish my children to be proud of me. . . . It is my conviction that they will be proud of me for having appeared in this motion picture."[29]

One group was not proud of Davis and the film. The Catholic Legion of Decency (CLD) stunned the film community in July 1956 by giving *Storm Center*, scheduled for August release, a "separate" classification. The CLD asserted that *Storm Center* was a "propaganda film" that offered "a warped, oversimplified and strongly emotional solution to the complex problem of civil liberties in American life." The classification, given for only the fifth time in twenty years, implied criticism on grounds other than morality—on which the CLD usually rated films. The action elicited a strong response, from others as well as Blaustein and Taradash. The Motion Picture Industry Council, in a statement loaded with irony considering its role in the clearance and blacklisting business, protested the rating as "a form of censorship with the purpose of dictating and controlling the content of motion pictures, contrary to American principles of freedom of thought and expression." The Catholic opinion weekly, *Commonweal*, also weighed in on the side of the film, criticizing the CLD for moving into political territory. Strangely enough, the DAR endorsed the film. Bette Davis broke her long-standing policy against making personal appearances to help counteract the CLD's rating. *Variety* columnist Joe Schoenfeld, who had agreed in advance to defend the film editorially if needed, called the Legion of Decency's action "indefensible."[30]

Schoenfeld's assistance was but a tiny part of the barrage of publicity prepared for the film. Numerous dignitaries and critics received invitations to advance screenings. Eleanor Roosevelt, for example, responded to a screening by touting *Storm Center* in her syndicated "My Day" column. "Washington Merry-Go-Round" columnist Drew Pearson not only organized a screening for members of Congress but also agreed to appear with Bette Davis in an advertising trailer for the film. Lawrence Lipskin of Columbia

Pictures International arranged highly successful previews for foreign correspondents. In addition, the Motion Picture Association of America—known for its defense of producers, even at the expense of freedom of expression—took the unusual step of distributing a brochure about *Storm Center* that included not only Eisenhower's "Don't Join the Book-Burners" speech but also the ALA's Library Bill of Rights. The ALA also contributed a *Storm Center* bookmark listing ten titles on free speech, book banning, and blacklisting to be distributed by theaters showing the film.[31]

LIBRARIANS AND OTHER CRITICS

The ALA did more. Intellectual Freedom Committee chairman John Henderson, of the Los Angeles County Public Library, who had appeared opposing Smart in the March 1955 Murrow show, served as a technical consultant on the script. While the film was still in production, both Blaustein and Taradash spoke to the February 1956 Midwinter Meeting of the ALA, and two thousand librarians attended a prerelease screening of the film at the annual summer conference. A letter from Bette Davis, expressing her hope that she had "reflected accurately" their "dedicated services" and had made communities more aware of the role of librarians, prefaced the showing.[32]

The librarians were not unanimous in their praise of the film, however. Of the 204 who returned comment cards at the ALA meeting, 33.8 percent rated the film "excellent," 32.4 percent rated it "good," 13.2 percent called it "fair," and 20.6 percent labeled it "poor." The publicist decided that it was "inadvisable to press for an ALA resolution endorsing" *Storm Center*, because a small number of "important librarians" seemed to be "quite violently opposed to the film" for reasons not elaborated. Nevertheless, the screening was deemed a success. Approving comments ranged from "powerful," "provocative . . . and worthy of serious consideration by all thinking Americans," "good dramatic entertainment," and "important message convincingly delivered" to "stand of librarian admirable" and "most people will look at librarians differently from now on." One enthusiastic respondent lauded Davis for elevating the library profession "to the level of accomplishment for which we have striven for 75 years" and promised to uphold "the mission of the freedom to read." Another was moved to reconsider a decision to leave the profession. On the negative side, librarians called the picture "exaggerated and unrealistic," "overdone," "lacking in psychological subtlety," and "sentimental." While some criticisms targeted the film's melodramatic nature and pat ending, others were aimed at the whole idea of the film. "This was a mountain out of a molehill," said one. "Why stir up things unnecessarily?" asked another. A third complained that the film misrepresented entirely "the problem of intellectual freedom."[33]

One librarian in attendance was "so impressed" that she wrote Taradash a note of thanks. She singled out the character of the librarian for particular praise: "principled but not having enough courage to stand up against the majority of her townspeople, dedicated to her profession, loving people in a sort of 'efficient' way, neither drab nor stylish or young or old, hurt as we all are by ostracism but very proud, finally in a crisis coming through." She hoped that through the film "we librarians will learn to be more brave and more outgoing." Paul Bixler wrote to a friend that *Storm Center* was a "flamboyant B picture (or maybe B+)." He was disappointed in the "screwy boy protagonist" and the "ending in which the building burns down and all is resolved." Nevertheless, he added, the film "gives a better representation of libraries and librarians" than previous films, and "its attitude on intellectual freedom is basically unexceptionable."[34]

Based on his monitoring of the status of the intellectual freedom credo of the library profession, Bixler would not have been surprised at the attitudes of some California librarians who had attended other screenings. Their letters reflected an ambivalence not only toward the movie but toward their profession as well. One felt the problem of book censorship was exaggerated in the film; another feared that the film "would bring to the attention of people that 'Communist' books were on the shelves of the public library." A third wrote that "we are all a little tired" of the Communist issue; she had hoped to be entertained, not informed. "It was a little too much of the real thing," she lamented. She wrote sadly of her profession: "Librarians, as a group, do not fight issues." In the Oakland Public Library, where she worked, a librarian "was fired for refusing to answer questions concerning an accusation . . . that she was a Communist." "If you want a little material for a new . . . film," she said, "you can write one on the apathy of her fellow-librarians." One male librarian excoriated female librarians, who, he said, show "no finesse in meeting such emergencies," are "just as conservative as any other group," and "slavishly" follow reviewers. He recommended a film on the role of library boards—"women who have leisure"—that base book selection decisions "not on intolerance but on smugness." Clearly those who were most intimately connected with libraries were not unanimous in their opinions of the film's, or their profession's, virtues.[35]

Lack of unanimity characterized reception of the film, except abroad, where it was greeted warmly. Lipskin passed along to Taradash "raves" about the film from Germany, Argentina, and Italy (where the film was dubbed in Italian). Some time before its U.S. debut, a novel, *Storm Centre*, sold thirty thousand copies in England and the film version opened to excellent reviews—and speculation that it would not be released in the United States. Domestic reviews and audience responses were far more mixed; some found fault with the plausibility of the story, others with the acting—particularly of the child who played Freddie—the direction, or the music. The ending, made more optimistic at the insistence of Columbia's Kahane, drew the most criticism. The courage of the production team won the most kudos. Several reviewers felt the "subject was outdated" or that the makers were "beating a dead horse"; others felt that its timeliness and thematic importance were the picture's greatest strengths. A few revealed the picture's continued pertinence with such comments as "Since when has Columbia gone communist?" and "The writer must have gone from pink to red."[36]

J. B. Matthews, professional anticommunist columnist for the Hearst newspapers and author of the 1952 *American Legion Magazine* article, "Did the Movies Really Clean House?" certainly thought so. His August 20, 1956, "Memorandum on 'Storm Center'" predicted that the movie's "undisguised propaganda blast" would earn "plaudits" from "the left-wing anti-anti-Communist front." Matthews attacked the film and quoted ALA materials to demonstrate "the obvious intention of the leadership of the librarians to launch, with the assistance of Columbia Pictures and on a grand scale, an intensive propaganda campaign for anti-anti-Communism." Using libraries for such a purpose was sure to "raise a storm of protest," he said. Finally, using the very tactics decried by the film, Matthews announced that Moll and Blaustein had signed the amicus curiae brief for the Hollywood Ten, "a savage attack" on the congressional committee for its investigation of the film industry.[37]

Another writer also remembered the Hollywood Ten and other beleaguered screen artists as he saw *Storm Center*. "I sat there thinking of the hectic days in 47–48," he wrote. "I was thinking of Carl Foreman and Sidney Buchman. Yes, I was even thinking of the overboard guys like Levitt and Trumbo and hoping they would see the picture. All the things I felt were left unsaid through those years, you guys said it in this picture. I salute you!"[38]

The Cannes Film Festival saluted *Storm Center* the following year. A jury awarded the film the first Chevalier de la Barre Prize as the 1956 film that best served "the cause of freedom of expression and tolerance." While it would hardly win an award for its quality as a film, it received worldwide recognition for its quality as a testament to both perseverance and courage. But it did not break the blacklist.[39]

ALICIA HULL AS RUTH BROWN?

A friend who had just seen the film wrote Ruth Brown in 1975 lamenting that Brown "didn't receive credit" for *Storm Center* or "something financially, as it was definitely your story." Although how she knew is not documented, certainly Brown told others that the film's story was based on her, and Taradash says that he got the idea from Darlene Anderson Essary's letter about the Ruth Brown case. There is no evidence to date that anyone associated with the film interviewed Brown or visited Bartlesville, but the filmmakers did have a copy of the Oklahoma Library Association's report on Brown's firing. Although certain elements of the film compare to elements of Brown's story, there are also certain glaring omissions and equally evident additions.[40]

Besides the major elements of the film, certain others also mirrored Brown's situation: Hull and Brown shared several personality traits as well as age and long service and a special relationship with children. Hull was depicted as being, like Brown, abrupt and direct, opinionated and stubborn, and warmer with children and teenagers than with adults. Ellerbe says Hull should have had children of her own, and Brown clearly assumed a maternal role with a number of the young people she hired. She adopted two young women. In each case, not unlike other children's librarians, the childless woman was assumed to play a maternal role within the library. Librarianship was regarded as an appropriate profession for women because it was an extension of the domestic, feminine sphere. In Hull's and Brown's stories, however, this role became a dangerous one, because in it the librarian could subvert children through books or magazines.[41]

In both the film and the real-life drama a citizens' committee brought the "subversive" materials to the attention of the council. In the film, however, unlike Brown's story, the committee remained offstage, simply the threat of dissatisfied voters, not the instigators and apparent moving force behind the attack on the librarian. Anti-intellectualism was an undercurrent in the Bartlesville episode as it was in the film. George Slater represented the kind of person who fears and suspects those whose intellectual interests and accomplishments he does not understand. Although highly educated people were important to Bartlesville's well-being, anti-intellectualism was latent, as Christopher's letter regarding the Ph.D.'s who were brought in without questioning their loyalty revealed.

Both Hull and Brown were summoned to go alone to a meeting with the city fathers—both middle-aged women with few defenses other than their wits facing a group of men with political power. In both cases there were no lawyers or recorders present. In both cases issues outside the challenged materials were brought into the discussion. In both cases these issues had to do with activities linked to the party line. In the actual as well as the fictional case, the women were fired immediately and the library turned over to someone else. In Brown's case, however, unlike Hull's, her assistant resigned in sympathy.

A group organized to try to reinstate Brown, just as it did in the film. In Brown's case, however, the group, composed mainly of women as determined as Hull's friend Eleanor Layton and as spunky as the mayor's daughter, Hazel Levering, persisted for more than two years and took her case to the Oklahoma Supreme Court. Neither they nor Brown were rewarded, however. Members of the Friends of Miss Brown, like both Brown and Hull, were ostracized by the townspeople. As she prepared to leave Bartlesville Brown talked about how tired she was of hearing the word *Communist*. Hull was persuaded by the destruction of the library—and some last-minute repentance—to remain in Kenport, her residence of many years; Brown sold her home and moved out of her community.

The film's most prominent departure from the Ruth Brown story is the hysterical Freddie Slater, used to highlight the damaging effects of red-scare tactics. Children do figure in the Brown story, although in a very different manner. Whereas in the film it is the red-scare tactics that harm Freddie, in Bartlesville the American Legion sought to portray Brown, as Freddie's father did, as the source of harm, a person who poisoned children's immature minds.

Most noticeably missing from *Storm Center* are Brown's interracial activities and the strong group of women of Bartlesville who also worked for racial equality and supported Brown. Essary's letter did not emphasize, although it mentioned, these two aspects. Considering the difficulties Taradash and Moll expected to confront in dealing with censorship and guilt by association, it is not remarkable that these aspects of the case were ignored. Constraints of the medium—the need to tell a story dramatically in under two hours—also would have limited the number of elements and the degree of complexity that could have been encompassed in the film. Interestingly, the film does show a hint of the feminism displayed by the women of Bartlesville. Hull is portrayed as a strong woman, accustomed to self-sufficiency, although, as Ellerbe points out, somehow diminished by widowhood and childlessness. Young, feisty Hazel Levering and the teacher Eleanor Layton are the only public voices of support for Hull other than Ellerbe. Laura Slater finally rebels against a cloddish husband. Lockridge is that rather unusual phenomenon in the 1950s, a divorcée not portrayed in film as a femme fatale. She ultimately rejects her suitor over principle. There is even an eerily modern ring to her rebuff of Paul Duncan: "You just don't get it, do you?"

Of course, many of the similarities between these cases can be attributed to the times and common experience, rather than to research or a deliberate attempt to use Brown's story. Hollywood, perhaps more than any other community scarred by charges of subversive influence, understood both the power of the "citizens' committee" like the American Legion, a huge factor in the Bartlesville case, and the power of the governmental entity using claims of subversion to political ends. It would understand the effects of tactics of assuming guilt by association, would have experienced the exaggeration of fears exemplified by Freddie Slater. Members of the Hollywood community could see, if not feel, the cooling of friendships, the loss of livelihood, and the deprivation of a sense of home and comfort that their colleagues—and Brown and her friends—had experienced. They had witnessed the disintegration of support for the blacklisted screen artists when those who might have supported them realized doing so might cause them to be branded "reds," just as Hull's supporters feared and as Brown's supporters experienced. In short, *Storm Center* was both the Ruth Brown story and the Hollywood story. It captured—albeit imperfectly and in monochrome—the Technicolor reality of the red scare.

CHAPTER SIX

"Only a Skirmish"

"We thought we had lost the battle, but it was only a skirmish."

—WILLIAM T. NELSON

The story of Ruth W. Brown's dismissal from the Bartlesville Public Library and the subsequent unsuccessful battle for her reinstatement and the control of the library has, as her friend Darlene Anderson Essary put it, "significance beyond the boundaries" of Bartlesville, Oklahoma. From an examination of the complex matrix of conditions and occurrences that brought about the controversy in Bartlesville emerges the importance of gender in this skirmish and in the nationwide battles. "McCarthyism," the discourse of guilt by association used to create fear and powerlessness, displays its utility as a weapon for those who fear loss of economic or political power. And books and magazines and the libraries that select them, organize them for use, and provide access to them appear as "exposed and vulnerable" arenas where opposing forces contend over cultural values. Brown's firing was the first to call forth an official response from the library profession, setting precedents and exposing weaknesses in both the ALA's intellectual freedom credo and its support system for librarians. Set in the middle of the country, in the middle of the century, the Bartlesville episode resonates across the years to remind us of those who fought the local skirmishes in the national struggles for African-American civil rights and for the freedom to read.[1]

BOUNDARIES

The battle lines in Bartlesville's skirmish had much to do with cultural boundaries. Brown's "boundaries," indeed the boundaries of white middle- and upper-class women generally, in Bartlesville as in the rest of the nation, were drawn by the community's understanding of the "place" of women.[2] The women of Bartlesville were keenly aware of their assigned roles as submissive, nurturant, moral, and domestic in a culture defined by the assertively masculine icons of outlaw, cowboy, athlete, and oilman in which the community reveled. The patriarchal families of the oil companies, especially of the dominant Phillips Petroleum Company, purposely cultivated and exploited those icons. In addition, the containment policies of the postwar period discouraged middle-class married women from working. As Paul Duncan told Martha Lockridge in *Storm Center*, when she married she would leave her job behind. Those (usually single) women who did work, out of necessity or desire, generally were limited in the occupations available to them. Unmarried women were likely to be secretaries or clerks, low-wage occupations necessitated by the development of modern office machinery and techniques, or teachers, an extension of their domestic child care role.

Ruth Brown was one of the women, mostly white and middle-class, who made up 88.8 percent of the allied profession of librarianship in 1950. For a salary less than a man would receive, she organized and maintained a comfortable homelike space where people, especially young people, went for wholesome enlightenment or entertainment. The professional role of the librarian gave communities low-cost female employees to provide healthy recreational and informational reading while it extended the margins of the domestic sphere without exploding them. The librarian's role did not transgress boundaries as long as the homelike space and the materials and activities organized in it remained safe, comforting, and submissive to the prevailing ideology—and as long as the librarian remained ladylike.[3]

However, Brown was, as she said, "unlibrarian like" and "indiscreet" both in what a friend called her "blunt, forthright way of talking" and in her actions. Although her selection of library materials was deemed to undermine the ideology of the dominant political group, it was her decision to move outside the private, domestic sphere into very public activity on behalf of integration— and to encourage other women to join her—that was seen as the real threat. Although the presence of a strong American Legion post frequently signaled potential problems for librarians during the McCarthy period, the Bartlesville post showed no interest in the library and its collection until Brown's interracial activities, and those of the YWCA, caught their attention. They then used their influence to suppress the activities of Brown and her (mainly) women friends.[4]

For women were the overwhelming majority of those working for integration in Bartlesville. The influx of Phillips scientists and engineers in the decade just preceding Brown's ouster had created a critical mass of educated young women, most of whom did not work outside the home but sought significant social involvement. As Bureau of Mines librarian Vern Hutchison remarked, Bartlesville was quite like a university town "where the division between 'town and gown' is so marked." The newcomers were better educated, more socially conscious, and more activist than the longtime Bartians; they did not consider themselves to be part of Bartlesville's wealthy elite, the "'best' people," as Gladys Gaddis described those opposing the YWCA's interracial activities. They more closely matched the profile of those Samuel Stouffer described in his research report, *Communism, Conformity, and Civil Liberties*, as "more tolerant of nonconformity"—young, well educated, from the North or West—than longtime Bartians, who tended to be less well educated and older and to originate from the South or the border states. Had the "little old single lady who loved her books" stayed within her expected role she would likely have been ignored. But Brown, emboldened by the company of other women who shared her concerns and commitments, transgressed both gender and racial boundaries not only by choosing an African-American doctor but also by openly socializing with a black woman at church and aggressively attacking the pattern of segregation in business. She thus raised the anxiety level of an already anxious conservative elite and made them determined to stop her, to reinforce the boundaries.[5]

Adding to their anxiety, Brown threatened to expose the community by talking to a reporter from a national publication. Her own account of her interview with the city commission makes plain her lack of submissiveness and her insistence on the rightness of her action in the face of overwhelming opposition. The city commission drew for Brown a circle of acceptable behavior and rhetoric and demanded that she stay within it. She declined, and threatened their authority. Like the city councilmen of *Storm Center*, they could not allow a "stubborn old woman" to best them; firing her was their only alternative.

Once fired (and even before) Brown's position in relation to the city commission was circumscribed by the political alliances available to her. In 1950 women did not belong to the same civic groups that men did; they were not expected to participate in the politicking that occurred in such men's venues as the Chamber of Commerce, Lion's Club, Kiwanis, or, in cold war Bartlesville, the American Legion. As Oliver Garceau noted in his 1949 *The Public Library in the Political Process*, "As the world has the habit of being run by males, the woman librarian is handicapped in opportunities to penetrate the councils of political power."[6] As a result, although Brown had a history of civic activity and was (as both she and others noted) an "institution" in the community, her status did not give her much protection. The circles of influence within which she operated—most obviously the YWCA, the AAUW, and the COPD—were circles of women and African Americans in a city in which pressure could easily be brought to bear on both groups by a mere handful of politically powerful men, especially those who controlled work, the managers of Phillips Petroleum (and to a lesser extent Cities Service and National Zinc). Thus the social, economic, and political structure of the highly patriarchal and paternalistic community meant that Brown's allies could easily be negated.

Strangely, the very aspect of librarianship that made it "appropriate" as an occupation for women, its relationship to children, added to Brown's vulnerability. There is no evidence that Brown ever attempted to inculcate in children anything other than a love for reading. Nevertheless, the American Legion's suggestion that she gave marked passages of subversive materials to young people raised the specter of a respected woman violating the trust of those who had sent children into her care. Like Freddie Slater's father and the women gossiping at the country club in *Storm Center*, some of Brown's opponents asserted that the community should be glad that its children would no longer come under her influence. It was much easier to persuade citizens to protect the "impressionable mind of formative years" from "subversive propaganda" than to persuade them that they ought to tell other adults what they should read. This twisting of Brown's role of provision of reading material into her alleged provision of communist propaganda is one example of the use of McCarthyism as a weapon of political control.

MCCARTHYIST DISCOURSE

As Hollywood screen artists discovered to their dismay, it was not difficult for groups like the American Legion and the chamber of commerce to link advocacy of a liberal social cause to the party line of the communists. These groups defined communism as a foreign ideology that undermined what they liked to call the American Way of Life. And although there was a significant group of Catholic anticommunists, there was a strong nativist and Christian—and generally in the South, Protestant—bias to the anticommunist literature, which reflected a fear of the Other. Thus anything critical of a racially segregated system in which white Anglo-Saxon

Protestant males held the political and economic power could be labeled subversive. Thus Brown's challenge to the racial status quo in Bartlesville, which threatened the economic and social order by proposing that the African-American women and men who labored in the kitchens and garages of Bartlesville might have the desire and the right to sit at the table rather than serve it, could easily be seen as communist. After all, communists had worked effectively for civil rights; therefore anyone who worked for civil rights must be a communist.

When the citizens' committee and its allies could not oust Brown because of her integrationist activities, they set about to prove her subversion a different way, by connecting her to magazines that right-wing groups had already set out to discredit. They not only linked these periodicals with the party line, they also linked them visually with communism by picturing them in the newspaper with a book called *The Russians*. Brown's purchase and circulation of these materials must mean that she endorsed the "communistic" ideas in them, they asserted. By the time the citizens' committee had asserted in print and in two public meetings that the library was stocked with communist books and magazines and had ostensibly documented that assertion with information from HUAC, Ruth Brown had become a communist threat.

The rumors that she and Gracey displayed pictures of Paul Robeson in the library and Douglass School, respectively, operated in the same way. Two assumptions underlay the rumors: that Robeson, who was critical of the United States, was a communist; and that only someone who was also a communist would display Robeson's picture. The group opposed to racial integration hinted that the COPD group that Brown helped to start was a communist cell group and that those associated with Brown, especially those from outside Oklahoma, had been sent down from the North to disrupt the peaceful life enjoyed by all Bartians. They used Joseph Kamp's pamphlet to charge communist influence in the YWCA and bring additional suspicion on Davis. Members of the same group hurled the epithet "Communist" at anyone who supported Brown at meetings. By implying Brown's disloyalty, the opponents of integration called her motives into question, made it dangerous for others to join her struggle for racial equality, and deprived her of her livelihood as well.

For McCarthyism to be most effective, others must observe the process of guilt by association and understand that it can happen to them. In spite of what appears to have been a clear understanding in the community that neither Brown nor any of the other participants in the effort for racial justice was a member of the Communist party or in any way disloyal to the United States, many of those who might have assisted Brown remained silent. The charges of subversion appear to have been designed to frighten potential supporters and diminish the already negligible power of "uppity" blacks and women. The opposition's use of McCarthyism said, in effect, that blacks and women who leave their "place" in the southern class and caste system are communist and subversive of the American Way of Life. To be a good American is to be docile and submissive and to stay within all the expected boundaries—including those of race and gender.

"AN EXPOSED AND VULNERABLE FRONT"

Like Ruth Brown and other female librarians, the library itself was (and is) "exposed and vulnerable."[7] Its vulnerability comes both from the importance and authority Americans accord the books, magazines, and other media that the library collects, organizes, and circulates and from its position as a public institution charged with the preservation and transmission of culture. From the days of the *New England Primer* and the pioneers reading their Bibles by candlelight, Americans, like their Old World predecessors, have been simultaneously reverential toward and fearful of the printed word. They have accorded books the power to do both great good and great harm. The metaphors for books and reading used in *Storm Center*, for example—food and nourishment (and "stuffing" or overeating), poison, and snakes suggestive of evil—are powerful ones. In the early days of their profession librarians themselves preached the need to protect their readers by carefully screening what they made available to them. By 1939, however, the ALA had adopted its Library Bill of Rights, which established the development of collections containing all points of view on controversial issues as a central jurisdiction of librarians. In 1948 the Library Bill of Rights was strengthened to assert more clearly its foundation on the values of pluralist democracy—values of diversity, tolerance, and openness—its resistance to a coercive notion of Americanism, and its opposition to censorship. The ALA articulated the importance of allowing citizens to decide for themselves what they should read, an idea Brown expressed in her interview with the city commission. These values were not universally accepted, however, not even by all librarians, many of whom could not relinquish their roles as protectors of taste and morals in exchange for the role of guarantor of access to ideas. Those who did accept them also acknowledged that reading, like freedom, was "dangerous" but that suppression of ideas was even more dangerous.[8]

Ideas that challenge the status quo and the texts (both print and nonprint) that hold them are perceived to be most dangerous at times of intense cultural change. Like educational institutions, libraries are charged with keeping and transmitting the culture of the community. When the cultural discourse is contested, the institutions charged with the transmission of culture become arenas in the contest. In Bartlesville the UDC, for example, in March 1950 presented to the city commission a resolution against the destruction of any historical documents or books on history. They had no evidence that any history books had been removed or harmed, but they understood—although they never explicitly made the connection—that a challenge to Jim Crow was a challenge to the traditional southern representation of history.[9] During the postwar decade, as the New Deal vision of the Roosevelt administration collided sharply with a newly ascendant conservative vision, challenges to library materials grew. The titles challenged, like the *Nation* and the *New Republic*, were invariably liberal in tone and content, and the challengers were inevitably right-wing. Libraries and librarians, with their stated commitment to collecting a diversity of views and eschewing a single view of Americanism, were bound to find themselves, in Archibald MacLeish's words, "strong points and pill boxes along that extended and dangerous frontier where the future of free institutions [was] being fought out, day after day, in minor skirmishes rarely noticed."[10]

THE AMERICAN LIBRARY ASSOCIATION

It is hard to reconcile the embattled but noble image of the librarian, painted in stirring patriotic colors by MacLeish, former Librarian of Congress, with the prevalent image of the good, gray librarian of midcentury. The typical librarian, both male and female, as described in Alice I. Bryan's 1952 research report, *The Public Librarian*, was "rather submissive in social situations" and lacked self-confidence. "Indiscreet" was not part of the lexicon by which librarians, especially female librarians, were described. In fact, female librarians have been characterized as discreet to a fault in book selection practices, "ruthless in their own censorship." Marjorie Fiske's 1959 classic, *Book Selection and Censorship*, depicted its mostly female subjects as anxious and fearful, avoiding challenges to library materials through self-censorship. How could self-censoring, submissive, anxious women "hold an exposed and vulnerable front through ten of the most dangerous years in American history"?[11]

How, indeed. Although some librarians, especially during the dangerous fifties, engaged in self-censorship, there is more to the story. There were many women librarians like Ruth Brown (among them Margery Quigley of Montclair, New Jersey, Julia Rothaus of San Antonio, Texas, and Mildred Harlan of Punxsatawney, Pennsylvania) who stood their ground in the face of a challenge to library materials. Elizabeth Haas of Baltimore, Jean Huot of Seattle, and Zoe Baur of Ephrata, Washington, resigned their jobs rather than sign loyalty oaths to which they were opposed. The first case regarding a loyalty program that was fought to the U.S. Supreme Court was that of Los Angeles County library worker Julia Steiner.

Women performed many unheralded acts of courage in the minor skirmishes over intellectual freedom.[12]

But the dismissal of Ruth W. Brown of Bartlesville, Oklahoma, was the first to which the ALA's young Intellectual Freedom Committee attempted to respond. Although the support it was able to offer was inadequate to save Brown's job, the committee provided information, mandated the first on-site investigation of a censorship episode, and assisted in publicizing the case nationwide. The difficulties its chairman, David Berninghausen, experienced in taking action led to a slight expansion of the committee's authority. It did not take up the racial issues underlying Brown's dismissal, however. Brown was disappointed: "I could not see then and have never understood why the ALA carefully seemed to avoid [the racial aspects of the case]," Brown wrote to the *Library Journal* in 1961. Still a CORE member at the age of seventy, she was nearing retirement from the Sterling Public Library in Colorado. In highlighting the censorship aspects of the case, in fact, the ALA unwittingly helped to obscure the issues of race, to nullify the attention Brown was trying to focus on segregation. The Intellectual Freedom Committee did not discuss whether access to libraries by African Americans could be considered under the rubric "rights of library users to freedom of inquiry" until a decade later. The association was not ready for the opportunity to embrace integration as an intellectual freedom issue. Ten years later, however, Everett T. Moore wrote in the *American Library Association Bulletin* that the Ruth Brown case did more "than any other in our time to shock librarians into examining their beliefs in intellectual freedom." It certainly was the first case to add access to libraries to the gradually expanding definition of intellectual freedom that the ALA is pledged to defend.[13]

WINNING THE STRUGGLE

It would be a mistake to exaggerate the importance of this episode or of the actions of Ruth Brown, Roosevelt Gracey, Clara Cooke,

Mary Ellen Street, Darlene Anderson Essary, Ida Rice, Anthony Andrews, and all the other women and men who decided that their actions could, or at least should, make a difference to Bartlesville, Oklahoma. After all, nothing much was changed by their actions. Bartlesville did not pull down its racial barriers; Ruth Brown did not keep her job; and the library was apparently "purged" of its alleged "pink" tint.

But it would be a mistake, too, to minimize its importance. The struggle for equal rights for African Americans was carried on in countless similar minor skirmishes all across the country. At times the movement toward greater freedom and equality was glacial. Sometimes advances were followed by retreats or defeats. But each act of courage, each breaching of boundaries, elicited a response— "made some think," as Brown said—and carried the struggle forward. Movements do not spring forth from the head of one person full blown. Just as many conditions and occurrences contributed to the events in Bartlesville in 1950, many events and conditions contributed to the flowering of the civil rights movement. It was people like Ruth Brown and Roosevelt Gracey who made Martin Luther King, Jr., possible.

The end of the century is marked by changes of a magnitude similar to those in the immediate postwar period. The end of the cold war has not only demanded a new role for the United States in the world, but it has seen an increase in the threat of terrorism, economic displacement, and rapidly changing family roles. The United States no longer has an external enemy on which to blame our alleged "moral decay," so we must discover new villains. The responses to the anxiety look and sound familiar—the search for scapegoats, contests over cultural values, and the move by conservative groups touting "family values" (rather than Americanism) to screen library materials. As the case of Ruth W. Brown and the Bartlesville Public Library demonstrates, when values are in conflict, those agencies entrusted with communicating cultural values, including libraries, become arenas of conflict, and the women and men whose professional jurisdiction is to build collections reflecting diversity of opinion and to make those collections available to all become vulnerable to attack. Perhaps it is time for those who love liberty and justice to be on guard and to remember that the battles for both equality and free inquiry are fought in myriad skirmishes in towns and cities we call home.

TELLING THE RUTH BROWN STORY

A Personal Journey

> *I tried to tell her how if you could not accept the past and its burden, there was no future, for without one there cannot be the other, and how if you could accept the past you might hope for the future, for only out of the past can you make the future.*

> —JACK BURDEN,
> in Robert Penn Warren, *All the King's Men*

> *All we have taught them is our rage.*

> —ROSE BEAN HICKS
> at the DouglassAires Reunion, 1994

For more than three years I have been piecing together the story of Ruth W. Brown. The journey I took as I tried to discover what had happened in Bartlesville nearly fifty years ago illustrates some of the issues with which a historian must grapple as she deals with highly politicized topics such as race, class, and gender. This epilogue lays out a kind of historian's path to allow readers to judge how I came to terms with issues of gathering data and constructing a narrative and how I grappled with my relationship to my subject and my responsibility to those whose history I tried to write.[1]

My path has not always been a straight and narrow one. Rather, it has been broadened by serendipity, diverted down blind alleys, intersected with surprises, and guided by reading in many areas. The set of questions with which I began has changed and deepened. The lenses of gender and race through which I first set out to examine this story have taken on a wider angle; I have tried to discover and represent the "interactive contextual model which considers ways in which factors of race, class, . . . and sex are expressed" in the Ruth Brown case. The matrices of community and professional organizations, the influence of business in a community, race and gender relations within reform movements, and contemporary representations of the Bartlesville conflict by the American Library Association, the national press, and Hollywood have taken on greater significance as I have worked to place the story in its rich social, cultural, and political context.[2]

I began this project at the urging of my University of Wisconsin–Madison colleague Wayne Wiegand. He knew that my twenty-four-year residence in Oklahoma gave me an understanding of the terrain (both literal and figurative) and some helpful contacts. What he may or may not have known fully was the standpoint from which I launched the project: I had a history of feminist political activism in Oklahoma and a history of civil rights activism as well. I could not be called "neutral" on issues of the historical oppression of African Americans or women. In fact, one reason I found this work worth doing was that it was an opportunity to center a woman in the library landscape of 1950 and to write both another woman and an early concern for racial justice into library history. I was interested in the case precisely because I have a political interest in the issues. I was either very well suited to this project or very ill suited, but there was no undoing who I was and am. I was very much aware that my telling of the story would be shaped—like all research, consciously or unconsciously—by my own ideology. Acknowledging that I was *not* an unbiased observer of the event, I worked reflexively throughout the project to minimize distortions my standpoint might cause. I not only had to defend against the tendency to interpret yesterday's discourse from today's perspective. In addition, I quickly became aware that this story had achieved mythic proportions and distortions that would test my ability to sort memory's wheat from its chaff and to resist sanctification of Ruth Brown. I also began to understand the full implications of the truism that "winners write history." This book represents the outcome of my struggles.[3]

FINDING THE STORY

Data gathering was my first challenge. It is generally true that the actions, attitudes, motives, and concerns of women, racial and ethnic minorities, and the poor have been inadequately represented in the archival record, which tends (or has tended) to preserve the documents of white middle- and upper-class men. For example, women's papers often have been buried in archives under their husbands' names. In addition, I believed that censorship was a mask behind which racism was hiding, and if that were true, the minimizing of racism in the episode's contemporary accounts was one of the case's most troublesome aspects. I could not once again leave the African-American community without voice. I had to listen for silences and also seek the voices of women and African Americans in a community that I believed was not likely to have recorded them. I feared that I would find little in the way of primary sources to supplement newspaper, magazine, and journal accounts. Although discovering them was difficult and time-consuming, to my surprise I ultimately found primary sources on Brown and the Bartlesville Public Library in collections from Wyoming to New Jersey to Washington, D.C., as well as in the closet of the Bartlesville Young Women's Christian Association and the minute book of the Bartlesville School Board.

This unexpectedly fruitful foray began with a call to the Bartlesville Public Library. The director, Jan Sanders, and the local history librarian, Joan Singleton, photocopied the library's file on Brown and put me in touch with Russell Davis, chairman of the library board that had been fired along with Brown. Davis provided two bits of invaluable information: first, Jason Talley, a fourteen-year-old from Joplin, Missouri, researching a History Day project on Brown several years before, had organized Davis's file on the episode and conveyed it to Pittsburg State University in Kansas; second, Pittsburg State had Brown's documents related to the case. Gene de Gruson, curator of Special Collections at Pittsburg State, sent me the Davis and Brown files in their entirety. These papers included letters to and from the city commission, letters to and from David K. Berninghausen (ALA Intellectual Freedom Committee chair), news coverage, Brown's account of the interrogation preceding her firing, and a report on the library's periodical collection, among other things. De Gruson also gave me the name and address of Brown's friend Margaret Varvel, who had deposited Brown's papers at Pittsburg State. Varvel, of course, led me to many other names.[4]

A newspaper article in the library's file led to a second cache of primary material. The article referred to Brown's membership in the Committee on Racial Equality, which I recognized as the Congress of Racial Equality. Hoping to find verification that Brown was a member, my research assistant went to the CORE papers at the State Historical Society of Wisconsin Library, where she discovered a substantial correspondence dating from 1946 to 1951 between Brown and George Houser, CORE executive secretary. The letters were full of revelations—of events, of Brown's motives, of Brown's personality, and (the biggest surprise) of Brown's two adoptive daughters. I had discovered primary source material aplenty to document Brown's perspective.

Later, with a trip of several weeks to Oklahoma, I was able to add different perspectives from other primary sources. The first was that of the YWCA. Its annual reports, as well as minutes of confrontational meetings, linked names and sentiments and showed a group of women banded together to meet their opposition. The records of school board meetings showed a very different picture, a picture of a divided African-American community. At the University of Oklahoma's Western History Collections—where I had gone on the chance that I might find some interesting information on Phillips Petroleum or the American Legion—I stumbled entirely serendipitously on the voice of the opposition in the papers of E. R. Christopher, postmaster, chairman of the replacement library board, and American Legion Americanism activist. Although Brown's opponents still were underrepresented in private documents (I had city commission meetings, letters to the editor, and public pronouncements, however), I suddenly had crucial pieces of evidence and perspectives that could only have been supplied by someone opposing Brown. I also had potent evidence of the intricacies of gender and race relations in the Bartlesville case.

The contents of the Christopher collection, however, revealed another important consideration in the use of archives: the questions of provenience and provenance, where and for what purpose a document was created and how it got where it is now.[5] Included in Christopher's file were three items that did not belong there: a letter from Roosevelt Gracey written to African-American teachers across Oklahoma in 1941, years before the Brown incident, which suggests that postmaster Christopher monitored Gracey's mail; both the negative and the positive of the photograph of sequestered magazines that appeared in a Bartlesville newspaper during the most turbulent part of the conflict; and a handwritten rough draft of a typed memo that Brown gave to the mayor during the city commission session that ended with her firing, stipulating that she would answer only in writing written questions about her personal life. This evidence, coupled with that from other sources (such as Russell Davis's letter to the mayor stating that he did not know how the picture was taken), certainly suggests that someone within the library had given Christopher both access to a locked area and something taken from Brown's trash can or desk. They also suggest more than the casual civic interest in the library that Christopher claimed. But without information from other files, the import of these pieces of paper or film would have been lost.

Another serendipitous event provided me with approximate dating for an undated register of Bartlesville Public Library borrowers. I badly wanted to know how early the register started, because some borrowers were identified as "(colored)" in red typewriter ribbon. As I studied the pages I came across a familiar name, Frank Hawkinson, and its accompanying address. Much to my surprise, a page later, at the same address, was Marguerite Hawkinson. I had forgotten that Marguerite, one of my dearest Ada, Oklahoma, friends, had lived in Bartlesville for two years in the 1920s with her young son, Frank, who later died in World War II. Now here was my friend, who had died two years earlier, in the pages of this register. I later confirmed with her brother the dates she had been in Bartlesville. And a man who as a youngster had been allowed to use Ruth Brown's typewriter remembered the red and black typewriter ribbon. So I knew that the register was hers and that it was begun before the mid-1920s.[6]

To add richness of detail, the perceptions and memories of participants, and the meanings they assigned to events, as well as to find voices not represented in the documentary evidence, I added interviews to the primary resources and the contemporary published reports. This kind of triangulation of method and data sources helped me to identify important threads I might have missed and corroborated—or challenged—the documentary evidence or newspaper stories.[7] The interviewing process was sometimes tedious and less than fruitful; it was also problematic from a number of perspectives. The Ruth Brown case has continued to hold interest in Bartlesville for more than forty years. Some people still do not want to discuss it for the same reason they did not want Brown raising issues of race in 1950: they believe it will bring the community bad publicity. This realization hinted at one of a growing list of interpretive elements—the role of community boosterism.[8]

I familiarized myself thoroughly with the documentary sources before I began interviewing. To give consent, each interviewee learned of the purpose of the interview and how the material would be used. My husband, Robby, operated the tape recorder, leaving me free to take notes and ask questions. Although I took a set of questions into each interview, the informant's answers often led to new questions, not strictly limited to the facts of the case; I wanted to understand the climate of 1950 Bartlesville and how the person being interviewed saw himself or herself fitting into the community. One interesting dilemma appeared early in the process. I discovered that each person's knowledge was limited to one, or perhaps two, aspects of a very complicated episode; to ask questions that made sense, I sometimes had to give considerable background information, perhaps in the process "leading the witness." I never figured out how to avoid this. Although it still concerns me, it did give me the opportunity to give something in exchange for the privilege of the interview.[9]

A second dilemma I encountered was how hard to press a participant to share painful memories.[10] Jean Jones, the African-American woman who had attended church with Brown, for example, told me quite bluntly that she had worked for a long time to forget the way white church members had treated her and was not sure she wanted to recall it. However, some interviewees found the experience of reliving this difficult period cathartic. But I could never know in advance how a participant would respond.

I listened for two opposite features in interview data: points of similarity or redundancy and points of difference. For example, I asked each interviewee some variation on the question of whether Phillips pressured its employees to be silent in the conflict, and repeatedly I got either direct answers from firsthand experience that Phillips had done so or, equally interesting, illustrative stories of the kind of influence that Phillips in general, and K. S. Adams in particular, had exercised. After two dozen interviews I had at least enough evidence to support an assertion that Phillips had pressured employees not to take Brown's part or participate in interracial activities (nevertheless, I was relieved when the Christopher papers gave me documentary evidence as well). The points of difference in interview data sometimes meant I had to reexamine what earlier sources—both print and interview—had revealed and then ask informants supplementary questions. While they did not always add to the record, sometimes interviews gave me hints about things to ask the next informant. Thus the process of interviewing was incremental and iterative; the story unfolded or developed in small pieces, some painfully culled from hours of transcriptions. Every new bit of information made it necessary to revisit earlier interviews because my filter had changed: I was now sensitive to and understood things that had not had meaning for me earlier. When additional interviews added no new insights I knew it was time to stop, as tempted as I was to ask for just one more.

Another interpretive dilemma arose when I realized through comparison with the documentary record that some interviewees had revised their memories—or the stories they are willing to share with an interviewer—in the light of the history that has followed the event. Because McCarthyism and racism have been discredited, they tried to throw in their lot with—or modify their stance toward—the very people they had formerly opposed. Their reconstructions illustrate the difficulty of adequately representing now-unpopular points of view. To the extent that stories of the past are modified to conform to today's expectations, it really is true that the winners write history.

A different kind of obstacle, that of gaining entrée into the African-American community, was overcome through happy coincidence and goodwill. Once I discovered the parts played by Gracey and the two young African-American women teachers, Mary Ellen Street and Clara Cooke, I was committed to make them visible. But I could not locate them and had no idea who to interview. One contact led to another. Bernice Brown, an African-American community elder, informed me that the triennial reunion of the graduates of the segregated Douglass School (which graduated its last high school class in 1957) was scheduled that very week in Bartlesville and that perhaps I could find people to interview there. Robby and I quickly visited the Westside Community Center to introduce ourselves to the reunion coordinator, James Abraham. When Abraham learned what we needed he asked if I would share my research in progress with the group in exchange for an opportunity to ask questions. I jumped at the chance and thereby discovered that we sometimes influence the present when we reconstruct the past.

Abraham had scheduled an hour and a half for our presentation and group interview with the DouglassAires. I briefly sketched

what I thought I had learned so far. When I tried to elicit information about Brown or Gracey, however, I got little response. So I
asked about health care in 1950 Bartlesville—a major concern of
Brown's CORE group—and the floodgates opened. Before long I
learned that the DouglassAires' earlier reticence was a result of
surprise: I had told them things about this episode they had not
known before. They were stunned to find that a disagreement over
the creation of the very Westside Community Center in which we
were sitting, and the amount of risk to take for integration, had
split the African-American community and helped to cost Gracey
his job. Many in the group felt that their parents had lied to protect
them, and they blamed themselves for having done substantially
the same thing with their children. Eva Chambers, with "tears
behind [her] eyes," confessed that she did not want to tell her
children that she had sat in an area designated "Colored." No one
likes to admit that another person made her "feel less than," she
explained; she had not known until that moment how angry she
still was. Like the others, she had not wanted to share those painful
memories. Thus, instead of teaching their children how far they
have come, Ruth Bean Hicks said, "All we have taught them is our
rage." About an hour later than scheduled, our program ended,
appropriately enough, with prayer that the process of healing
begun that day would continue.[11] Although the healing begun
among the DouglassAires was an unanticipated consequence of
the research process, nevertheless it demonstrated in convincing
fashion that the discovery of one's own history can be liberating. I
renewed my commitment to seeing the invisible and hearing the
silences in history.

TELLING THE STORY

With three big boxes full of photocopies, photographs, and hundreds of pages of transcripts, I continued to try to make sense of the
events in Bartlesville in the early years of the cold war. I had begun
my research journey with a commitment to focus on the censorship

and anticommunism in this case through the lenses of race and gender. I had almost immediately discovered that anticommunism had given an excuse and a rhetoric for attacks on library materials but that those attacks were actually a way to attack Brown for her activities on behalf of racial justice. I discovered that women were central to the story in many ways; the YWCA, the American Association of University Women's Racial Problems Study Group, the wives of Phillips employees, the women of the Anti group, the African-American women teachers, and the women of the Friends of Miss Brown all emerged from the data to force more than a "notable woman" approach to this piece of history. Instead I had to examine the whole pattern of gender relations, including men's and women's networks and the strongly masculine and patriarchal corporate culture of Phillips Petroleum, within the Bartlesville community.[12]

This pattern of gender relations included the problematic relations of African-American domestic servants with their employers, as well as the relations among women and men, blacks and whites, within the CORE group. Thus my focus on race complicated my examination of gender issues. And neither race nor gender could quite be separated from issues of class: it was "the best people," as Mrs. Preston Gaddis made clear, who were dead set against racial integration, not the "young matrons and working people" of the community, as YWCA director Elizabeth Davis characterized the YWCA's supporters.[13]

All these factors of gender, race, and class had to be set within the state and national context. Not only did I have to consider how fervent anticommunism and such events as the Korean War affected the community, I also had to look at intellectual freedom issues and gender and race relations within libraries and the library profession. The national programs of local organizations such as the American Legion, the DAR, CORE, the NAACP, the YWCA, and the AAUW had to be considered, as did other instances in which the *Nation* and the *New Republic* had been targets of censors. Into this complex web of issues, movements, and organizations I had to place the personalities, the actors, of this particular story.

According to the data I have gathered, these events happened, and I believe that my interpretation of why these events happened as they did, when and where they did, is as truthful an interpretation as I can make it. No one other person, however, has stood in a place to be able to see the events and hear the voices as I have seen and heard them. Someone else, looking at the same data, might see the events from a different angle and hear different tones in the voices. The story I construct, as I warned, is colored by my decision to center the women and to be sensitive to the impact of race, gender, and class relations in these events.

In constructing my representation of the case of Ruth W. Brown and the Bartlesville Public Library, I am to a degree constrained and influenced by the actors' constructions and subsequent reconstructions of their actions. Not only Brown's enemies but her friends and Brown herself may well have reconstructed, wittingly or unwittingly, their experience so as to fit them most comfortably. When Brown recorded the executive session with the city commissioners, was she aware of how her record might be used? Was she thinking of newspaper coverage? court evidence? a historian in the 1990s? How did that influence what she wrote? And how did her motivation differ when she wrote to George Houser of CORE? In interpreting the documentary evidence as well as the interview data, I must remind myself that we are all constantly reinventing ourselves.

I must also remind myself that words that sound racist today—"colored woman," for example—did not sound so to many people in 1950; I have to remember that "feminist" was not a concept that Brown would have known (although today we would surely call her one) and that anticommunism (although not the virulent, McCarthy variety) was a perfectly acceptable liberal position. Although there is evidence that the anticommunist crusade was a top-down campaign and that the American Legion played an active role nationally in carrying it out, the cold war really did frighten many people; much anxiety was genuine.[14] Anxious people of goodwill, not just evil demagogues, could be encouraged to see communists under every rock. I must not read understandings of the 1990s into the world of 1946. I must resist the temptation to write the present into the past. The most important questions I must ask myself—and the reader must ask of my story—are those of integrity and rigorousness. Does the evidence gathered, as well as the method for gathering and presenting the evidence, support the interpretations I have made? Is the story credible? Does this account of Ruth Brown's experience ring true? Those who have seen a shorter version of this story have told me that it does.

Because I chose a research subject about which I care deeply, and the individual through whose story I chose to look at the subject was and is intensely interesting to me, I have been concerned since the outset with my relationship to Ruth Brown. As I listened to her slightly acid tongue and heard of her "prickly" habit of hanging up the phone without saying good-bye, as I learned that she loved bird-watching and listening to music (though she could not play an instrument herself), as I discovered how she mentored bright young people into librarianship and fought to adopt two young women left orphaned by the death of their mother, I came to know and admire her. But I also saw that she had something of the do-gooder, the desire to leave her mark, to be significant, to act rather than be acted on, that may have propelled her as much as her undeniable hatred of racism and her support for free inquiry. By getting to know her well I was able to discover her warts, to understand how she could inspire anger in "the chief oily words hand rubbing anti," irritation in the Episcopal priest, and anxiety in her elder daughter. While I was initially very concerned that such close involvement with Brown would lead me to be uncritical of her, I found instead that it led me to an appreciation of the complexity of human beings and an understanding of the importance of a sense of agency in people's lives.

My growing awareness of how a rather insignificant episode in a small city in a sparsely populated state nearly half a century ago reveals so much that is significant has made me feel an enormous sense of responsibility to the story and to all those who have helped me to tell it. The episode demonstrates much about the dynamics of censorship and the concerns it hides or reveals. It shows that individual librarians have been more courageous than the library profession as a whole in confronting racism and free access to ideas. The evidence shows that Bartlesville's elite used McCarthyist discourse to contain Brown's transgressions of the boundaries of gender and race. It reveals that the contemporary representations of the story, from those of the local newspaper to the ALA's reports to the film *Storm Center*, all minimized or ignored the racial aspects of the case. In an effort to defeat censorship they obscured more thoroughly than did Brown's enemies her true concern about intellectual freedom, a concern that all people have access to ideas. Thus I feel a very personal responsibility to give voice to the women and African Americans who have for so long been unheard. I hope I have told their story right.

ABBREVIATIONS

AAUW — American Association of University Women Collection, Bartlesville Public Library, Bartlesville, Oklahoma

Academy — Storm Center File, Center for Motion Picture Research, Academy of Motion Picture Arts and Sciences, Beverly Hills, California

ACLU — American Civil Liberties Union Archives, Seeley G. Mudd Manuscript Library, Princeton University, Princeton, New Jersey

ALA — American Library Association Archives, University of Illinois, Urbana-Champaign

BCC — Bartlesville City Commission Minutes, City Clerk's Office, Bartlesville, Oklahoma

Bixler Papers — Paul Bixler Papers, Antiochiana, Olive Kettering Library, Antioch College, Yellow Springs, Ohio

BPL — Bartlesville Public Library Local History Collection

Brown Papers — Ruth W. Brown Papers, Special Collections, Pittsburg State University, Pittsburg, Kansas

City Clerk — City Clerk's File, City of Bartlesville

CORE — Congress of Racial Equality Papers 1941–67, State Historical Society of Wisconsin, Madison

Davis Papers — Russell Davis Papers, Pittsburg State University

DKB — David K. Berninghausen Papers, University Library, University of Minnesota, Minneapolis

ERCC — E. R. Christopher Collection, Western History Collections, University of Oklahoma Library, Norman

Ericksen Papers — Ellen Brown Ericksen Papers, personal collection, Collinsville, Oklahoma

Frantz Papers — Evelyn Frantz Papers, in the possession of the author

NAACP — National Association for the Advancement of Colored People File, Archives and Manuscripts Reading Room, Library of Congress, Washington, D.C.

NBC — National Broadcasting Company Radio Broadcast Transcript File, Library of Congress

ODL — Working Files, Oklahoma Department of Libraries, Oklahoma City, Oklahoma

Ogilvie Papers — Lois Ogilvie Papers, personal collection, Santa Barbara, California

OLA — Oklahoma Library Association Files, Oklahoma State Archives, Oklahoma Department of Libraries

Phillips — Phillips Petroleum Company Archives, Bartlesville, Oklahoma

PCPL — Ponca City Public Library Archives and accession books, Ponca City, Oklahoma

Sark — Elmer Sark Collection, Bartlesville Public Library

School Board — School Board Minute Book, Bartlesville Public School Administration Building, Bartlesville, Oklahoma

SHSW — *Storm Center* File, Wisconsin Center for Film and Theater Research, State Historical Society of Wisconsin

Supreme Court — Oklahoma Supreme Court Files, Oklahoma State Archives

Taradash Papers — Daniel Taradash Papers, American Heritage Center, University of Wyoming, Laramie

YWCA — Young Women's Christian Association Archives, YWCA Building, Bartlesville

NOTES

INTRODUCTION

1. Cole and Norton, *A Red Herring*.

2. Egerton, *Speak Now Against the Day*; Sullivan, *Days of Hope*.

3. Sipuel v. Board of Regents of the University of Oklahoma, 332 U.S. 631 (1948); McLaurin v. Oklahoma Regents for Higher Education, 339 U.S. 637 (1950); Cross, *Blacks in White Colleges*; Egerton, *Speak Now Against the Day*; Fisher, *A Matter of Black and White*.

4. Meier and Rudwick, *CORE*, chaps. 1, 2.

5. Egerton, *Speak Now Against the Day*, 415; United States, President's Committee on Civil Rights, *To Secure These Rights, the Report of the President's Committee on Civil Rights*.

6. Egerton, *Speak Now Against the Day*; Sullivan, *Days of Hope*, 105.

7. May, *Homeward Bound*.

8. For the "creation" of McCarthyism, see Theoharis, *Seeds of Repression*; Freeland, *The Truman Doctrine and the Origins of McCarthyism*. For examinations of the motives for the loyalty program, Executive Order 9835, see McCullough, *Truman*, 551–53; and Theoharis, *Seeds of Repression*, 102, 103. See Bontecou, *The Federal Loyalty-Security Program*, for an examination of Truman's loyalty program and subsequent executive orders and legislation; the text of the various executive orders can be found in appendix 1.

9. Lewis Wood, "90 Groups, Schools Named on U.S. List as Being Disloyal," *New York Times*, December 5, 1947.

10. Ralph S. Brown's *Loyalty and Security* looks at not only the federal program but programs applied to state and private sector employees as well.

11. See Schrecker, *No Ivory Tower*, for the effects of McCarthyism on higher education. Public school teachers, especially in New York City, were also singled out for special scrutiny.

12. Fried, *Nightmare in Red*, 21.

13. Ibid., 85. For this period, see also Caute, *The Great Fear*.

14. Fried, *Nightmare in Red*, 35, 85; two case studies that provide examples of this are McCormick, *This Nest of Vipers*, and Carleton, *Red Scare!*

15. Irons, "American Business and the Origins of McCarthyism."

16. Schrecker, *Many Are the Crimes*, chap. 1.

17. Fried, *Nightmare in Red*, 27.

18. Michael Wallis, *Oil Man*.

19. McCormick, *This Nest of Vipers*, 1–4, posits a similar idea of why McCarthyism takes root.

20. Robbins, *Censorship and the American Library*.

21. This was the committee's official name. It became known as the House Un-American Activities Committee, or HUAC, through usage.

CHAPTER 1. "AMERICA'S IDEAL FAMILY CENTER"

1. *Polk's Bartlesville (Washington County, Okla.) City Directory, 1950*, 8. The quotation in the chapter title is from p. 7. Additional historical information on Bartlesville and the surrounding area is drawn also from Williams, *Bartlesville*; Teague, *History of Washington County and Surrounding Area*; and Washington County Historical Society, *Pictorial History of Bartlesville*. Angie Debo's *And Still the Waters Run* is still the definitive work on how white land, oil, and railroad interests conspired to deprive these Indians of their land and culture; Dennis McAuliffe's *The Deaths of Sybil Bolton* personalizes the fate of the Osage Indians through the story of the investigation of the death of one young Osage woman.

2. Wertz, *Phillips*, 96; Frank Phillips's story is told by Michael Wallis in *Oil Man*; for the Cow Thieves and Outlaws Reunions, see 264–71.

3. Wallis, *Oil Man*, 108. Many of the images associated with Oklahoma culture are here wrapped into one: the cowboy, the Indian, the outlaw, and the oil man. See Stein and Hill, *The Culture of Oklahoma*, especially Stein and Hill's "The Culture of Oklahoma," 198–235.

4. Wallis, *Oil Man*, 185.

5. Williams, *Bartlesville*, 93.

6. Wallis, *Oil Man*, 143–44, 428–31; Brooks Spies, interview with author, Bartlesville, Okla., June 19, 1995.

7. "Mr. Phillips 66" is a reference to the Phillips 66 brand name.

8. Wallis, *Oil Man*, 376.

9. Ibid., 438–66.

10. U.S. Bureau of the Census, *Census of Population: 1950*, vol. 2: *Characteristics of the Population*, pt. 36, *Oklahoma* (hereafter cited as *Census of Population: 1950*), table 36–53; nearly every interview I conducted over two years referred to the dominant, and complex, role of Phillips in the community's life.

11. Descriptions of Bartlesville in 1950 are derived from the sum of my research, maps, and the study of aerial photographs provided by the Phillips Petroleum Company Archives, Susan Box, Archivist; *Census of Population: 1950*, table 36–61 (this figure is the median income for families and unrelated individuals, including African Americans).

12. *City Directory, 1950*, 7.

13. *City Directory, 1950*; Betty Rausch Frey, transcript in Bartlesville Women's Network, *Taproots*, 1:29–49 (hereafter cited as *Taproots*); information about Alberta Bradstreet comes from both the *City Directory* and Ellen Brown Ericksen, interview with author, Collinsville, Okla., July 7, 1994, and July 20, 1995.

14. Donald E. Koppel, interview with author, Bartlesville, Okla., July 13, 1994; Lois Straight Johnson, oral history transcript, *Taproots*, 1:9–10; Roy and Carolyn Price-Barton, interview with author, Bartlesville, Okla., August 2, 1994.

15. Details are taken from *City Directory, 1950*.

16. The role of white landlords is discussed in William Nelson, autograph manuscript, [January 5, 1991], Davis Papers; *Census of Population: 1950*, tables 36–49, 36–53, 36–59, 36–108, 36–109; it is difficult to be precise about income figures because available data are not directly comparable; *Census of Housing: 1950*, vol. 1: *General Characteristics*, pt. 5, *North Carolina–Tennessee*, tables 36–27, 36–58; additional figures and analysis of the problems of the African-American community are found in R. T. Gracey, "Community Survey: Bartlesville, Oklahoma," March 17, 1947, Frames 564–66, Group 22, Series 3: Exec. Secy's File, CORE.

17. DouglassAires, interview with author, Bartlesville, Okla., July 22, 1994. While this is a group interview, whenever I can attribute information to individuals, I do so.

18. Description of inferior medical services for African Americans comes from *Taproots*, 1:47, and from DouglassAires, group interview; Goble, "The Southern Influence on Oklahoma."

19. Smallwood and Phillips, "Black Oklahomans and the Question of 'Oklahomaness,'" 50–51.

20. Williams, *Bartlesville*, 42; it is probably not a coincidence that the doctor in Laura Ingalls Wilder's *Little House on the Prairie* is Dr. Tann; Wilder's book is set in Kansas, not far north of Bartlesville in land that

once belonged to the Osage tribe; Goble, "The Southern Influence on Oklahoma," 284–85; Smallwood and Crispin, "Black Oklahomans and the Question of Oklahomaness," 51–54; for Jim Crow, see Woodward, *The Strange Career of Jim Crow*; Oklahoma Territory was roughly the western half of the state, populated by Indians such as the Apache and Nez Perce, removed from western lands; Indian Territory was the eastern half of the state, to which the Five Civilized Tribes (from the southeastern United States) were removed. Oklahoma's statehood ceremony included the symbolic marriage of Oklahoma Territory and Indian Territory; Oklahoma means "Land of the Red Man."

21. Goble, "The Southern Influence of Oklahoma," 288–89; Smallwood and Crispin, "Black Oklahomans and the Question of Oklahomaness," 57, 58.

22. Smallwood and Crispin, "Black Oklahomans and the Question of Oklahomaness," 58–59; Scales and Goble, *Oklahoma Politics*, 106–7.

23. Scales and Goble, *Oklahoma Politics*, 109, shows a photo of an initiation of new Klansmen near Bartlesville. Assorted newspaper clippings, Ku Klux Klan folder, Bartlesville Public Library. A number of whites I interviewed said that the Tulsa race riots made no impact on Bartlesville; *City Directory, 1924*, 276.

24. Sullivan, *Days of Hope*, 100.

25. Smallwood and Crispin, "Black Oklahomans and the Question of Oklahomaness," 60.

26. Sullivan, *Days of Hope*, 87.

27. Meier and Bracey, "The NAACP as a Reform Movement, 1909–1965," 21; Request to reactivate Bartlesville charter, September 24, 1940; Membership list, July 6, 1942, Box C 154, RG 2; Annual Report of Branch Activities—1944, Box C 273, RG 3; all NAACP; Frey, oral history transcript, *Taproots*, 1:47 (I can find no confirmation of this memory).

28. Sipuel v. Oklahoma State Board of Regents, 332 U.S. 631 (1948); McLaurin v. Oklahoma Regents for Higher Education, 339 U.S. 637 (1950); Cross, *Blacks in White Colleges*; Egerton, *Speak Now Against the Day*.

29. Salmond, "'The Great Southern Commie Hunt.'"

30. Fried, *Nightmare in Red*, 35, 85; for Oklahoma's loyalty oaths and the American Legion's role in pushing them through the legislature, see Robinson, *Anti-Sedition and Loyalty Investigations in Oklahoma*. See also Schrecker, *Many Are the Crimes*, for a discussion of the anticommunist apparatus and its purposes.

31. Phillips Petroleum Company, "The Road We've Traveled"; *Census of Population: 1950*, table 36–53; U.S. Bureau of the Census, *Sixteenth Census of the United States: 1940—Population*, vol. 2: *Characteristics of the Population*, pt. 5, *New York–Oregon*, 918; one indication of the many points of origin of

the college-educated women is the roster of the American Association of University Women, Minutes, AAUW.

32. Shera, *Foundations of the Public Library*.

33. "The Bartlesville Public Library: The Services and Facility. A Study by the League of Women Voters, Bartlesville, Oklahoma," 2, BPL.

34. Oklahoma Library Commission, *Oklahoma Libraries, 1900–1937*, 20–21. This history indicates that contrary to the later League of Women Voters pamphlet, the Tuesday Club did not run a library of its own; the difference is probably a matter of semantics.

35. Ibid.

36. Oklahoma Library Commission, Report, 1948, 23, 26, 27; Oklahoma Library Commission, *Oklahoma Libraries, 1900–1937*, 20–21.

37. Oklahoma Library Commission, *Oklahoma Libraries, 1900–1937*, 21; Ericksen interview; Diploma, Alva Normal School, Ericksen Papers; *Sooner Nineteen-Fifteen*, 34; Mildred Holliday Dryer Creasy, interview with author, Cincinnati, Ohio, November 4 and 5, 1994.

38. Mary Nan Meade, oral history transcript, *Taproots*, 1:60; Ruth Fisher Putnam, telephone interview with author, April 18, 1994; Joanne Bennett, oral history transcript, *Taproots*, 1:86.

39. Ruth W. Brown to Ellen [Brown Ericksen], December 26 [n.d. but after 1962], Ericksen Papers; James Henderson, telephone interview with author, March 24, 1994; Elmo Olson to Miss Brown, February 15, 1939, Ericksen Papers. Olson died in the Battle of the Bulge.

40. Ericksen interview; Dryer Creasy interview; Henderson interview.

41. Canonical Parish Register, St. Luke's Episcopal Church, Bartlesville, Okla.; "U. of L. Opening Second Semester," undated Bartlesville *Morning Examiner* clipping labeled Spring 1946, BPL; Program, Oklahoma Library Association, Norman, February 20, 1930, Box 1, OLA.

42. Oklahoma Library Commission, *Oklahoma Libraries, 1900–1937*, 201; "Oklahoma Library Association, Weatherford—Nov. 10–12, 1931," Box 1, OLA. Observant readers will note that Brown reports more volumes in the 1930s than in the late 1940s. One conclusion to draw from this is that poor support over an extended period resulted in failure to replace books worn out in use; another possibility is that Brown was imprecise or deliberately inaccurate in her reporting.

43. "New Books at the Library," unidentified newspaper clipping, June 4, 1939, BPL; Henderson interview; Oklahoma Library Commission, *Reports, July 1, 1936–June 30, 1937, July 1, 1937–June 30, 1938*, 58; Grimshaw, "Ruth Brown," 2139; "A Typical Day in the Library: What the Public Likes in Reading Matter Is Checked by Miss Brown and Staff," newspaper clipping from unidentified source, May 1932, BPL.

44. Henderson interview; Naomi Stocker Gordon, telephone interview with author, April 20, 1994; Brown, "Remember Bartlesville."

45. Ericksen interview; Henderson interview; Columbia University summer school catalogs (various years); Margaret Varvel, interview with author, Corvallis, Ore., March 20, 21, 1994; Odie McReynolds, interview with author, Bartlesville, Okla., July 14, 1994; Odie McReynolds, in *Taproots*, 2:35–36, said that they made a connection between the war against fascism and their own activism; "Affiliation Blank," Frame 555, Group 22, and Ruth W. Brown to Congress of Racial Equality, November 18, 1946, Frame 1293, Group 47, both Series 3: Exec. Secy's File, CORE; "Proposed Constitution of the Bartlesville Committee on Practice of Democracy," n.d., Ogilvie Papers.

46. Buckler, "The CORE Way"; Meier and Rudwick, *CORE*. Brown to Congress of Racial Equality, November 18, 1946, Frame 1293, Group 47; Brown to George W. Houser, January 20, 1947, Frame 562, Group 22; "Affiliation Blank," Frame 555, Group 22; Brown to Houser, February 11, 1950, Frame 606, Group 22; all Series 3: Exec. Secy's File, CORE.

47. [Annual Report 1947], Frame 664; Brown to Houser, September 22, 1947, Frame 567; Group 22, Series 3: Exec. Secy's File, CORE; Robert Jennings, interview, with author, Bartlesville, Okla., July 8 and August 9, 1994.

48. William Nelson, autograph manuscript, Davis Papers; Betty Frey, *Taproots*, 1:47.

49. Mrs. Robert Ogilvie, "Bartlesville Racial Problems Study Group," *Oklahoma Division Bulletin, American Association of University Women* 19 (Fall 1948): 2, AAUW; Minutes of the Executive Board Meeting, Bartlesville Branch, December 2, 1947, Minutes, vol. 3, AAUW; Lynn, *Progressive Women in Conservative Times*, 40–67; Elizabeth C. Davis, *Annual Report*, September 1, 1950, YWCA; "YW Established in 1921," clipping from *Bartlesville Examiner-Enterprise*, July 31, 1970, YWCA File, BPL; Department of Data and Trends, National Board of the YWCA, *Toward Better Race Relations*; the Interracial Charter appears on 179–80; "Voting Begins on Policies of YWCA," *Bartlesville Examiner-Enterprise*, April 19, 1950.

50. Ogilvie, "Bartlesville Racial Problems Study Group," 1–3; "Bartlesville Branch, 1948–1949," [annual report], lists an average of a dozen members in each of eleven study groups; a membership list contains 105 names, AAUW; for the national AAUW's contradictory attitude and behavior regarding integration, see Levine, *Degrees of Equality*, esp. chap. 6; Lois Ogilvie, telephone interview with author, July 29, 1996.

51. Lois Ogilvie to Houser, March 17, 1948, Frame 573; Houser to Ogilvie, March 22, 1948, Frame 574; Brown to Houser, May 20, 1948, Frame 577; Brown to Houser, June 2, 1948, Frame 578; all Group 22, Series 3: Exec. Secy's File, CORE.

52. Gleason, *The Southern Negro and the Public Library*, discusses the factors leading to the development of libraries as well as the status of library service to African Americans in thirteen southern states, including Oklahoma, in 1939. Other sources that deal with the development of library services in the South are Barker, *Libraries of the South*; Wilson and Wight, *County Library Service in the South*; Wilson, *Geography of Reading*; and Wilson and Milczewski, *Libraries of the Southeast*; Malone, "Accommodating Access"; Du Mont, "Race in American Librarianship," 488.

53. Gleason, *The Southern Negro and the Public Library*.

54. Wilson and Milczewski, *Libraries of the Southeast*, 284.

55. Cresswell, "Last Days of Jim Crow in Southern Libraries"; Dickey, "A History of Public Library Service for Negroes in Jackson, Mississippi, 1950–1957," 16, 30. Similar patterns can be seen, for example, in Montgomery and Bessemer, Alabama, and Columbus, Georgia. See Grayson, "A History of Public Library Service for Negroes in Montgomery, Alabama"; Fonville, "A History of Public Library Service to Negroes in Bessemer, Alabama"; and Crittenden, "A History of Public Library Service to Negroes in Columbus, Georgia, 1831–1959." These theses are part of a series of at least fifteen done at Atlanta University, mostly under the direction of Dean Virginia Lacy Jones. See also Shockley, *A History of Public Library Services to Negroes in the South, 1900–1955*.

56. Gleason, *The Southern Negro and the Public Library*, 74.

57. Oklahoma Library Commission, *Reports*, 1948, 31.

58. Oklahoma Library Commission, *Oklahoma Libraries, 1900–1937*, 167; Oklahoma Library Commission, *Reports*, 1948, 31.

59. Oklahoma Library Commission, *Oklahoma Libraries, 1900–1937*, 167–68.

60. Ibid., 169; Oklahoma Library Commission, *Reports*, 1948, 31.

61. Oklahoma Library Commission, *Oklahoma Libraries, 1900–1937*, 168.

62. Oklahoma Library Commission, *Reports*, 1942, 21–22.

63. Ibid., 1938, 52–53; 1940, 15; and 1942, 22; "The Community (Attucks) Library," Attucks Library Folder, Ponca City—City of, Vertical File, PCPL.

64. Oklahoma Library Commission, *Reports*, 1948, 31.

65. Ibid., 1923, 11, 43; Oklahoma Library Commission, *Oklahoma Libraries, 1900–1937*, 167, 169. For the relative usefulness of schools as branch libraries or deposit stations, see Gleason, *The Southern Negro and the Public Library*.

66. Oklahoma Library Commission, *Reports*, 1948, 31; Oklahoma Library Commission, *Oklahoma Libraries, 1900–1937*, 166.

67. Holden, "The Color Line in Southern Libraries," 3.

68. Gleason, *The Southern Negro and the Public Library*, 82–85; Danton, "South Does Less Restricting."

69. Gleason, *The Southern Negro and the Public Library*, 83.

70. Bernice Brown, Marie Littles Wilson, and Rose Bean Hicks, Doug-lassAires interview.

71. Annotated list of periodical titles held in the Bartlesville Public Library, included with the first report of the Library Board to the City Commission, April 25, 1950, Davis Papers; "Report on City Library Is Made by Citizens Group," *Bartlesville Examiner-Enterprise*, May 28, 1950.

72. Danton, "South Does Less Restricting"; "First Southern Library Has Opened Doors to Negroes," *Library Journal* 73 (August 1948): 1070. See Malone, "Accommodating Access," for Louisville's history of service to African Americans.

73. "Intellectual Freedom," *American Library Association Bulletin* 41 (15 October 1947): 393; U.S. President's Committee on Civil Rights, *To Secure These Rights*; Jenkins, "Everyday Resistance "; Robbins, *Censorship and the American Library*, esp. chap. 2.

74. Ruth W. Brown to George Houser, July 25, 1948, Frames 580-81, Group 22, Series 3: Exec. Secy's File, CORE.

CHAPTER 2. HASTENING THE DAY

1. Brown to Houser, August 1, 1948, Frame 584, Group 22, Series 3: Exec. Secy's File, CORE.

2. Meier and Rudwick, *CORE*, 64.

3. Robbins, *Censorship and the American Library*.

4. Membership Directory, March 16, 1948, Ogilvie Papers; Member-ship list, July 6, 1942, Box C 154, RG 2, NAACP; city directories.

5. Membership Directory, March 16, 1948, Ogilvie Papers; Bartlesville Branch, 1947–48, and Bartlesville Branch, 1948–49, all AAUW, BPL. Arrivals in Bartlesville have been determined through use of city directories. Janice and William Nelson, also connected with Phillips, were also COPD members at some time, but they were not in Bartlesville in 1948.

6. Membership Directory, Ogilvie Papers; city directories.

7. Membership Directory, Ogilvie Papers; Lois Ogilvie, telephone interview with author, July 29, 1996. Brown to Houser, February 11, 1950, Frames 606–7; Brown to Houser, February 25, 1949, Frame 588; both Group 22, Series 3: Exec. Secy's File, CORE. Robert Davis does not appear in the membership directory or in the city directories, but his address is the same as that for Clifford and Sadie Gibbs, so one can conclude at least that he is one of the African-American members of the group.

8. Brown to Houser, February 25, 1949, Frame 588, Group 22; People at the CORE Convention, 1949, Frame 1044, Group 28; Brown to Houser, July 3, 1949, Frames 595–98, Group 22; all Series 3: Exec. Secy's File, CORE. George Houser, telephone interview with author, February 20, 1994.

9. F. E. Condon to Houser, March 11, 1950, Frame 615; Brown to Houser, July 8, 1949, Frame 594; Houser to Brown, July 19, 1950, Frame 600; Brown to Houser, February 11, 1950, Frame 605; all Group 22, Series 3: Exec. Secy's File, CORE.

10. Lois Ogilvie interview; Richard Rodgers, telephone interview with author, August 20, 1995; Brown to Houser, July 1, 1950, Frames 628–31, Group 22, Series 3: Exec. Secy's File, CORE; Jean Jones, telephone interview with author, November 7, 1995.

11. J. B. Dixon, telephone interview with author, July 12, 1995; Preston Gaddis, interview with author, Bartlesville, Okla., July 14, 1994; Ogilvie interview.

12. See Caute, *The Great Fear*; Fried, *Nightmare in Red*; and Schrecker, *Many Are the Crimes*, for surveys of the period; although individuals and some newspaper accounts report that Brown had a picture of Robeson in the library, she denied that she did; the same rumors abounded concerning Gracey and Douglass School. For an in–depth discussion of the Smith Act trials, see Belknap, *Cold War Political Justice*.

13. Davis, *Annual Report*, September 1, 1950, YWCA.

14. Ibid.

15. [Darlene Anderson Essary] to Freda Kirchwey, Editor, *Nation*, July 26, 1950, Davis Papers; published as "Patriotism in Bartlesville," *Nation* (August 12, 1950): 155–56; "A Call to Action during Brotherhood Month," *Bartlesville Examiner-Enterprise*, February 1,1950, evening edition; Brown to Houser, February 2, 1950, Frame 602, Group 22, Series 3: Exec. Secy's File, CORE.

16. Brown to Houser, February 2, 1950, Frame 602, Group 22, Series 3: Exec. Secy's File, CORE. I cannot identify Street and Cooke with certainty, but they were teachers, unmarried, relative newcomers, and officers in the CORE group, factors that match Brown's description of her companions most closely and make them the most likely to have shared Brown's penchant for action. In her February 11, 1950, letter to Houser, Brown commented that because "the two young teachers and I are always wanting to do instead of talk I think they all feel we must be held back." Part of the description of the visit to Hull's comes from James R. Patterson, "Her Zeal for Complete Democracy Costs a Librarian Her Job," *Kansas City Star*, (November 19, 1950).

17. Brown to Houser, February 2, 1950, Frame 602; Brown to Houser, February 11, 1950, Frame 604; both Group 22, Series 3: Exec. Secy's File, CORE.

18. "Telephone Poll Results," *Minute Record, Board of Education, Bartlesville, OK*, 103, School Board; Brown to Houser, February 11, 1950, continued February 16, 1950, Frame 603–9; F. E. Condon to Houser, March 11, 1950, Frame 615; Brown to Houser, July 25, 1948, Frames 580–81; all Group 22, Series 3: Exec. Secy's File, CORE.

19. Minutes of Adjourned Regular Meeting of the Board of Commissioners of the City of Bartlesville, Oklahoma, February 16, 1950, 1, BCC; "February 16, 1950 the first protest was made against me . . . " [undated manuscript written after July 25, 1950], Brown Papers. The Warren pamphlet, which I have not yet been able to locate, is cited in Mays, "McCarthyism in Oklahoma," 23. "City Fathers Discuss Union at Meeting," *Bartlesville Examiner-Enterprise*, February 17, 1950; "Friends of Miss Brown" to Dear Friends, mimeographed letter, August 21, 1950, Brown Papers; city directories; "K. S. Adams Elected President of Chamber of Commerce," *Bartlesville Examiner-Enterprise*, June 23, 1950; Davis, *Annual Report*, September 1, 1950, app. 12, 19, YWCA.

20. City directories; Canonical Parish Register, St. Luke's Episcopal Church, Bartlesville, Okla.

21. City directories; Richard Kane, interview with author, Bartlesville, Okla., July 13, 1994.

22. Kane interview; Russell W. Davis, interview with author, Bartlesville, Okla., July 8, 1994. I cannot establish with certainty how often the library board had been meeting, as I cannot locate the minutes of the "old" library board and memories vary considerably. "Board Hears Report on Library Affairs," *Bartlesville Examiner-Enterprise*, March 2, 1950; "Library Board Report," *Bartlesville Examiner-Enterprise*, March 7, 1950.

23. Philip Lorenz, interview with author, Bartlesville, Okla., July 14, 1994; "Library Quiz Brings Hot Clash," *Bartlesville Examiner-Enterprise*, March 7, 1950; Charles W. Varvel, letter to the editor, *Bartlesville Examiner-Enterprise*, March 12, 1950; Minutes of the Regular Meeting of the BCC, March 6, 1950, 1; John H. Purnell, ". . . and by the way" [column], *Bartlesville Examiner-Enterprise*, March 8, 1950; Brown to Houser, March 11, 1950, Frames 611–14, Group 22, Series 3: Exec. Secy's File, CORE.

24. James Spivey, telephone interview with author, March 23, 1995; William Nelson, autograph manuscript, January 5, 1991, Davis Papers; Lorenz interview.

25. "Board Removes 'Red' Literature; Action Delayed," *Daily Oklahoman*, March 10, 1950; Lucy Ann Babcock to Russell W. Davis, March 9, 1950, Davis Papers; photo with caption, *Bartlesville Examiner-Enterprise*, March 9, 1950; Herbert E. Winn, interview with author, Bartlesville, Okla., July 18, 1994; "To the Board of the Commissioners of the City of Bartles-

ville, Oklahoma" [Report of Library Board], Davis Papers. Both the positive and the negative of the picture are in ERCC.

26. Robert Manuel, letter to editor, *Bartlesville Examiner-Enterprise*,
March 26, 1950; Frank E. Condon to Houser, March 11, 1950, Frame 615;
Brown to Houser, March 11, 1950, Frames 611–14; both Group 22, Series 3:
Exec. Secy's File, CORE; Russell W. Davis to David K. Berninghausen,
March, 15, 1950, DKB.

27. Davis, *Annual Report*, September 1, 1950, secs. 1 and 2, YWCA;
Spivey interview.

28. Kamp, *Behind the Lace Curtains of the YWCA*; Davis, *Annual Report*,
September 1, 1950, secs. 1, 2, App. 5–12, YWCA; "Joseph P. Kamp," *Look*,
April 12, 1950, 6; "Citizens Criticize Y.W.C.A. Policies at Public Meeting,"
Bartlesville Examiner-Enterprise, April 4, 1950; "YWCA Body Gives Policy
Statement," *Bartlesville Examiner-Enterprise*, April 5, 1950.

29. Davis, *Annual Report*, September 1, 1950, secs. 1 and 2, YWCA.

30. "Voting Begins on Policies of YWCA," *Bartlesville Examiner-
Enterprise*, evening edition, April 19, 1950; Davis, *Annual Report*, September
1, 1950, app. 12, YWCA.

31. Davis, *Annual Report*, September 1, 1950, app. 17, YWCA.

32. Ibid., secs. 1 and 2, 5, YWCA.

33. Ibid., 2, YWCA; "Segregation Is Burning Issue at Bartlesville," *The
Black Dispatch* [City Edition], March 18, 1950.

34. Minutes of the Adjourned Regular Meeting of the BCC, March 13,
1950, BCC; "Mrs. Lichenheld Is DAR Guest Speaker," *Bartlesville Examiner-
Enterprise*, April 6, 1950.

35. Kane interview; "To the Board of Commissioners of the City of
Bartlesville, Oklahoma" [Report of the library board], [April 24, 1950], 3,
Davis Papers.

36. Russell W. Davis to Committee on Intellectual Freedom, March 15,
1950, DKB; James F. Gourley to Davis, March 9, 1950, Davis Papers;
Clarence S. Paine to Davis, April 21, 1950, City Clerk's File; Loose Leaf
Accession Book, July 1945–July 1949 and July 1949–October 1954, PCPL.

37. Robbins, *Censorship and the American Library*; Berninghausen, "The
Case of the *Nation*"; Berninghausen to Russell W. Davis, March 24, 1950,
DKB; Jenkins, "Everyday Resistance."

38. "To the Board of the Commissioners of the City of Bartlesville,
Oklahoma," 1–3, Davis Papers.

39. Ibid., 3–4.

40. Don V. Purington to Russell W. Davis, April 25, 1950; R. H. Hudson
to Davis, May 5, 1950; George W. Cade to Davis, May 8, 1950; William
Nelson, autograph manuscript; all Davis Papers.

41. "No Fireworks at Library Meeting"; Minutes, Adjourned Regular Meeting, BCC, May 25, 1950, 1.

42. "No Fireworks at Library Meeting"; "To: Mayor Hudson and the Members of the Bartlesville City Commission from the Citizens Committee" [Report], [May 25, 1950], City Clerk's File; "Report on City Library Is Made by Citizens Group," *Bartlesville Examiner-Enterprise*, May 28, 1950.

43. "To: Mayor Hudson and the Members of the Bartlesville City Commission"; "Report on City Library Is Made by Citizens Group."

44. [Untitled draft of American Legion resolution, approved by the executive committee], February 27, 1950, ERCC; Minutes, Adjourned Regular Meeting, BCC, May 25, 1950, 1.

45. Brown to Houser, May 22, 1950, Frames 622–26, Group 22, Series 3: Exec. Secy's File, CORE; Spivey interview.

46. Brown to Houser, May 22, 1950, Frames 622–26, Group 22, Series 3, Exec. Secy's File, CORE.

47. Minutes, Adjourned Regular Meeting, BCC, June 14, 1950, 2; Ordinance No. 1453, published in *Bartlesville Examiner-Enterprise*, June 16, 1950; Davis to Lee Erhard, June 22, 1950, Davis Papers.

48. Eva Sanderson to Davis, July 8, 1950, Davis Papers; "New Library Board Named; New Fire Chief Appointed," *Bartlesville Examiner-Enterprise*, July 11, 1950; E. R. Christopher to Joseph J. Lawler, Assistant Postmaster General, September 12, 1950, ERCC. Christopher's membership on national legion committees can be traced through the *Proceedings* of the various years' national conventions, published as part of the U.S. Congress Serial Set. Characterizations of the new library board and of Donald T. Koppel come from an interview with him in Bartlesville, Okla., July 13, 1994. Canonical Parish Register, St. Luke's Episcopal Church, Bartlesville, Okla.

49. Brown to Houser, July 11, 1950, Frames 628–31, Group 22, Series 3: Exec. Secy's File, CORE; Brown's account of Condon's transfer is substantiated by the written recollections of William Nelson, autograph manuscript, Davis Papers, and Francis E. Condon, telephone interview, August 5, 1994. Condon went into university teaching.

50. Brown, "July 25, 1950, City Manager's Office . . . ," Brown Papers. In some instances, I have added stage directions based on her notes to capture the flavor of the document.

51. Brown, "July 25, 1950, City Manager's Office . . . ," Brown Papers; Paul Hood, "Collision of Ideas Fans Violent Fuss," *Sunday Oklahoman*, November 5, 1950; Minutes of Adjourned Regular Meeting, BCC, July 25, 1950, 1.

52. "City Library Chief Fired Tuesday Night," *Bartlesville Examiner-Enterprise*, July 26, 1950; "City Librarian Is Relieved of Duty by Commissioners," *Bartlesville Record*, July 26, 1950; Minutes of Regular Meeting,

August 7, 1950, BCC, 5; To Members Bartlesville Library Board from [E. R.] Christopher, July 19, 1950, ERCC.

53. "City Library Still Open; Miss Brown Has Statement," *Bartlesville Examiner-Enterprise*, July 27, 1950.

54. Russell W. Davis to Mrs. J. R. Dale and Lucy Ann Babcock, July 27, 1950, Davis Papers.

CHAPTER 3. THE MANY FRIENDS OF MISS BROWN

1. Mrs. Lee Still to City Commissioners, July 28, 1950, City Clerk's File; Brown to Houser, August 11, 1950, Frames 631–34, Group 22, Series 3: Exec. Secy's File, CORE.

2. "Miss Brown Is Backed by Committee in Her Battle to Regain Library Post," *Bartlesville Examiner-Enterprise*, September 11, 1950; "Just Friends Backing Mrs. [*sic*] Brown's Suit," *Bartlesville Record*, September 17, 1950; Bob Snair, "Many Issues Involved in Bartlesville Library Case," reprinted in *University Daily Kansan*, January 15, 1951, from the *Bartlesville Record*; Davis interview; "City Woman Says She Is Not Group Member," *Bartlesville Examiner-Enterprise*, September 22, 1950; Ericksen interview; The Friends of Miss Brown to "Dear Friend," March 12, 1951, Brown Papers; Davis, *Annual Report*, September 1, 1950, app. 12, 3; Achtemeier, *The Meaning and the Mystery*.

3. [Essary] to Kirchwey, Editor, *Nation*, July 26, 1950, Davis Papers, published as "Patriotism in Bartlesville"; James F. O'Neill to E. R. Christopher, September 15, 1950, ERCC; John D. Upham, telephone interview with author, July 9, 1998.

4. "U.S.A. or U.S.S.R.?" [advertisement], *Bartlesville Examiner-Enterprise*, July 30, 1950.

5. Regular Meeting of the Board of Commissioners, August 7, 1950, BCC; M. P. Matuszak to John D. Upham, September 18, 1950, Ruth Brown file, BPL; Brown to Houser, August 11, 1950, Frames 631–34, Group 22, Series 3: Exec. Secy's File, CORE; Max K. Gilstrap, "Battles of Bartlesville."

6. [Darlene Anderson Essary] to David K. Berninghausen, August 1, 1950, copy in Library Censorship—Bartlesville folder, ACLU; Brown to Houser, August 11, 1950, Frames 631–34, Group 22, Series 3: Exec. Secy's File, CORE.

7. Brown to Houser, August 11, 1950, Frames 631–34, Group 22, Series 3: Exec. Secy's File, CORE; "City Will Not Hire Special Counsel in Library Action," *Bartlesville Examiner-Enterprise*, September 13, 1950; "Ex-City Librarian Sues City for Job," *Bartlesville Examiner-Enterprise*, September 12, 1950.

8. "District Judge Disqualifies in City Library Job Lawsuit," *Bartlesville Examiner-Enterprise*, October 2, 1950; "Former City Librarian Denied Reinstatement," *Bartlesville Enterprise*, November 9, 1950.

9. "Casualty of the Hysteria," *CORE-lator* (October 1950), Ogilvie Papers; Houser to Brown, August 3, 1950, Frame 637; Houser to Brown, September 1, 1950, Frame 641: all Group 22, Series 3: Exec. Secy's File, CORE; "Just Friends Backing Mrs. [*sic*] Brown's Suit," *Bartlesville Record*, September 17, 1950; Brown to Houser, September 22, 1950, Frame 647, Group 22, Series 3: Exec. Secy's File, CORE.

10. Naomi Stocker Gordon telephone interview; Abbott Gould to George Soll, October 3, 1950; Soll to Gould, October 6, 1950; John Upham to Gould, October 9, 1950; Berninghausen to Gould, October 19, 1950; all ACLU.

11. "Private Censors Ban Magazines," *Civil Liberties*, October 1, 1950, unpaged clipping, Brown Papers; Lewis, *"Friday Is a Great Day"*; Robert W. Orr to Clerk of City Commissioners, December 23, 1950, City Clerk's File; James C. Adams to the Editor, *Bartlesville Examiner-Enterprise*, January 28, 1951; Ruth W. Brown to American Civil Liberties Union, December 18, 1950, ACLU.

12. Henderson, "Ruth Brown's Dismissal Shocks Former Bartlesville Resident."

13. For the development of the ALA's intellectual freedom position from 1939 until this episode, see Robbins, *Censorship and the American Library*, esp. chaps 1, 2; American Library Association, "The Library Bill of Rights"; for its development in the 1950s see Robbins, "Champions of a Cause."

14. John Mackenzie Cory to Ruth Warncke, January 22, 1951, DKB; for the controversy over loyalty programs in libraries, see Robbins, "After Brave Words, Silence."

15. Cory to Berninghausen, August 3, 1950; Berninghausen to Intellectual Freedom Committee, Personnel Board, and Executive Board, August 1, 1950; Berninghausen to Cory, January 19, 1951; all DKB.

16. Berninghausen to Cory, January 19, 1951, DKB; Rutherford D. Rogers to Mayor E. S. Dunaway, January 17, 1951, City Clerk's File; Berninghausen to Brown, August 3, 1950, DKB; [Frances Kennedy] to Mrs. Marable, September 11, 1950, Box 9, OLA; for a complete discussion of Berninghausen's effort to launch state committees, see Robbins, *Censorship and the American Library*, chap. 2.

17. Minutes of OLA Executive Board Meeting, September 9, 1950; Esther Mann McRuer to Gertrude B. Davis, September 16, 1950; Mary Hays Marable to Frances Kennedy, September 13, 1950; all OLA.

18. Clarence S. Paine to McRuer, September 12, 1950, Box 9, OLA.

19. Davis to McRuer, September 19, 1950, Box 9, OLA.

20. Kennedy to McRuer, September 21, 1950; McRuer to Kennedy, September 23, 1950; Kennedy to McRuer, November 15, 1950; [McRuer] to Clarence Graham, January 22, 1951; all Box 9, OLA.

21. Frances Kennedy, interview with author, Oklahoma City, July 6, 1994; Kennedy to Marable, September 11, 1950; Kennedy to McRuer, November 15, 1950; Kennedy to McRuer, December 4, 1950; [McRuer] to Clarence Graham, January 22, 1951; McRuer to O.L.A. Executive Board, January 22, 1951; McRuer to Kennedy, January 22, 1951; all Box 9, OLA; "Former City Librarian Denied Reinstatement," *Bartlesville Examiner-Enterprise*, November 9, 1950.

22. Earle to Chris, January 18, 1951, ERCC; Imogene Patrick, "Legion Official Takes a Walk at Church Talk," *Daily Oklahoman*, January 19, 1951; "Library Scrap Is Revived in Public Debate," Guthrie *Leader*, January 19, 1951; both Bartlesville Historical Folder, ODL; Harold C. Price, Jr., telephone interview with author, December 11, 1994.

23. McRuer to O.L.A. Executive Board, January 22, 1951, Box 9, OLA; "Library Dispute at Bartlesville Subject of Forum," *Oklahoma City Times*, January 15, 1951, ERCC; McRuer to J. L. Rader, January 22, 1951; Rader to McRuer, January 31, 1951; Essary to McRuer, February 14, 1951; McRuer to Gaston Litton, February 7, 1951; Lee Spencer to McRuer, February 7, 1951; Mary Ann Wentroth to McRuer, February 13, 1951; Frances Lander Spain to Kennedy, February 14, 1951; Willard Watson to McRuer, February 23, 1951; Christopher to Editorial Offices, Oklahoma Librarian, March 6, 1951; all Box 9, OLA.

24. For example, Jack Heaney, "Dismissal of Bartlesville Librarian Scored by Board," *Tulsa World*, January 20, 1951; "Library Group Assails Ouster at Bartlesville," *Oklahoma City Times*, January 22, 1951; "Library Issue Puts Heat on B'Ville Group," *Miami (Okla.) News-Record*, January 22, 1951; "Bartlesville Condemned on Library Tiff," *Tulsa Tribune*, January 22, 1951; "State Library Group Raps Citizens' Committee Action," *Bartlesville Examiner-Enterprise*, January 22, 1951.

25. Kennedy, Marable, Ralph Hudson, and McRuer, "Report of the Intellectual Freedom Committee of the Oklahoma Library Association on the Bartlesville Public Library," January 8, 1951, Brown Papers.

26. Ibid.; the report was also published in the *Oklahoma Librarian* 1 (Winter 1950–51): 7, 17, and as "Censorship in Bartlesville," *American Library Association Bulletin* 45 (March 1951): 87–90.

27. For example, Arthur T. Hamlin to Kennedy, March 6, 1951; and Joseph C. Pray to Marable, April 28, 1951; both Box 9, OLA. McRuer to Litton, February 8, 1951; John B. Freeman to Litton, February 14, 1951; Business Meeting, March 16, 1951; all Box 9, OLA.

28. "Former City Librarian Denied Reinstatement," *Bartlesville Enterprise*, November 9, 1950; Miriam Matthews to David K. Berninghausen, November 30, 1950; Marion E. Hawes to Berninghausen, November 27, 1950; both DKB.

29. Ruth Warncke to John Mackenzie Cory, January 5, 1951; Cory to Warncke, January 22, 1951; both DKB. Helen A. Ridgway to Darlene Anderson Essary, February 19, 1951; Ridgway to Thurman S. Hurst, February 19, 1951; all Box 11, OLA.

30. Berninghausen to Cory, January 19, 1951; DKB; Rutherford D. Rogers to Mayor E. S. Dunaway, January 17, 1951, City Clerk's File; Cory to Rogers, Berninghausen, and Hazel B. Timmerman, n.d. but after January 29, 1951, DKB.

31. "Resolutions," *American Library Association Bulletin* 45 (March 1951): 94; Cory, Memo to Members, *American Library Association Bulletin* 45 (February 1951): 45; Ridgway to Essary, February 10, 1950, Box 9, OLA; Everett T. Moore, "Bartlesville and After," *American Library Association Bulletin* 54 (November 10, 1960): 815.

32. "National Groups Eye Library Row," undated clipping, *Oklahoma City Times*, Box 9, OLA; Jeanette Hopkins, "State Library Censor Battle Pledged Help," unidentified clipping, May 15, 1951, Box 11, OLA.

33. Robert D. Snair, "Black Eyes and Bartlesville," with an introduction by John A. Bannigan, *Daily Kansan*, January 15, 1951; "City Wins Court Library Decision," *Bartlesville Enterprise*, September 16, 1952; State ex rel Brown et al. v. Dunnaway [sic] et al., 207 Okla. 144 or 248 P. 2d 232.

34. Bob Snair, "Many Issues Involved in Bartlesville Library Case?" reprinted from *Bartlesville Record* in *University Daily Kansan*, January 15, 1951; F. A. Behmyer, "Librarian Fights for Job Lost over Criticism of Journals Chosen," *St. Louis Post-Dispatch*, October 16, 1950.

CHAPTER 4. THE CLEANUP:
BARTLESVILLE AND ITS LIBRARY AFTER BROWN

1. Business meeting of the Library Board, City of Bartlesville, Oklahoma, August 1, 1950, Box 13, ERCC; Minutes of the Regular Meeting of the Bartlesville City Commission, August 7, 1950, 5–6, BCC.

2. Minutes of the Regular Meeting of the Bartlesville City Commission, August 7, 1950, 5–6, BCC; Business meeting of the Library Board, August 1, 1950, Box 13, ERCC; "For your information," August 1, 1950, City Clerk's File; Minutes of the Regular Meeting of the Bartlesville City Commission, March 6, 1950, 7–8, BCC.

3. Life Membership Program, December 4, 1951, Box 83; Minutes of the Department Americanism Commission Meeting, January 15, 1951; both ERCC. American Legion, *Proceedings of the 29th National Convention* (1948), 166; *Proceedings of the 30th National Convention* (1949), 158; *Proceedings of the 33d National Convention* (1952), 144; and *Proceedings of the 34th National Convention* (1953), 139; all Box 72, ERCC. "Department Americanism Chairmen"; Robert B. Porta to Christopher, March 20, 1950; list enclosed with letter; all Box 72, ERCC. Christopher to Joseph J. Lawler, September 12, 1950, Box 13, ERCC.

4. Christopher to W. C. Sawyer, August 17, 1950, Box 13, ERCC.

5. Anthony Andrews protested the fate of the magazines at the October 3, 1950 meeting; John Upham and Tom Tarr brought up the magazines again at the November 7 meeting; Andrews, Upham, and Gladys Spies attended the December 5, 1950, meeting, according to Minutes of the Library Board; Christopher to Members of the Library Board, [n.d. but during Christopher's term as chairman], Box 1, ERCC. The contents of this list are nearly identical to, although in a different order from, the "Recommended Book List, National Americanism Division, National Headquarters, The American Legion," February 15, 1951, Box 72, ERCC, and includes the titles listed in the pamphlet, *How You Can Fight Communism*, 12; Christopher to Members of the Bartlesville Library Board, [n.d. but a month following the previous letter], Box 1, ERCC. I have tried, without success, to locate accessions books of the Bartlesville Public Library so as to judge the balance of the collection before Brown's ouster and to determine which and how many of the books Christopher suggested were purchased.

6. Proceedings of the Midwinter Meeting of the American Library Association: Council Meetings, January 31, 1951, February 3, 1951, 315, 316, Box 3, RG 1/1/1, ALA; "Notes Made at A.L.A. Mid-winter," *Library Journal* 76 (March 1, 1951): 396; Alice G. Higgins, "Intellectual Freedom," *American Library Association Bulletin* (October 15, 1947): 394; "Current Attacks," *American Library Association Bulletin* 42 (February 1948): 58.

7. Proceedings of the Midwinter Meeting American Library Association, 311–12. The Peoria case is described in Berninghausen, *The Flight from Reason*, 37–45; and Berninghausen, "Film Censorship," *American Library Association Bulletin* 44 (December 1950): 447–48. Information about the Robeson concert and the attacks on the black American Legion post comes from documents in the Peoria, Illinois, Chapter file, NAACP; Rorty, "The Libraries in a Time of Tension," 35.

8. Laurence J. Kipp, "Report from Boston," *Library Journal* 77 (November 1, 1952): 1843–46, 1887; Rorty, "The Attack on Our Libraries," 543; McCormick, *This Nest of Vipers*; "The Legion and the Libraries," *Shreveport*

Times, January 4, 1953, clipping in Folder 9, Box 1, Bixler Papers. Mildred Harlan to David H. Clift, February 14, 1955; Harlan to Paul Bixler, July 6, 1955; "Dear Library Board," *Legion News* 8 (June 1955): 1, 4; Free Library Association Board of Directors to Executive Committee John Jacob Fisher Post No. 62, January 12, 1956; Harlan to Bixler, February 11, 1956; Harlan to John D. Henderson, February 18, 1956; Henderson to Harlan, March 1, 1956; all Folder 25, Box 1, Bixler Papers. Paul Bixler, "Legionnaire 'Assults' Public Library," *Newsletter on Intellectual Freedom* 4 (January 1956): 4.

9. Rorty, "The Libraries in a Time of Tension," 31.

10. American Legion, *Proceedings of the 34th National Convention*, 139; *Counterattack* 6 (July 11, 1952): 1–4, copy in Folder 11, Box 1, Bixler Papers; Kuhn, "Why You Buy Books That Sell Communism"; "Ten Best Books," *American Legion Magazine*, 51 (May 1952): 29.

11. Business Meeting of the Library Board, August 1, 1950, 11–12; Fred A. Walker to Christopher, August 4, 1950; Wilma Ingram to Christopher, August 19, 1950; all Box 13, ERCC.

12. Christopher to Mary Mathis, November 6, 1950; Mathis to Christopher, November 15, 1950; Christopher to Mathis, December 5, 1950; all Box 13, ERCC.

13. Brown to Houser, April 21, 1951, Frame 662, Group 22, Series 3: Exec. Secy's File, CORE. Christopher to Mathis, April 21, 1951; Christopher to Edward W. Barron, May 23, 1951; both Box 1, ERCC.

14. Christopher to Barron, May 23, 1951, Box 1, ERCC.

15. "Miss Gatlin Is Appointed Head Librarian Here," *Bartlesville Examiner-Enterprise*, June 24, 1951; [Library Board Meeting Minutes,] March 5, 1952, Library Board; American Legion, *Proceedings of the 33d National Convention*, 139.

16. Christopher to D. F. Wiegel, July 31, 1952, Box 1, ERCC; [Library Board Meeting Minutes], October 7, 1952, Library Board.

17. Adjourned Regular Meeting of the Board of Commissioners, November 2, 1952, BCC; Minutes of Library Board, October 7, 1952, Library Board; *City Directory, 1950*; Herbert E. Winn, interview with author, Bartlesville, Okla., July 10, 1994; "Herbert Winn Appointed to Library Post," *Bartlesville Examiner-Enterprise*, September 1, 1953; Minutes of Library Board, August 11, 1953, Library Board.

18. Brown to Houser, September 5, 1950, Frame 642, Group 22, Series 3: Exec. Secy's File, CORE.

19. Brown to Houser, September 12, 1950, Frame 643, Group 22, Series 3: Exec. Secy's File, CORE.

20. Advertisement, *Bartlesville Examiner-Enterprise*, September 24, 1950, found in Box 13, ERCC; Spencer Prentiss, interview with author, Bartlesville, Okla., July 22, 1994; Brown to Houser, January 6, 1951, Frame 660, Group 22, Series 3: Exec. Secy's File, CORE.

21. Brown to Ellen Brown Ericksen, February 22, 1951, Ericksen Papers.

22. Brown to Houser, April 21, 1951, Frame 662, Group 22, Series 3: Exec. Secy's File, CORE.

23. Brown to Houser, April 21, 1951, Frame 662, Reel 9, Series 3: Exec. Secy's File 22, CORE; Minutes, April 10, 1950, 106; Minutes, June 12, 1950, 117; Minutes, January 8, 1951, 144; January 22, 1951, 144–57; all School Board. Spivey interview.

24. Minutes, February 2, 1951, 145–46, School Board.

25. Minutes, February 14, 1951, 152; March 8, 1951, 153; and March 12, 1951, 157; all School Board. William Nelson, autograph manuscript, Davis Papers.

26. Paul J. Parker, interview with author, Bartlesville, Okla., July 18, 1994.

27. Nelson, autograph manuscript, Davis Papers; Katrina Cade, interview with author, Tulsa, Okla., July 15, 1994; Francis E. Condon, telephone interview.

28. Davis, *Annual Report*, September 1, 1951, 4, YWCA; Cade interview; McReynolds interview; Varvel interview; Nelson, autograph manuscript, Davis Papers.

29. Upham interview.

30. John S. Athens for Whit Y. Mauzy to Christopher, August 10, 1950; Christopher to Athens, August 16, 1950; Andrews to Joseph J. Lawler, August 21, 1950; all Box 13, ERCC.

31. Christopher to Lawler, September 12, 1950, Box 13, ERCC.

32. *"CONFIDENTIAL REPORT"* attached to Christopher to Lawler, September 12, 1950; K. S. Adams to Lawler, September 8, 1950; both Box 13, ERCC. Schrecker, *Many Are the Crimes*, includes discussion of anti-intellectualism in anticommunism and of the use of the concept of dupes.

33. Nelson, autograph manuscript, Davis Papers; Upham interview.

34. K. S. Adams to Adolph Dryer, April 16, 1951, with note on the back in Mildred Holliday's hand, Ericksen Papers.

35. Behymer, "Librarian Fights for Job Lost."

36. Spies interview.

37. Davis, *Annual Report*, September 1, 1950, YWCA; "K. S. Adams Awarded Scroll as Outstanding Legionnaire," *Bartlesville Enterprise*, August 12, 1952, clipping, Sark.

38. Spivey interview; Ogilvie interview; McReynolds interview; Varvel interview; Nelson autograph manuscript, Davis Papers.

39. Jennings interview; "Women in Oil," *Philnews* 3/54, Darlene Anderson, Attorney—Bartlesville (label on photograph) Neg. 2522, courtesy of Corporate Archives, Phillips Petroleum, Bartlesville, Okla.; Darlene

Anderson to Vera Andrews, November 2, 1956, Ericksen file; Boyle, "Spit in the Devil's Eye," 327–29.

40. Davis, *Annual Report*, September 1, 1951, 1:1, YWCA.

41. Ibid., 3.

42. Ibid.; "YWCA Groups Bid Goodbye to Miss Betty Davis," *Bartlesville Record*, July 19, 1951; "Y.W. Groups to Honor Miss Davis," *Bartlesville Examiner-Enterprise*, July 22, 1951; "Betty Davis Is Honoree at Buffet Supper," *Bartlesville Examiner*, July 24, 1951; all clippings in YWCA Scrapbook, June 24, 1951–March 26, 1961, YWCA.

43. Martha A. Good, recorder, *Annual Report*, September 15, 1952, 1:1, YWCA; Evelyn Sherrill, *DouglassAires Homecoming 1994* [souvenir program], inside front and back covers; Good, *Annual Report*, September 15, 1953, 1, YWCA.

44. Good, *Annual Report*, September 15, 1953, 1, YWCA.

45. Brown, "Three Years in a Negro School in Mississippi," typescript, Brown Papers; Evelyn M. Frantz, telephone interview with author, August 20, 1995; Frantz, letter to the author, September 7, 1995.

46. Brown, "Three Years in a Negro School in Mississippi."

47. Ibid.

48. Ibid.; Brown to "Dear Evelyn," June 2, 1953, Frantz file in possession of the author.

49. Beth McElwain, telephone interview with author, July 28, 1994.

50. Bernia Barrows, telephone interview with author, June 4, 1994; McElwain interview.

51. McElwain interview.

52. Brown to Ellen, various dates, Ericksen file; Dryer Creasy, telephone interview with author, January 26, 1994; Tom Dryer and Ellen Dryer, interviews with author, November 4, 1994. Holly Dryer to Evelyn Frantz, December 20, 1975; Ellen Brown Ericksen to Maud Clark, December 14, 1975; both Frantz file. "Service in Remembrance of These Whose Mortal Remains Were Bequeathed for the Furtherance of Medical Education and Research in Oklahoma," April 23, 1978, Ericksen file.

CHAPTER 5. "FIGHTING MCCARTHYISM THROUGH FILM": THE RUTH BROWN EPISODE ACCORDING TO HOLLYWOOD

1. Essary, "Hush-Hush in Bartlesville"; Daniel Taradash, telephone interview with author, April 18, 1994; Taradash, Comments on Box 3, mimeographed communication sent to the author, April 15, 1994, 1. *Storm Center*, starring Bette Davis, a Phoenix Production for Columbia Pictures,

1956; written in 1951 by Daniel Taradash and Elick Moll; directed by Daniel Taradash; produced by Julian Blaustein.

2. Ceplair and Englund, *The Inquisition in Hollywood*, 290. Ceplair and Englund's book is the most comprehensive of a number dealing with HUAC's investigations of Hollywood and about blacklisting in the entertainment industry more generally. They demonstrate that the Hollywood communists and liberals of the thirties and forties were targeted not because HUAC believed they actually posed a threat to the security of the United States but because they were effective in supporting the causes of the Popular Front— such as unionism, racial justice, and antifascism—to which they were committed. See also Hellman, *Scoundrel Time*; Kanfer, *The Journal of the Plague Years*; Navasky, *Naming Names*; and Faulk, *Fear on Trial*.

3. American Legion, *Proceedings of the 33d National Convention*, 144. E. R. Christopher was a member of the national Un-American Activities Committee.

4. It was, and still is, legal to be a communist. As Ceplair and Englund demonstrate, the Hollywood communists were targeted because they were effective activists in liberal and radical causes; virtually no one thought that they posed a threat of any kind, even to the content of films, over which the producers had control. See also Schrecker, *Many Are the Crimes*.

5. The events immediately leading up to and including the 1951 hearings are discussed in Ceplair and Englund, *The Inquisition in Hollywood*, 361–97. Robinson's testimony is discussed on 364–65.

6. Ceplair and Englund, *The Inquisition in Hollywood*, 386–97, discuss the role of the American Legion, ABC, and Aware, Inc., in the graylist and in clearance procedures. John Henry Faulk's blacklisting by and his 1956 lawsuit against Aware, Inc., is the subject of his *Fear on Trial*.

7. American Legion, *Proceedings of the 30th National Convention*, 69–70; and *Proceedings of the 31st National Convention*, 74, 72; Combs, "How Communists Make Stooges out of Movie Stars."

8. Matthews, "Did the Movies Really Clean House?"; Ceplair and Englund, *The Inquisition in Hollywood*, 389–92; American Legion, *Proceedings of the 34th National Convention*, 138–39; Robinson, "How the Reds Made a Sucker out of Me."

9. Taradash, " 'Storm Center' Course: Forthcoming Drama Followed Rugged Trail before Reaching the Screen," *New York Times*, October 14, 1956; Essary, "Hush-Hush in Bartlesville." Taradash confirmed that the story came from Essary's letter in a telephone interview with the author. See the series of letters and memos in Box 24, Taradash Papers.

10. Three out of four of the organizations in the script were actual, although defunct, Popular Front organizations; the fourth was invented, with a name similar to an actual organization, according to two interoffice

communications from Roger Mayer of Columbia to Blaustein and Taradash, August 31 and September 9, 1955, Box 33, Taradash Papers.

11. All quotes in the plot summary are taken from *Storm Center* (1956), written by Daniel Taradash and Elick Moll; directed by Daniel Taradash; produced by Julian Blaustein; a Phoenix Production for Columbia Pictures. The screenplay was turned into a paperback book in England, *Storm Centre*, written by Gordon Lansborough.

12. Taradash, "Comments on Box 3," 1; Taradash, "'Storm Center' Course"; notes on script, probably in Stanley Kramer's hand, Box 81; all Taradash Papers.

13. Taradash, "'Storm Center' Course"; Taradash, "Comments on Box 3," 1; Taradash, [I've played a lot of horses] untitled manuscript, 3, Box 24, Taradash Papers.

14. "Original Agreement," March 25, 1951, Box 81; [Taradash] to Dear Stanley, [n.d. but probably March 1951], Box 81; both Taradash Papers.

15. Taradash, "Comments on Box 3"; Kramer to Taradash, April 19, 1951, Box 81, Taradash Papers; The MPAPAI published Ayn Rand's *Screen Guide for Americans*, which listed such guidelines as "Don't Smear the Free Enterprise System" and "Don't Glorify the Collective," as well as "Don't Deify the Common Man" and "Don't Smear Industrialists," according to Ceplair and Englund, *The Inquisition in Hollywood*, 211–15; Caute, *The Great Fear*, 502; American Legion, *Proceedings of the 33d National Convention*, 40, 46; [Taradash] to [Kramer], April 28, 1951, Box 81, Taradash Papers.

16. Kramer to Taradash, May 1, 1951, Box 81, Taradash Papers.

17. Ceplair and Englund, *The Inquisition in Hollywood*, 367, 371, 373; Kanfer, *A Journal of the Plague Years*, 133; Spoto, *Stanley Kramer*, 75; Sayre, *Running Time*, 176. The Kramer-Foreman break up and the "diminished Fifth" are both treated in Navasky, *Naming Names*, 157–61. Kramer maintained that it was not Foreman's failure to inform that caused him to force Foreman out but Foreman's secretive behavior, which Kramer found threatening. Foreman went into exile in Great Britain, where he wrote scripts under assumed names, started a production company, and became a leader in the British film industry. He collaborated on the Academy Award–winning *Bridge on the River Kwai* but received no credit for it in the United States. He returned to the United States after twenty-three years in Great Britain.

18. Taradash to Kramer, May 26, 1951; Kramer to Taradash and Moll, June 7, 1951; both Box 81, Taradash Papers; Taradash and Moll, *The Library*, FIRST DRAFT, September 15, 1951, "SEK's copy" in manuscript on upper right-hand corner of cover sheet, Box 61, Taradash Papers; Taradash, "Comments on Box 3," 1; "Pickford Gets 50G Cash, Plus %, for Kramer Pic," *Variety* (daily), November 21, 1951, Academy.

19. David H. Clift to Clarence R. Graham, December 6, 1951; Clift to Kramer, December 6, 1951; Clift to Mary Pickford, December 6, 1952; Kramer to Clift, December 11, 1951; all Box 2, RG 2/1/28, ALA. "Mary Pickford Signs for 'The Library' Her First Film Since 'Secrets' in 1933," *New York Times*, November 19, 1951; Irving Reis to David K. Berninghausen, February 1, 1951 [1952], Research Folder, Box 43, Taradash Papers.

20. Reis to Berninghausen, February 1, 1951 [1952], Research Folder, Box 43, Taradash Papers; American Library Association. Intellectual Freedom Committee, "Propaganda and Pressures"; Reis to Taradash, February 11, 1952, Box 81, Taradash Papers.

21. Reis to Taradash, February 11, 1952, Taradash Papers; Ceplair and Englund, *The Inquisition in Hollywood*, 386; Caute, *The Great Fear*, 503; Taradash, "I've played a lot of horses," 3, Box 24 (the version of this article, "Storm Center Course," that appeared in the *New York Times* did not include this sentence); Dorothy M. Drake to Reis, August 4, 1952, Box 33, Taradash Papers.

22. "Mary Pickford Hops out of Stan Kramer's 'Fire' because It Isn't Tinted," *Variety* (daily), September 19, 1952; Taradash, "Comments on Box 3"; [Taradash], "Re: Kramer complaints," [after September 19, 1952], Box 81, Taradash Papers.

23. "Kramer Signs Stanwyck for Ex-Pickford Role," *Hollywood Reporter*, September 25, 1952; "Kramer May Temporarily Shelve 'Circle of Fire,'" *Variety* (daily), November 21, 1952; Taradash, "'Storm Center' Course."

24. Dwight D. Eisenhower, quoted in Edward T. Folliard, "Ike Urges 'Don't Join the Book-Burners' in Plea for Freedom," *Washington Post*, June 15, 1953. For more on the overseas libraries and McCarthy and librarians' and publishers' *Freedom to Read* statement, see Robbins, *Censorship and the American Library*, 75–83; and Robbins, "The Overseas Libraries Controversy and *The Freedom to Read*." Examples of librarians' use of Eisenhower's speech include an offprint from *Wilson Library Bulletin* 28 (September 1953) that featured on the front page both the speech and a letter to the ALA conference from Eisenhower that reiterated the importance to democracy of the freedom to read.

25. Taradash, "'Storm Center' Course"; Taradash places the Eisenhower speech incorrectly in 1954.

26. According to the *Los Angeles Times*, October 23, 1955, Taradash and Blaustein formed the company specifically to make *Storm Center*, but other documents are less clear. *Bell, Book and Candle* was certainly part of the deal with Columbia. Initially *Guard of Honor* was as well, but Phoenix apparently did not make it.

27. Taradash, "Comments on Box 3"; Taradash, "'Storm Center'" Course;" Taradash interview.

28. "Taradash Says 'Library' Will Be More Anti-Red than 'Usual,'" *Variety* (daily), July 6, 1955, Academy.

29. Taradash and Moll to Hedda Hopper, [telegram] September 2, 1955; Mrs. Anne Smart to Mrs. Gary Merrill, August 30, 1955, both Box 33, Taradash Papers. Anne Smart, "What to Look for in the Library of *Your School*," [1955], Folder 29, Box 1, Bixler Papers; Bette Davis to Smart, [after August 30, 1955], Box 33, Taradash Papers. Smart's campaign was featured in "Book Banning," an April 1955 segment of Murrow's "See It Now" series. Three of the six titles she featured dealt with race relations. Her list bears many of the names found on American Legion lists from 1950 and 1951. In 1955 the ALA reported that her list was being circulated by the national defense chairman of the national Daughters of the American Revolution to local chapters. See Grace T. Stevenson to Paul H. Bixler, March 11, 1955, Folder 29, Box 1, Bixler Papers. Smart also told Davis—inaccurately—that the film was funded in part by the Fund for the Republic, an offshoot of the Ford Foundation run by Robert Maynard Hutchins; many of the activities of the fund supported civil liberties. It had recently given a $5,000 award to the Jeanes Library of the Plymouth Meeting in Pennsylvania for its support of Mary Knowles, a librarian called before the Senate Internal Security Subcommittee. It also funded the ALA's *Newsletter on Intellectual Freedom*. For more detail on Smart, the Fund for the Republic, and Knowles and the Plymouth Meeting controversy, see Robbins, *Censorship and the American Library*, 86–92. Smart's list did include some people who were, or had been, communists, such as Howard Fast.

30. "Legion of Decency 'Separately' Classifies Col's 'Storm Center,'" *Variety* (daily), July 10, 1956; Aline Mosby, "'Storm Center' Draws Protest," *Hollywood Citizen-News*, July 21, 1956; "MPIC Hits Legion for 'Storm' Rating," *Hollywood Reporter*, July 23, 1956; all Academy. Ceplair and Englund, *The Inquisition in Hollywood*, 359; Arthur Wilde to Staff, June 18, 1956, Box 24, Taradash Papers; Taradash, "Comments on Box 3," 4. "Commonweal Deplores Legion of Decency Act of Political Opinion"; "Bette Davis Revises Views on Personals; Legion Hurt 'Storm'"; both *Variety* (weekly), August 8, 1956. Joe Schoenfeld, "Time and Place" [column], *Variety* (daily), July 11, 1956, Academy.

31. Eleanor Roosevelt, excerpt from "My Day," June 11, 1956, Box 24, Taradash Papers. Jonas Rosenfield, Jr., to Drew Pearson, June 28, 1956; "Trailer for 'Storm Center'"; Lawrence Lipskin to Taradash, July 3, 1956; Gordon Lansborough to Taradash, August 10, 1956; Lipskin to All Branches, June 22, 1956; all Box 33, Taradash Papers. "DeBra's Brochure Touts 'Storm' Film," *Variety* (weekly), August 8, 1956; Arthur H. DeBra to Dear Friend and accompanying brochure, July 1956; "Storm Center" [bookmark], Academy.

32. *Proceedings of the 1956 Midwinter Meeting, American Library Association*, February 1–2, 1956, Chicago, Box 4, RG 1/1/1, ALA; John D. Henderson to Paul H. Bixler, March 6, 1956, Folder 18, Box 1, Bixler Papers; Bette Davis to Dear Friend, June 18, 1956, Box 33, Taradash Papers.

33. Lois Weber to Taradash and Jonas Rosenfield, June 18 [1956], Box 33, Taradash Papers.

34. Helga Eason to Taradash, July 2, 1956, Box 33, Taradash Papers; Paul Bixler to George Bidinger, July 17, 1956, Folder 1, Box 1, Bixler Papers.

35. Bixler was editor of the *Newsletter on Intellectual Freedom* from 1952 to 1956. He helped set up several intellectual freedom conferences; he often said it was the librarian of the small public library who needed assistance to understand and act on the Library Bill of Rights. For discussion of the years in which Bixler was secretary of the Intellectual Freedom Committee, see Robbins, *Censorship and the American Library*, 69–89. Sidney Michaelson to Taradash, July 26, 1956; Etheleeda Davis to Taradash, September 13, 1956; both Box 33, Taradash Papers. The librarian was Rebecca Wolstenhomme, fired from her job in 1954 after refusing to answer questions posed to her by HUAC; she won reinstatement in 1959. See Robbins, "After Brave Words, Silence"; John Montgomery to Taradash, September 12, 1956, Box 33, Taradash Papers.

36. Lipskin to Taradash, July 3, July 26, and July 27, 1956, with attachments; Gordon Lansborough to Taradash, August 10, 1956; Lipskin to All Branches, June 22, 1956; "British Reviews of Storm Center" [undated mimeographed excerpts]; "Opinions on 'Storm Center'" and other numerous letters and reviews; all Box 33, Taradash Papers. Lansborough complained that early release of *Storm Centre* in England hurt sales of the book. Ava Boswan to Taradash, September 21, 1956; Robert T. Stellar to Taradash, September 11, 1956; Jonas Rosenfield to Taradash and Julian Blaustein, with attached Wingate (Brooklyn) High School film reviews, June 18, 1956; "Breakdown of preview cards Storm Center #2," March 6, 1956; all Box 33, Taradash Papers. Numerous additional reviews are found in the "Storm Center" file, Academy.

37. J. B. Matthews, *Memorandum on "Storm Center,"* August 20, 1956, Box 33, Taradash Papers.

38. Jerry Davis to Julian and Dan, [n.d.], Box 33, Taradash Papers. See Ceplair and Englund, *The Inquisition in Hollywood*, for discussion of the individuals named. Foreman, Buchman, and Levitt all were blacklisted following HUAC's second 1951–53 Hollywood probe; Trumbo was blacklisted and went to prison as one of 1947's Hollywood Ten.

39. "U.S. Movie Cited for Award," *New York Times*, May 17, 1957. See Ceplair and Englund, *The Inquisition in Hollywood*, 418–29 and Kanfer, *The Journal of the Plague Years*, 276–79 for a discussion of the end of the

blacklist. Only about 10 percent of those affected managed to salvage their careers.

40. Ruth H. to Ruth Brown, August 26, 1975, Ericksen Papers.

41. The metaphors for reading in *Storm Center* include eating (Freddie stuffs himself with words and has no room for food), poison (food gone bad), and snakes (which connote the threat of too much knowledge as well as the evil of communism).

CHAPTER 6. "ONLY A SKIRMISH"

1. Archibald MacLeish, "A Tower Which Will Not Yield." MacLeish uses the battle image extensively in talking about the fight to maintain free communications and the role of the libraries and librarians as "pill boxes" or "exposed and vulnerable front[s]" in the battle. The war metaphor was commonly used by librarians during the McCarthy era and reflects their sense of embattlement and their elevation of the importance of the freedom to read. MacLeish, a former Librarian of Congress, was an articulate spokesman for librarians in this role.

2. It should be noted that African-American and poor white women were expected to work outside the home, caring for the homes of middle- and upper-class whites.

3. For a concise discussion of the ways in which the Victorian Cult of True Womanhood with its ideas of separate private and public spheres for women and men and the Progressive Era propensity for social reform informed the role of women in waged library work, see Jenkins, "'Since So Many of Today's Librarians Are Women"; the figure 88.8 percent comes from p. 243 (app. A, Census Figures on U.S. Librarians, 1870–1990).

4. Evelyn M. Frantz to Ellen Ericksen, January 11, 1976, Ericksen Papers; Preston Gaddis, E. R. Christopher, W. D. McGinley, and Mayor Dunaway were all active members of the American Legion, as was K. S. Adams. It was a primary identification for Gaddis and Christopher, and an important one for the others.

5. Davis, *Annual Report*, September 1, 1950, 1 and 2, 4–5, app. 12, 3, YWCA; Vern Hutchison to Mary Hayes Marable, July 31, 1951, Brown Papers; Stouffer, *Communism, Conformity, and Civil Liberties*; Kane interview.

6. Garceau, *The Public Library in the Political Process*, 114.

7. MacLeish, "A Tower Which Will Not Yield," 652; MacLeish also was chairman of the Ad Hoc Committee to End the Ban on the *Nation*.

8. American Library Association and American Book Publishers Council, *The Freedom to Read*.

9. Cherokee Chapter, United Daughters of the Confederacy to City Commissioners, March 11, 1950, Davis Papers. See other examples of the UDC's efforts to control the interpretation of history in Bailey, "Free Speech and the 'Lost Cause' in Texas."

10. MacLeish, "A Tower Which Will Not Yield," 652.

11. Bryan, *The Public Librarian*, 42–43; Garceau, *The Public Library in the Political Process*, 131; Fiske, *Book Selection and Censorship*. In her *Apostles of Culture*, Dee Garrison claims that feminization led to both censoriousness and a lack of leadership in the American library profession. MacLeish, "A Tower Which Will Not Yield," 652.

12. For a persuasive analysis of the reasons that men's names are usually associated with intellectual freedom while women are deemed censorious, see Jenkins, " 'Since So Many of Today's Librarians Are Women.' " In my own research, I have found only one man who lost a librarian position over questions of loyalty, Phillip Martineau of Williams College, who was job hunting when he was called before one of the investigating committees. Although he was not charged with any offense, all his job offers were withdrawn.

13. Brown, "Remember Bartlesville"; Brown to Ellen [Brown Ericksen], [n.d. but after 1961], Ericksen Papers. For ALA's history in regard to race, see Du Mont, "Race in American Librarianship "; and Moon, "The Silent Subject." Moore,"Bartlesville, and After"; Wiegand, "Tracing the Concept of Freedom of Access to Information in American Library History."

EPILOGUE. TELLING THE RUTH BROWN STORY: A PERSONAL JOURNEY

1. The concept of the ethnographer's path is a common one in anthropology; see Sanjek, "On Ethnographic Validity," 394–400.

2. Nissenbaum, "The Month before 'The Night before Christmas,' " describes the process of historical research as a series of fortunate accidents, interpretations and reinterpretations, and ongoing syntheses; my experience has been very similar. Lerner, "Reconceptualizing Differences Among Women," 116.

3. The feminist scholar, by definition, engages in research that sheds light on the historic roles (and oppression) of women; feminist research derives from a political perspective and commitment. According to Plummer, *Documents of Life*, 123, the selection of the problem to be investigated is the first use of the researcher's theoretical perspective. I use "ideology" here to mean the web of understandings, beliefs, and discourses that shape one's construction of experience; it places one in relation to the

dominant social order. See Eagleton's *Ideology*. No one can escape having an ideology; one can only escape being reflexive about it. For the importance of systematic reflexity, see Lather, "Issues of Validity in Openly Ideological Research," 66–67.

4. Jason Talley and his mother, Susan, were also willing to discuss their experience traveling to Bartlesville to do research. Jason's History Day project in Missouri was disqualified because the story and his research were not believed. Two ninth graders from Marietta, Oklahoma, also created a History Day project on this episode, a videotape called "Red Herring."

5. Handlin, "Using Historical Sources," 31–32.

6. Ralph Espach, telephone interview with author, August 4, 1994.

7. A primary reason for using oral histories and interviews as research tools is to hear voices that would otherwise be silenced. Because these voices are not represented in documentary evidence, however, in historical research they must be used with care. Triangulation is discussed in Lather, "Issues of Validity in Openly Ideological Research," 67, 69, 72.

8. Boosterism refers to a community's selling of itself as a desirable place to live, work, or build a business. It generally emphasizes the natural resources and beauty of a location and/or the cultural and civic resources, such as a good workforce, excellent schools, and a "family atmosphere." See Cronon, *Nature's Metropolis*, for theories of boosterism.

9. Oakley, "Interviewing Women," asserts that this giving back is an important part of the process. Like her, I found that because I chose to regard those who assisted me as participants in the research process rather than subjects of the research, the research took on the character of a shared enterprise.

10. This issue was the topic of an interesting discussion at the forum "Oral Histories of Jim Crow" at the 10th Berkshire Conference on the History of Women, Chapel Hill, N.C., June 1996. Participants came down, as I ultimately did, on the side of encouraging individuals—even pushing them—to discuss painful memories, but they insisted as well that the privacy and integrity of the individual had to be respected.

11. DouglassAires interview, especially Marlene Johnson Gilkey, Marie Littles Wilson, Eva Chambers, Rose Bean Hicks, Ida Dailey, Bernice Brown, and Arnetta Nash.

12. See Hildenbrand, "Some Theoretical Considerations on Women in Library History," for a discussion of Lerner's perspectives (in "Placing Women in History") on the history of women—including the "notable woman" perspective—as they apply to library history.

13. See Tucker, *Telling Memories among Southern Women*; Rollins, *Between Women*; and Jones, *Labor of Love, Labor of Sorrow*; Meier and Rudwick, *CORE*; Marx and Useem, "Majority Involvement in Minority Movements "; Davis, *Annual Report*, September 1, 1950.

14. Schrecker, *Many Are the Crimes*.

BIBLIOGRAPHY

PRIMARY SOURCES

Interviews

Andrews, Anthony and Frances, July 8 and August 9, 1994, Bartlesville, Oklahoma

Barrows, Bernia, telephone interview, June 14, 1994

Cade, Katrina, July 15, 1994, Tulsa, Oklahoma

Carlson, Frances Varvel, August 9, 1994, Bartlesville, Oklahoma

Condon, Francis E., telephone interview, August 5, 1994

Davis, Russell, July 8 and 21 and August 9, 1994, Bartlesville, Oklahoma

Dixon, J. B., M.D., telephone interview, July 12, 1995

DouglassAires (Rose Bean Hicks, Bernice Brown, Eva Chambers, Ida Dailey, Marlene Johnson Gilkey, Marie Littles Wilson, Arnetta Nash), July 22, 1994, Bartlesville, Oklahoma

Dryer, Ellen, D.V.M., November 4 and 5, 1994, Cincinnati, Ohio

Dryer, Tom, M.D., November 4, 1994, Cincinnati, Ohio

Dryer Creasy, Mildred Holliday, telephone interview, January 26, 1994, November 4 and 5, 1994, Cincinnati, Ohio

Ericksen, Ellen Brown, July 7, 1994, July 20, 1995, Collinsville, Oklahoma

Espach, Ralph, telephone interview, August 4, 1994

Frantz, Evelyn M., telephone interview, August 20, 1995

Frey, Elizabeth "Betty," July 21, 1994, Bartlesville, Oklahoma

Frey, Fred, July 21, 1994, Bartlesville, Oklahoma

Gordon, Naomi Stocker, telephone interview, April 20, 1994

Gaddis, Preston, July 14, 1994, Bartlesville, Oklahoma

Henderson, James, telephone interview, March 24, 1994
Houser, George, telephone interview, February 20, 1994
Jennings, Robert, July 8, August 9, 1994, Bartlesville, Oklahoma
Jones, Jean, telephone interview, November 7, 1995
Kane, Richard, July 13, 1994, Bartlesville, Oklahoma
Kennedy, Frances, July 6, 1994, Oklahoma City, Oklahoma
Koppel, Donald T., July 13, 1994, Bartlesville, Oklahoma
Lorenz, Phillip, July 14, August 9, 1994, Bartlesville, Oklahoma
McElwaine, Beth, telephone interview, July 28, 1994
McReynolds, Odie, July 14, 1994, Bartlesville, Oklahoma
Ogilvie, Lois, telephone interview, July 29, 1996
Parker, Paul J., July 18, 1994, Bartlesville, Oklahoma
Prentiss, Spencer, July 22, 1994, Bartlesville, Oklahoma
Price, Harold C., Jr., telephone interview, December 11, 1994
Price-Barton, Roy and Carolyn, August 2, 1994, Bartlesville, Oklahoma
Putnam, Ruth Fisher, telephone interview, April 18, 1994
Rodgers, the Reverend Richard, telephone interview, August 20, 1995
Spies, Brooks, June 19, 1995, Bartlesville, Oklahoma
Spivey, the Reverend James, telephone interview, March 23, 1995
Stewart, Jimmy, August 1, 1994, Oklahoma City, Oklahoma
Stocker, Allan, July 20, 1994, Bartlesville, Oklahoma
Stocker, Joseph, telephone interview, April 20, 1994
Taradash, Daniel, telephone interview, April 18, 1994
Upham, John D., telephone interview, July 9, 1998
Varvel, Margaret, March 20, 21, Corvallis, Oregon; 9 August 9, 1994, Bartlesville, Oklahoma
Winn, Herbert E. "Gene" and Sarah, July 10, 1994, Bartlesville, Oklahoma

Archives and Manuscripts

American Assocation of University Women Collection (scrapbooks and minute books), Bartlesville Public Library
American Civil Liberties Union Archives, Seeley G. Mudd Manuscript Library, Princeton University, Princeton, N.J.
American Library Association Archives, University of Illinois, Urbana-Champaign
Bartlesville City Commission Minutes, City Clerk's Office, Bartlesville, Oklahoma
Bartlesville Public Library Board Minutes (new board), City Clerk's Office, Bartlesville, Oklahoma
Bartlesville Public Library local history collection, Bartlesville, Oklahoma

Bartlesville Young Women's Christian Association Archives, YWCA Building, Bartlesville, Oklahoma

Berninghausen, David K., Papers. University Library, University of Minnesota, Minneapolis

Bixler, Paul, Papers. Antiochiana, Olive Kettering Library, Antioch College, Yellow Springs, Ohio

Brown, Ruth W., Papers. Special Collections, Pittsburg State University, Pittsburg, Kansas

Christopher, E. R., Collection. Western History Collections, University of Oklahoma Library, Norman

City Clerk's File. City of Bartlesville

Congress of Racial Equality Papers 1941–67. State Historical Society of Wisconsin, Madison

Davis, Russell, Papers. Special Collections, Pittsburg State University

Ericksen, Ellen Brown, Papers. Personal collection, Collinsville, Oklahoma

Frantz, Evelyn, Papers. In the possession of the author

National Association for the Advancement of Colored People File, Archives and Manuscripts Reading Room, Library of Congress, Washington, D.C.

National Broadcasting Company Radio Broadcast Transcript File, Library of Congress

Ogilvie, Lois, Papers. Personal collection, Santa Barbara, California

Oklahoma Department of Libraries working files, Oklahoma Department of Libraries, Oklahoma City, Oklahoma

Oklahoma Library Association Files, Oklahoma State Archives, Oklahoma Department of Libraries

Oklahoma Supreme Court files, Oklahoma State Archives, Oklahoma Department of Libraries

Phillips Petroleum Company Archives, Bartlesville

Ponca City Public Library Archives and accession books, Ponca City, Oklahoma

Sark, Elmer, Collection, Bartlesville Public Library, Bartlesville

St. Luke's Episcopal Church, Canonical Parish Register, Bartlesville

School Board Minute Book, Bartlesville Public School Administration Building, Bartlesville

Storm Center File, Center for Motion Picture Research, Academy of Motion Picture Arts and Sciences, Beverly Hills, California

Storm Center File, Wisconsin Center for Film and Theater Research, State Historical Society of Wisconsin, Madison

Taradash, Daniel, Papers. American Heritage Center, University of Wyoming, Laramie

Newspapers

Bartlesville Examiner-Enterprise (and the *Examiner* and the *Enterprise*)
Bartlesville Record
Black Dispatch (Oklahoma City)
Christian Science Monitor
Daily Oklahoman
Kansas City Star
New York Times
Oklahoma City Times
St. Louis Post-Dispatch
Tulsa Eagle
Tulsa World
Tulsa Tribune

SECONDARY SOURCES

Books, Articles, and Other Materials

Achtemeier, Elizabeth Rice. *The Meaning and the Mystery: A Biography of
F. E. Rice of Phillips Petroleum Company*. Richmond, Va.: Achtemeier,
1979.
American Legion. *Proceedings of the 29th National Convention of the American
Legion*. Washington, D.C.: Government Printing Office, 1948.
————. *Proceedings of the 30th National Convention of the American Legion*.
Washington, D.C.: Government Printing Office, 1949.
————. *Proceedings of the 33d National Convention of the American Legion*.
Washington, D.C.: Government Printing Office, 1952.
————. *Proceedings of the 34th National Convention of the American Legion*.
Washington, D.C.: Government Printing Office, 1953.
American Library Association. "The Library Bill of Rights." *American
Library Association Bulletin* 42 (July–August 1948): 285.
————. Committee on Intellectual Freedom. "Propaganda and Pressures."
Chicago: The Committee, [1951].
American Library Association and American Book Publishers Council.
The Freedom to Read. Chicago: The Associations, 1953.
Bailey, Fred A. "Free Speech and the 'Lost Cause' in Texas: A Study of
Social Control in the New South." *Southwestern Historical Quarterly* 97,
no. 3 (1994): 453–77.
Barker, Tomie Dora. *Libraries of the South*. Chicago: American Library
Association, 1936.

Bartlesville Women's Network. *Taproots: Transcription of the Bartlesville Women's Network Oral History Network.* 3 vols. Bartlesville, Okla.: The Network, 1994, 1996, 1998.

Belknap, Michael R. *Cold War Political Justice: The Smith Act, the Communist Party, and American Civil Liberties.* Westport, Conn.: Greenwood Press, 1977.

Berninghausen, David K. "The Case of the *Nation.*" *American Scholar* 19 (Winter 1949): 44–55.

————. "Film Censorship." *American Library Association Bulletin* 44 (December 1950): 447–48.

————. *The Flight from Reason: Essays on Intellectual Freedom in the Academy, the Press, and the Library.* Chicago: American Library Association, 1975.

Bixler, Paul. "Legionnaire 'Assults' Public Library." *Newsletter on Intellectual Freedom* 4 (January 1956): 4.

Bontecou, Eleanor. *The Federal Loyalty-Security Program.* Ithaca, N.Y.: Cornell University Press, 1953.

Boyle, Sarah Patton. "Spit in the Devil's Eye: A Southern Heretic Speaks." *Nation,* October 20, 1956, 327–29.

Brown, Ralph S. *Loyalty and Security: Employment Tests in the United States.* New Haven: Yale University Press, 1958.

Brown, Ruth W. "Remember Bartlesville" [letter to the editor], *Library Journal* 86 (February 15, 1961): 730.

Bryan, Alice I. *The Public Librarian.* New York: Columbia University Press, 1952.

Buckler, Helen. "The CORE Way." *Survey Graphic* 35 (February 1946): 50–52.

Carleton, Don E. *Red Scare! Right-wing Hysteria, Fifties Fanaticism, and Their Legacy in Texas.* Austin: Texas Monthly Press, 1985.

Caute, David. *The Great Fear: The Anti-Communist Purge under Truman and Eisenhower.* New York: Simon and Schuster, 1978.

Ceplair, Larry, and Steven Englund. *The Inquisition in Hollywood: Politics in the Film Community, 1930–1960.* Garden City, N.Y.: Anchor Press, 1980.

Chamber of Commerce of the United States. *Communist Infiltration in the U.S.: Its Nature and How to Combat It.* Washington, D.C.: The Chamber, 1946.

————. *Program for Community Anti-Communist Action.* Washington, D.C.: The Chamber, 1948.

Cole, John, and Kristi Norton. *A Red Herring.* Marietta, Okla.: High School, 1987. Produced under the direction of Ann Cleary, librarian.

Combs, R. E. "How Communists Make Stooges out of Movie Stars." *American Legion Magazine,* (May 1949): 14, 15, 42–46.

Cresswell, Stephen. "Last Days of Jim Crow in Southern Libraries." *Libraries and Culture* 31 (Summer–Fall 1996): 557–73.

Crittenden, Juanita Louise Jones. "A History of Public Library Service to Negroes in Columbus, Georgia, 1831–1959." Master's thesis, Atlanta University School of Library Service, 1960.

Cronon, William. *Nature's Metropolis: Chicago and the Great West.* New York: W. W. Norton, 1991.

Cross, George Lynn. *Blacks in White Colleges: Oklahoma's Landmark Cases.* Norman: University of Oklahoma Press, 1975.

Danton, Emily Miller. "South Does Less Restricting." *Library Journal* 73 (July 1948): 990–92.

Debo, Angie. *And Still the Waters Run: The Betrayal of the Five Civilized Tribes.* 2d ed. Princeton: Princeton University Press, 1972.

Department of Data and Trends, National Board of the YWCA. *Toward Better Race Relations.* Edited by Margaret Hiller, field worker Dorothy Sabiston. New York: Woman's Press, 1949.

Dickey, Pennie Williams. "A History of Public Library Service for Negroes in Jackson, Mississippi, 1950–1957." Master's thesis, Atlanta University School of Library Service, 1960.

Du Mont, Rosemary Ruhig. "Race in American Librarianship: Attitudes of the Library Profession." *Journal of Library History, Philosophy, and Comparative Librarianship* 21 (Summer 1986): 288–309.

Eagleton, Terry. *Ideology: An Introduction.* London: Verso, 1991.

Egerton, John. *Speak Now Against the Day: The Generation before the Civil Rights Movement in the South.* New York: Alfred A. Knopf, 1994.

Essary, Darlene Anderson. "Hush-Hush in Bartlesville." *Saturday Review* 33 (September 30, 1950): 23.

———. "Patriotism in Bartlesville." *Nation,* August 12, 1950: 155–56.

Faulk, John Henry. *Fear on Trial.* Austin: University of Texas Press, 1983.

Fisher, Ada Lois Sipuel, with Danney Goble. *A Matter of Black and White: The Autobiography of Ada Lois Sipuel Fisher.* Norman: University of Oklahoma Press, 1996.

Fiske, Marjorie. *Book Selection and Censorship: A Study of School and Public Libraries in California.* Berkeley: University of California Press, 1959.

Fonville, Emma Ruth. "A History of Public Library Service to Negroes in Bessemer, Alabama." Master's thesis, Atlanta University School of Library Service, 1962.

Freeland, Richard M. *The Truman Doctrine and the Origins of McCarthyism: Foreign Policy, Domestic Politics, and Internal Security, 1946–1948.* New York: Alfred A. Knopf, 1972.

Fried, Richard. *Nightmare in Red: The McCarthy Era in Perspective.* New York: Oxford University Press, 1990.

Garceau, Oliver. *The Public Library in the Political Process: A Report of the Public Library Inquiry.* New York: Columbia University Press, 1949.

Garrison, Dee. *Apostles of Culture: The Public Librarian and American Society, 1876–1920.* New York: Free Press, 1979.

Gleason, Eliza Atkins. *The Southern Negro and the Public Library.* Chicago: University of Chicago Press, 1941.

Goble, Danney. "The Southern Influence on Oklahoma." In *"An Oklahoma I Had Never Seen Before": Alternative Views of Oklahoma History,* edited by Davis D. Joyce, 280–301. Norman: University of Oklahoma Press, 1994.

Grayson, Bessie Rivers. "A History of Public Library Service for Negroes in Montgomery, Alabama." Master's thesis, Atlanta University School of Library Service, 1965 .

Grimshaw, Ivan Gerould. "Ruth Brown." *Library Journal* 75 (December 15, 1950): 2139.

Handlin, Oscar. "Using Historical Sources." In *Clio's Craft: A Primer of Historical Methods,* edited by Terry Crowley, 25–41.Toronto: Clopp Clark Pittman, 1988.

Hellman, Lillian. *Scoundrel Time.* Boston: Little, Brown, 1976.

Henderson, James W. "Ruth Brown's Dismissal Shocks Former Bartlesville Resident." *Library Journal* 75 (October 15, 1950): 1810–11.

Higgins, Alice G. "Intellectual Freedom." *American Library Association Bulletin* (October 15, 1974): 394.

Hildenbrand, Suzanne. "Some Theoretical Considerations on Women in Library History." *Journal of Library History* 18 (Fall 1983): 382–90.

Hildenbrand, Suzanne, ed. *Reclaiming the American Library Past: Writing the Women In.* Norwood, N.J.: Ablex, 1996.

Holden, Anna. "The Color Line in Southern Libraries." *New South* 9 (January 1954): 1–4.

National Americanism Commission of the American Legion. *How You Can Fight Communism.* Indianapolis: The Commission, [1949].

Irons, Peter H. "American Business and the Origins of McCarthyism: The Cold War Crusade of the United States Chamber of Commerce." In *The Specter: Original Essays on the Cold War and the Origins of McCarthyism,* edited by Robert Griffith and Athan Theoharis, 74–89. New York: New Viewpoints, 1974.

Jenkins, Christine. "Everyday Resistance: American Children's Librarians and Censorship in Cold War America." Paper presented at Berkshire Women's History Conference, Chapel Hill, June 1996.

———. " 'Since So Many of Today's Librarians Are Women . . . ': Women and Intellectual Freedom in U.S. Librarianship, 1890–1990." In *Reclaiming the American Library Past: Writing the Women In,* edited by Suzanne Hildenbrand, 221–24. Norwood, N. J.: Ablex, 1996.

Jones, Jacqueline. *Labor of Love, Labor of Sorrow: Black Women, Work, and the Family, from Slavery to the Present*. New York: Vintage Books, 1995.

Kamp, Joseph P. *Behind the Lace Curtains of the Y.W.C.A.* New York: Constitutional Education League, 1949.

Kanfer, Stephan. *The Journal of the Plague Years*. New York: Atheneum, 1973.

Kipp, Laurence J. "Report from Boston." *Library Journal* 77 (November 1, 1952): 1843–46. 1887.

Kuhn, Irene Corbally. "Why You Buy Books That Sell Communism." *American Legion Magazine* (January 1951): 19, 53–55, 58–63.

Lansborough, Gordon. *Storm Centre*. London: Panther Books, [1956]. Based on a script by Daniel Taradash and Elick Moll.

Lather, Patti. "Issues of Validity in Openly Ideological Research: Between a Rock and a Soft Place." *Interchange* 17 (Winter 1986): 66–72.

Lerner, Gerda. "Placing Women in History: Definitions and Challenges." In Lerner, *The Majority Finds Its Past: Placing Women in History*, 145–49. New York: Oxford University Press, 1979.

———. "Reconceptualizing Differences Among Women." *Journal of Women's History* 2 (Winter 1990): 106–22.

Levine, Susan. *Degrees of Equality: The American Association of University Women and the Challenge of Twentieth-Century Feminism*. Philadelphia: Temple University Press, 1995.

Lewis, Philip. *"Friday Is a Great Day": A Radio Program for the American Civil Liberties Union Commemorating the 159th Anniversary of the Bill of Rights, December 15, 1950*. Transcript of radio program aired on NBC, December 13, 1950, Motion Picture, Broadcasting, and Recorded Sound Division, Library of Congress, Washington, D.C.

Lynn, Susan. *Progressive Women in Conservative Times: Racial Justice, Peace, and Feminism, 1945 to the 1960s*. New Brunswick, N.J.: Rutgers University Press, 1992.

McAuliffe, Dennis. *The Deaths of Sybil Bolton: An American History*. New York: Times Books, 1994.

McCormick, Charles H. *This Nest of Vipers: McCarthyism and Higher Education in the Mundel Affair, 1951–1952*. Urbana: University of Illinois Press, 1989.

McCullough, David. *Truman*. New York: Simon and Schuster, 1992.

MacLeish, Archibald. "A Tower Which Will Not Yield." *American Library Association Bulletin* 50 (November 1956): 649–54.

Malone, Cheryl Knott. "Accommodating Access: 'Colored' Carnegie Libraries, 1905–1925." Ph.D. dissertation, University of Texas, 1996.

Marx, Gary T., and Michael Useem. "Majority Involvement in Minority Movements: Civil Rights, Abolition, Untouchability." *Journal of Social Issues* 27 (1971): 81–104.

Matthews, J. B. "Did the Movies Really Clean House?" *American Legion Magazine* (December 1951): 12–13, 49–56.

May, Elaine Tyler. *Homeward Bound: American Families in the Cold War Era.* New York: Basic Books, 1988.

Mays, Blane. "McCarthyism in Oklahoma: The Case against Ruth Brown of Bartlesville." *Oklahoma State Historical Review* 3 (Spring 1982): 17–28.

Meier, August, and John H. Bracey, Jr. "The NAACP as a Reform Movement, 1909–1965: 'To Reach the Conscience of America.'" *Journal of Southern History* 65 (February 1963): 2–30.

Meier, August, and Elliott Rudwick. *CORE: A Study in the Civil Rights Movement, 1942–1968.* New York: Oxford University Press, 1973.

Moon, Eric. "The Silent Subject." *Library Journal* 85 (December 15, 1960): 4436–37.

Moore, Everett T. "Bartlesville, and After." *American Library Association Bulletin* 54 (November 1960): 815–17.

Navasky, Victor. *Naming Names.* New York: Penguin, 1980.

Nissenbaum, Stephen. "The Month before 'The Night before Christmas.'" In *Humanists at Work: Disciplinary Perspectives and Personal Reflections,* 43–78. Chicago: University of Illinois at Chicago, 1989.

Oakley, Ann. "Interviewing Women: A Contradiction in Terms." In *Doing Feminist Research,* edited by Helen Roberts, 30–51. London: Routledge & Kegan Paul, 1981.

Oklahoma Library Commission. *Oklahoma Libraries, 1900–1937: A History and Handbook. Published in Observance of the Thirtieth Anniversary of the Organization of the Oklahoma Library Association.* Oklahoma City: The Commission, 1937.

———. *Reports of the Oklahoma Library Commission and Survey of Libraries of Oklahoma.* Oklahoma City: The Commission, various dates, 1919–49.

Plummer, Ken. *Documents of Life: An Introduction to the Problem and Literature of a Humanistic Method.* London: George Allen & Unwin, 1983.

Polk's Bartlesville (Washington County, Okla.) City Directory. Dallas, Tex.: R. L. Polk, various dates.

Phillips Petroleum Company. "The Road We've Traveled: A 75-Year Journey" [poster]. Bartlesville, Okla.: The Company, [1992].

Robinson, Edward G. "How the Reds Made a Sucker out of Me." *American Legion Magazine* (October 1952): 11, 62, 64–68, 70, 71.

Robbins, Louise S. "After Brave Words, Silence: American Librarianship Responds to Cold War Loyalty Programs, 1947–1957." *Libraries and Culture* 30 (Fall 1995): 345–65.

———. *Censorship and the American Library: The American Library Association's Response to Threats to Intellectual Freedom, 1939–1969.* Westport, Conn.: Greenwood Press, 1996.

———. "Champions of a Cause: American Librarians and the Library Bill of Rights in the 1950s." *Library Trends* 45 (Summer 1996): 28–49.

———. "The Overseas Libraries Controversy and *The Freedom to Read*: U.S. Librarians and Publishers Confront Sen. Joseph McCarthy." Paper presented at the International Federation of Library Association Round Table on Library History conference "Books, Libraries, Reading, and Publishing in the Cold War," Paris, France, June 1998.

Robinson, James A. *Anti-Sedition and Loyalty Investigations in Oklahoma.* Norman, Okla.: Bureau of Government Research, 1956.

Rollins, Judith. *Between Women: Domestics and Their Employers.* Philadelphia: Temple University Press, 1985.

Rorty, James. "The Attack on Our Libraries: Defending 'Freedom to Read' at the Grass-Roots." *Commentary* (June 1955): 541–49.

———. "The Libraries in a Time of Tension: The Legion and Its Demands." *Commentary* (July 1955): 30–37.

Salmond, John A. "'The Great Southern Commie Hunt': Aubrey Williams, the Southern Conference Educational Fund, and the Internal Security Subcommittee." *South Atlantic Quarterly* 77 (1978): 433–52.

Sanjek, Roger, ed. *Fieldnotes: The Making of Anthropology.* Ithaca: Cornell University Press, 1990.

Sayre, Nora. *Running Time: Films of the Cold War.* New York: Dial Press, 1982.

Scales, James R., and Danney Goble. *Oklahoma Politics: A History.* Norman: University of Oklahoma Press, 1982.

Schrecker, Ellen W. *Many Are the Crimes: McCarthyism in America.* Boston: Little Brown, 1998.

———. *No Ivory Tower: McCarthyism and the Universities.* New York: Oxford University Press, 1986.

Shera, Jesse H. *Foundations of the Public Library: A Social History of the Public Library Movement in New England from 1629 to 1855.* Chicago: University of Chicago Press, 1949.

Sherrill, Evelyn, ed. *DouglassAires Homecoming 1994* [souvenir program]. Bartlesville, Okla.: DouglassAires, July 20–24, 1994.

Shockley, Ann Allen. *A History of Public Library Services to Negroes in the South, 1900– 1955.* Dover, Del.: Delaware State College, n.d.

Smallwood, James M., and Crispin A. Phillips. "Black Oklahomans and the Question of 'Oklahomaness': The People Who Weren't Invited to Share the Dream." In *The Culture of Oklahoma*, edited by Howard F. Stein and Robert F. Hill, 48–67. Norman: University of Oklahoma Press, 1993.

Sooner Nineteen-Fifteen. Norman: University of Oklahoma, 1915.

Spoto, Donald. *Stanley Kramer: Film Maker.* New York: G. P. Putnam's Sons, 1978.

State ex rel Brown et al. v. Dunnaway [*sic*] et al. 207 Okla. 144 or 248 P. 2d 232 (1952).

Stein, Howard F., and Robert F. Hill. *The Culture of Oklahoma*. Norman: University of Oklahoma Press, 1992.

———. "The Culture of Oklahoma: A Group Identity and Its Images." In *The Culture of Oklahoma*, edited by Howard F. Stein and Robert F. Hill, 198–235. Norman : University of Oklahoma Press, 1992.

Stouffer, Samuel. *Communism, Conformity, and Civil Liberties*. New York: Doubleday, 1955.

Sullivan, Patricia. *Days of Hope: Race and Democracy in the New Deal Era*. Chapel Hill: University of North Carolina Press, 1996.

Teague, Margaret Withers. *History of Washington County and Surrounding Area*. Bartlesville, Okla.: Bartlesville Historical Commission, 1967–68.

"Ten Best Books." *American Legion Magazine* 51 (May 1952): 29.

Theoharis, Athan. *Seeds of Repression: Harry S Truman and the Origins of McCarthyism*. Chicago: Quadrangle Books, 1971.

Tucker, Susan. *Telling Memories among Southern Women: Domestic Workers and Their Employers in the Segregated South*. New York: Schocken Books, 1988.

United States. Bureau of the Census. *Census of Housing: 1950. Vol. 1: General Characteristics, Part 5, North Carolina-Tennessee*. Washington, D.C.: Government Printing Office, 1953.

———. *Census of Population: 1950*. Vol. 2: *Characteristics of the Population, Part 36, Oklahoma*. Washington, D.C.: Government Printing Office, 1952.

———. *Sixteenth Census of the United States: 1940—Population*. Vol 2: *Characteristics of the Population, Part 5, New York-Oregon*. Washington, D. C.: Government Printing Office, 1942.

United States. President's Committee on Civil Rights. *To Secure These Rights, the Report of the President's Committee on Civil Rights*. New York: Simon and Schuster, 1947.

Wallis, Michael. *Oil Man: The Story of Frank Phillips and the Birth of Phillips Petroleum*. New York: Doubleday, 1988.

Washington County Historical Society. *Pictorial History of Bartlesville*. Bartlesville, Okla.: The Society, 1979.

Wertz, William C., ed. *Phillips: The First 66 Years*. Bartlesville, Okla.: Phillips Petroleum Company, 1983.

Wiegand, Wayne A. "Tracing the Concept of Freedom of Access to Information in American Library History." In *Buch und Bibliothekswissenschaft im Informationszeitalter: Internationale Festschrift für Paul Kaegbein sum 65 Geburtstag*, edited by Englebert Plassman, Wolfgang Schmitz, and Peter Vodosek, 313–21. Munich: K.G. Saur, 1990.

Wilder, Laura Ingalls. *Little House on the Prairie*. Uniform ed. New York: Harper, 1953.

Williams, Albert Rhys. *The Russians: The Land, the People, and Why They Fight*. New York: Harcourt Brace, 1943.

Williams, Joe. *Bartlesville: Remembrances of Time Past, Reflections of Today*. Bartlesville, Okla.: TRW Reda Pump Division, 1978.

Wilson, Louis Round. *Geography of Reading*. Chicago: American Library Association and University of Chicago Press, 1938.

Wilson, Louis Round, and E. A. Wight. *County Library Service in the South*. Chicago: University of Chicago Press, 1935.

Wilson, Louis Round, and Marion A. Milczewski, eds. *Libraries of the Southeast: A Report of the Southeastern States Cooperative Library Survey, 1946–47*. Chapel Hill: Southeastern Library Association by the University of North Carolina Press, 1949.

Woodward, C. Vann. *The Strange Career of Jim Crow*. 3d rev. ed. New York: Oxford University Press, 1974.

INDEX

materials, 8–9, 103, 163, 168;
organizations against, 35
Rader, Jesse L., 90–91, 107
Randolph, A. Philip, 54
Reading: metaphors for, 160
Reda Pump, 13
Red Channels, 102, 131
Red Masquerade, 102
Red Menace, The, 131
Red scare, 153
Reis, Irving (director), 141–43, 145
Religion: in Bartlesville, 16, 49
Removal of materials, 133–34. *See
also Censorship; Nation; New
Republic*; Subversive materials
Ribble, Audrey (Mrs. J. M.), 56
Rice, Ida (Mrs. F. E.), 62, 78, 164
Ridgway, Helen, 95
Riggs, Alta R., 74
Rise of Russia in Asia, The, 102
Roberts, George, 112–13
Robeson, Paul, 23, 51–52, 72, 103,
159
Robinson, Edward G., 130, 132
Rodgers, Richard, 51
Rogers, Lela, 129
Rogers, Rutherford D., 94
Roosevelt, Eleanor, 21, 145; actions
for racial equality, 21; support
for *Storm Center*, 146
Roosevelt, Franklin D., 6, 21
Roosevelt, Theodore, 19
Rorty, James, 105
Rose, Ernestine, 34
Rosenberg, Ethel, 130
Rosenberg, Julius, 130
Rotary Club, 15, 116
Rothaus, Julia, 162
Rowland, Alton, 71, 74
Russians, The, 59, 159
Rustin, Bayard, 37, 54–56, 64, 100,
114, 160

St. Louis Post-Dispatch, 97
Sandburg, Carl, 145
Sanders, Jan, 168
Santa Fe Railroad, 11
Saturday Review, 78, 128. *See also*
Essary, Darlene Anderson,
Saturday Review letter
Sawyer, W. C. ("Tom"), 100
Schoenfeld, Joe: support for *Storm
Center*, 146
School of Library Service
(Columbia University, 34
Scott, H., Rev., 48
Scott, T. P., 36, 63, 113, 122
"See It Now," 145, 147
Segregation, 50, 64; of community
facilities, 4, 18, 50–53, 61–64; in
libraries, 33, 43–44; in the mili-
tary, 5, 23, 46, 55; and racial
tension, 20; in schools, 22, 38;
Senate Bill Number One, 19;
supported in Bartlesville, 119
Selection of materials, 156, 159;
guided by lists, 100–106. *See also*
Book selection; Lists
Self-censorship, 162
Seminole Indians, 18
Senate Bill Number One, 19
Senate Subcommittee on Internal
Security, 23
Separate but equal, 38
Sheridan, Don, 34–35
Sheridan, Ida Helen, 34
Shipman, James T. (District
Judge), 83
Shreveport Times, 104
Singleton, Joan, 168
Sipuel, Ada Lois, 22, 24
Sipuel case, 36
Sissons, Anne (Mrs. Frank), 56, 63
Slater, Freddie, 134–37, 149, 152–53
Slater, George, 134, 136–37, 151, 158